COMMUNITY AND COLLECTIVE RIGHTS

This book presents an argument for the existence of moral rights held by groups and a resulting account of how to reconcile group rights with individual rights and with the rights of other groups. Throughout, the author shows applications to actual legal and political controversies, thus tying the normative theory to actual legal practice. The author presents collective moral rights as an underlying normative explanation for various legal norms protecting group rights in domestic and international legal contexts. Examples at issue include rights held by indigenous peoples, by trade unions, and by religious and cultural minority groups. The account also bears on contemporary discussions of multiculturalism and recognition, on debates about reasonable accommodation of minority communities, and on claims for third generation human rights. The book will thus be relevant both to theorists and to legal and human rights practitioners interested in related areas.

Volume 2 in the series Law and Practical Reason

Law and Practical Reason

The intention of this series is that it should encompass monographs and collections of essays that address the fundamental issues in legal philosophy. The foci are conceptual and normative in character, not empirical. Studies addressing the idea of law as a species of practical reason are especially welcome. Recognising that there is no occasion sharply to distinguish analytic and systematic work in the field from historico-critical research, the editors also welcome studies in the history of legal philosophy. Contributions to the series, inevitably crossing disciplinary lines, will be of interest to students and professionals in moral, political, and legal philosophy.

Volume 1: The Normative Claim of Law
Stefano Bertea

Community and Collective Rights

A Theoretical Framework for Rights held by Groups

Dwight Newman

·HART·
PUBLISHING

OXFORD AND PORTLAND, OREGON
2011

Published in the United Kingdom by Hart Publishing Ltd
16C Worcester Place, Oxford, OX1 2JW
Telephone: +44 (0)1865 517530
Fax: +44 (0)1865 510710
E-mail: mail@hartpub.co.uk
Website: http://www.hartpub.co.uk

Published in North America (US and Canada) by
Hart Publishing
c/o International Specialized Book Services
920 NE 58th Avenue, Suite 300
Portland, OR 97213-3786
USA
Tel: +1 503 287 3093 or toll-free: (1) 800 944 6190
Fax: +1 503 280 8832
E-mail: orders@isbs.com
Website: http://www.isbs.com

British Library Cataloguing in Publication Data
Data Available

ISBN: 978-1-84113-228-0

Typeset by Hope Services Ltd, Abingdon
Printed and bound in Great Britain by
Lightning Source UK Ltd

Acknowledgements

This books stems originally from a DPhil thesis completed in the Oxford University Faculty of Law. I thank first and foremost Timothy Endicott for his dedicated and patient supervision of the doctoral project. He was an excellent guide in the methods of legal philosophy, a firm but fair critic following his careful reading of drafts, and an important mentor. I thank Joseph Raz and Chris McCrudden, who each took on supervision of my work for a term through exchange supervisions and who each carefully analysed several chapters and pressed me onward on key issues. I thank John Gardner and Peter Oliver, who acted as examiners, for their careful examination and discussion of the thesis product and their very helpful and encouraging suggestions. I also thank Sandy Fredman and Ray Davern for their scrutiny of part of the thesis at the MPhil stage. At the publication stage, I thank Richard Hart for his receptiveness to the project, the anonymous reviewers for their helpful comments, and Hart's publications team for their efficiency and skill.

I have also learned from many audiences. I had the opportunity (with thanks to the Rhodes Trust, to St John's College, and to the Oxford Faculty of Law for travel funding) to present pieces of this work at different points in time at the Oxford Jurisprudence Discussion Group and Oxford Human Rights Discussion Group, at an International Law and Ethics Conference Series (ILECS) meeting in Belgrade, at the University of Antwerp's International Conference on Religious Identity and Cultural Pluralism, at the Wits Workshop on Law and Society at the University of the Witwatersrand, at the Law University of Lithuania (now Mykolas Romeris University) in Vilnius, at Leuven's Centre for Ethics, Social, and Political Theory, and at Centre of Canadian Studies conferences in Edinburgh. At the risk of excluding others whose names I did not catch, I thank the following for important questions on those occasions: Cathi Albertyn, Jovan Babic, Nick Barber, Samantha Besson, Paul Bou-Habib, Herman de Dijn, Avigail Eisenberg, Vladimir Gligorov, John Haldane, Jonathan Klaaren, Evelina Kurgonaite, Dimitrios Kyritsis, James Morauta, Dragan Milovanovic, Jorge Menezes Oliveira, John O'Dowd, Zoran Oklopcic, Harry Papadopoulos, Amir Paz-Fuchs, Irma du Plessis, Danny Priel, Prince Saprai, Patricia White, Burleigh Willkins and Steve Winter. I also thank the following for helpful bibliographical suggestions: Jeffrey Brand-Ballard, Nick Bunnin, Tomas Castillo, Matthew Harding, Santiago Legarre, Banu Paksoy, Oonagh Reitman, Irit Samet-Porat, Mike Sanderson, Henry Shue, Delaine Swenson, John Tasioulas and Shlomit Wallerstein.

For commenting in written form or engaging in other extended dialogues, I extend special thanks to Gerry Bradley, Rob Edger, John Finnis, Sébastien

Grammond, Les Green, Peter Jones, Maris Köpcke-Tinturé, David Miller, Jim Nickel, Ken Norman, George Rainbolt, Denise Réaume, Helder de Schutter, Ron Stevenson and John Whyte. I must also single out Will Kymlicka, who was both gracious and helpful in response to my critique of his arguments when I presented at a session he attended. As a great philosopher once told me, we have been most influenced by and learned the most from the writers whose works we most criticise.

Predecessor forms of two chapters have appeared as journal articles: 'Collective Interests and Collective Rights' (2004) 49 *American Journal of Jurisprudence* 127; and 'Exit, Voice, and "Exile": Rights to Exit and Rights to Eject' (2007) 57 *University of Toronto Law Journal* 43–47. I also published a predecessor form testing some of the arguments from chapter one in 'Putting Kymlicka in Perspective: Canadian Diversity and Collective Rights' in Stepehen Tierney (ed) *Accommodating Cultural Diversity: Contemporary Issues in Theory and Practice* (Aldershot, Ashgate, 2007). I thank the editors and others involved in these different processes.

I also thank the Rhodes Trust and Canada's Social Sciences and Humanities Research Council (SSHRC) for the scholarships that funded my doctoral work, and SSHRC in particular for awarding my doctoral work the Taylor Prize as the best SSHRC-funded doctorate of the pertinent year. I thank the University of Saskatchewan College of Law for the academic environment in which I have completed the book form of this work as a faculty member and the McGill Faculty of Law for hosting me as a semester-long visitor within their rich intellectual community while I was thinking about some related themes.

Finally, I thank my spouse, Simonne Horwitz, for her caring and support throughout the journey.

Contents

Table of Cases

African Commission on Human Rights

Australia

Canada

European Court of Human Rights

India

Inter-American Court of Human Rights

International Court of Justice

South Africa

United Kingdom ....

United States of America

Table of Legislation

Bolivia

Canada

Ecuador

European Union

Moldova

Poland

Russia

South Africa

Spain

United Kingdom

United States of America

Table of Conventions, Treaties etc

I

The Existence of Collective Moral Rights

1

Introduction

I. THE MORAL PLAUSIBILITY OF COLLECTIVE RIGHTS

SOMETIME IN THE not-too-remote past, people identifying as members of some cultural, ethnic, or religious group had their land and rights brutally stripped away, and many were harmed or killed. We cannot identify the lawful heirs of the precise individuals who suffered. Today, people who identify as members of this same cultural, ethnic, or religious group claim an entitlement to some compensation, ongoing protection, or benefit. We feel some intuitive sympathy with their claim. Why?

A constitutional text contains a clause granting the citizens of some state 'freedom of association'. Union activists say this clause should be read so as to give unions some powers not otherwise possessed by their members. Religious activists similarly claim that this clause protects some entitlement on their part to engage in communal acts of worship. We say that judges should be prepared to listen to these arguments. Why?

A province with distinctive linguistic and cultural features holds a referendum in which a majority of its population vote to secede from the larger state of which it had been a part. The government officials of this province claim that it is entitled to secede, notwithstanding that some people within it object that some of their interests will be adversely affected. In at least some circumstances, we will still agree with the government officials. Why?

Posing these questions has presumed certain intuitions. Someone claiming not to share these intuitions might object that the questions identify nothing to explain. But even if you do not share these intuitions, many people do, and it is worth exploring whether they might be right. If this motive has not convinced you, then consider that many of the intuitions have been legally entrenched in various ways.[1] Given that legal norms often express moral norms, the various

[1] For example, Constitution Act 1982 (Canada) (schedule B to Canada Act 1982 (UK) c 11) s 35 (protecting Aboriginal rights); Charter of Fundamental Rights of the European Union [2000] OJ C364/1 art 12 and Constitution of the Republic of South Africa Act 108 of 1996 s 23 (providing explicitly for union rights); Constitution of Poland 1997 art 25, Constitution of the Republic of Spain 1978 art 16, Constitution of the Republic of Moldova 1994 art 31(2) (granting equality, autonomy, organisational rights to religious bodies); *Reference re Secession of Quebec* [1998] 2 SCR 217 and Clarity Act SC 2000 c 26 (recognising forms of right to secession). See also eg RR Garet 'Communality and Existence: The Rights of Groups' (1983) 56 *Southern California Law Review* 1001 (using group rights in explicating American constitutional law); JE Magnet *Modern Constitutionalism: Identity, Equality and Democracy* (Toronto,

situations and states in which such intuitions are entrenched also give them moral plausibility and make them worthy of closer examination.

In this book, I seek to offer a foundation and framework that will assist in the resolution of such questions, specifically by arguing on a non-relativistic basis for the claim that groups hold moral rights. I thus seek to offer an articulated justification and examination of collective moral rights. Specifically, I have three purposes, each addressed in one of the Parts: (I) to offer a justification of the claim that collectivities have moral rights; (II) to use the rationales undergirding this justification to elucidate the conditions collectivities must meet to hold rights legitimately, conditions that avert widespread conflicts between collective rights and individual rights and that identify certain collectivities (and not others) as legitimate rights-holders; and (III) to begin to examine what these principles imply for how to appropriately accommodate collective moral rights in legal and political orders, examining principled reasons for and against interference with collectivities so as to bring them into compliance with the conditions identified in Part II.

I offer in this book a theory of irreducibly collective moral rights. 'Collective rights' here denote rights held by collectivities rather than by individuals.[2] In saying this, and in making my claims, I use the term 'collectivity' in a specific sense. A *set* is a collection of persons that one would identify as a different set if the included persons changed. A *collectivity* is a collection of persons such that one would still identify it as the same collectivity were some or all of the included persons to change (provided some other conditions were met) and such that the included persons properly identify themselves non-trivially as members of this collectivity.[3] It is thus a number of persons gathered together and perceived for at least some purposes as forming a single unit. The corresponding adjective is *collective*.

The term *group* is commonly used for certain kinds of collectivities, those where there is particularly strong member identification. The term is typically applied to collectivities such as ethnic, national, religious, and linguistic groups. I shall generally use the term 'collectivity' so as to avoid particularistic connotations, though other theorists have used the term 'group' and I may do so for fluidity in discussing their views. *Community*, likewise, may seem like a potentially loaded term; however, in chapter two, I will analyse the property of *community* present in certain collectivities, developing an account of collectivities that have responsibilities and thus a capacity for rights. I will thus sometimes call collectivities of

Butterworths 2004) 193ff (using group rights in explicating Canadian constitutional law); V Van Dyke *Human Rights, Ethnicity, and Discrimination* (Westport, Greenwood 1985) 213–15 (identifying factors behind ascription of group rights in various legal contexts).

[2] *Cf* P Jones 'Human Rights, Group Rights, and Peoples' Rights' (1999) 21 *Human Rights Quarterly* 80, 84–86 (using the terms differently, with the term 'corporate rights' referring to those held by the group itself).

[3] *Cf* R Bhargava, 'The Majority-minority Syndrome and Muslim Personal Law in India', in M Seymour (ed) *The Fate of the Nation-State* (Kingston, McGill-Queen's University Press, 2004) 327, 333–36.

the sort under discussion *communities*. I will also be particularly interested in something I will call the *Community Conditions*, the moral conditions enunciated in Part II for collectivities to hold rights legitimately.

Many collectivities stand between individuals and the larger political community, in forms as diverse as families, cultural and religious groups, and trade unions or corporations, so an argument that some of these collectivities have moral rights adds importantly to our understanding. Although one can identify some already-existing collectivities, my argument will not refer exclusively to pre-existing collectivities. In Part II, I will turn to evaluate what collectivities do or could hold rights legitimately – including with some reference to membership control, thereby envisioning possible alterations to existing collectivities. This book thus seeks to make a general case.

II. CONTEXT OF THIS ARGUMENT

The project in this book develops a case that has not been made at sufficient length. Although numerous theorists' works have contained stray references to group rights or collective rights,[4] relatively few have developed their analysis further,[5] despite a gradually growing literature attentive to related issues. Joseph Carens has described an appealing ideal of evenhandedness between groups, to which I will return at a later stage of the argument, but he has also explicitly acknowledged that he has not offered a full theory of how to apply this principle in conjunction with other relevant

[4] For three examples, see: R Dworkin *Taking Rights Seriously* (London, Duckworth, 1978) 82 ('Arguments of principle justify a political decision by showing that the decision respects or secures some individual or group right') 91n; J Finnis, *Aquinas: Moral, Political, and Legal Theory* (Oxford, Oxford University Press, 1998) VI.2 n10 (referring to the property rights of 'particular individuals or groups'), VII.7 n127 (referring to control of non-basic goods by '*private* persons and groups', seemingly adding the 'groups' element to the quote from Aquinas under discussion); JW Harris 'Human Rights and Mythical Beasts' (2004) 120 *Law Quarterly Review* 428, 428 ('A person, group, corporation, people or state is said to have a right'). *Cf* DG Newman 'Collective Interests and Collective Rights' (2004) 49 *American Journal of Jurisprudence* 127, 127.

[5] Four notable book-length works skirting the topic have left many questions unanswered: M Galenkamp *Individualism Versus Collectivism: The Concept of Collective Rights*, 2nd edn (Rotterdam, Gouda Quint, 1998) (in this second edition, abandoning any argument for collective moral rights, largely based on practical difficulties with collective legal rights); N López Calera *¿Hay derechos colectivos? Individualidad y socialidad en la teoriá de los derechos* (Barcelona, Ariel, 2000) (mostly summarizing related literature); D Ingram *Group Rights: Reconciling Equality and Difference* (Lawrence, University Press of Kansas, 2001) (raising interesting issues but without a fully developed general theoretical framework); JM Valadez *Deliberative Democracy, Political Legitimacy, and Self-Determination in Multicultural Societies* (Boulder, Westview, 2001) (making an argument within the proper approach to deliberative democracy, not developing a wider account of collective rights). Collections of short works that inherently make points limited by the length of the pieces they contain include: (1991) 4 *Canadian Journal of Law & Jurisprudence* 2 (special issue on collective rights); (1994) 4 *Lekton* 1 (special issue edited by Daniel Weinstock); J Baker (ed), *Group Rights* (Toronto, University of Toronto Press, 1994); C Sistare, L May and L Francis (eds) *Groups and Group Rights* (Lawrence, University Press of Kansas, 2001); K de Feyter and G Pavlakos (eds) *The Tension Between Group Rights and Human Rights: A Multidisciplinary Approach* (Oxford, Hart Publishing, 2008); P Jones (ed), *Group Rights* (Aldershot, Ashgate, 2009) (the Jones collection reprinting a number of classic articles in the area, including my 'Collective Interests and Collective Rights' (n 4)).

principles.[6] Bhikhu Parekh (whose view on the point is also adopted by Tariq Modood[7]) has stated some moral principles for collective rights, to which I will return in some significant agreement, but his account based on cultural diversity does not justify the specific restraints that he puts on collective rights[8] and thereby calls for further discussion on how to ground a general account of collective rights. Anna Moltchanova's recent book discusses in detail some issues related to group rights in more general terms and will be an interesting reference point in parts of my argument but does not ultimately provide a general theory since she chooses to focus more narrowly on issues of national self-determination.[9]

Indeed, one can describe an underdeveloped literature on group rights despite the theoretical attention the highly prominent writings of Will Kymlicka have drawn to related issues. Despite occasional misunderstandings otherwise, Kymlicka has actually proceeded based on a refusal to analyse collective rights in the sense of rights actually held by groups, as opposed to his model of 'group-differentiated rights' held by members of groups.[10]

Kymlicka has been more concerned to develop a liberal egalitarian justification for multicultural policies, and his work has spawned a whole field of writing on 'liberal multiculturalism', which Kymlicka became ready at one point to assert had become a 'consensus' position.[11] Writers like Anne Phillips took up this position, adapted it to additional concerns about groups affected by multiculturalist policies, and developed visions of multicultural politics focused on the rights of individuals.[12] However, both security issues and other shifts in thinking have led some now to propose even that we are in an era of 'post-multiculturalism'.[13] The

[6] JH Carens, *Culture, Citizenship, and Community: A Contextual Exploration of Justice as Evenhandedness* (Oxford, Oxford University Press, 2000) 12–14.

[7] See T Modood, *Multicultural Politics: Racism, Ethnicity and Muslims in Britain* (Minneapolis, University of Minnesota Press, 2005) 171–73.

[8] See eg B Parekh, *Rethinking Multiculturalism: Cultural Diversity and Political Theory* (London, Macmillan, 2000) 213–18

[9] See A Moltchanova, *National Self-Determination and Justice in Multinational States* (Heidelberg, Springer, 2009).

[10] W Kymlicka *Multicultural Citizenship* (Oxford, Clarendon, 1995) 35; W Kymlicka 'Individual and Community Rights' in J Baker (ed) *Group Rights* (Toronto, University of Toronto Press, 1994) 18. *Cf* W Kymlicka *Liberalism, Community and Culture* (Oxford, Clarendon, 1989) 138–39.

[11] W Kymlicka, *Politics in the Vernacular: Nationalism, Multiculturalism, and Citizenship* (Oxford, Oxford University Press, 2001) 39. *Cf* N Glazer, *We Are All Multiculturalists Now* (Cambridge MA, Harvard University Press, 1997). See also A Xanthaki, *Indigenous Rights and United Nations Standards: Self-determination, Culture, Land* (Cambridge, Cambridge University Press, 2007) 27ff (discussing encouragement of multiculturalism policies in international law).

[12] See A Phillips, *Multiculturalism without Culture* (Princeton, Princeton University Press, 2007) 162–66. See also G Mahajan, *Identities and Rights: Aspects of Liberal Democracy in India* (New Delhi, Oxford University Press, 2001) 179 (advocating the implementation of group rights for egalitarian purposes to counter pre-existing patterns of discrimination).

[13] *Cf* W Kymlicka, *Multicultural Odysseys: Navigating the New International Politics of Diversity* (Oxford, Oxford University Press, 2007) 119–21, 191; Christopher McCrudden, 'Multiculturalism, Freedom of Religion, Equality, and the British Constitution: the *JFS* case considered' (2011) *International Journal of Constitutional Law* (forthcoming). For an important and more specific discussion of the implications of terrorism concerns for various rights policies, see AN Guiora, *Freedom from Religion: Rights and National Security* (Oxford, Oxford University Press, 2009).

argument I make is not based on egalitarian concerns but simply the just claims of groups, and it is not specifically related to multiculturalism, although it has implications for which multicultural claims should be supported and which rejected.

Kymlicka's general approach, I might add, has held significant sway over other authors who have stated more general arguments on group rights, and they have not broken from Kymlicka's assumptions in ways that it first appeared they might. Eric Mitnick's writing in the American context follows on Kymlicka's idea of 'group-differentiated rights', with these rights then held largely by individuals.[14] The argument of Neus Torbsico Casals is similarly ultimately framed to a significant extent in terms of Kymlicka's arguments (with some reconciliation with arguments of Charles Taylor).[15] Michel Seymour's impressive recent French-language account of group rights similarly remains tied to some of Kymlicka's key assumptions in terms of being committed to an explicitly 'liberal' account in which a right-holding group must specifically advance its members' freedom[16] – in addition to excluding many groups from attention – although I will return to discuss Seymour further periodically throughout the book, for his work contains many subtleties and important arguments.

In a bibliographical essay, Linda Cardinal wrote several years ago that '[t]here are still no comprehensive studies of the anthropological, historical, legal, philosophical, or social and political foundations of collective rights'.[17] Her claim has remained surprisingly accurate even in the context of additional writing in recent years.[18] The theoretical gap in present understandings is most notable in the specific lack of theoretical analysis probing the existence of moral rights held by groups. As Eric Posner and Adrian Vermeule note, widespread beliefs that there are collective moral rights have received 'few philosophically sophisticated defenses'.[19]

Certain reasons irrelevant to the truth of the claims may have discouraged theorists from offering these defences and exploring fully the possibility of collective rights. At an international level, the formulation of rights theories has taken place against the backdrop of rights instruments framed after international conflict that seemed spurred on by the claims of national groups.[20] There has also

[14] E Mitnick, *Rights, Groups and Self-Invention: Group-Differentiated Rights in Liberal Theory* (Aldershot, Ashgate, 2006).

[15] NT Casals, *Group Rights as Human Rights: A Liberal Approach to Multiculturalism* (Dordrecht, Springer, 2006), especially 148ff.

[16] M Seymour, *De la Tolérance à la Reconnaissance: Une théorie libérale des droits collectifs* (Montréal, Boréal, 2008).

[17] L Cardinal, 'Collective Rights in Canada: A Critical and Bibliographical Study' (2000) 12 *National Journal of Constitutional Law* 165, 165.

[18] See DG Newman, 'Recent Work: Collective Rights' (2007) 48 *Philosophical Books* 221.

[19] EA Posner and A Vermeule 'Reparations for Slavery and Other Historical Injustices' (2003) 103 *Columbia Law Review* 689, 707.

[20] A Addis 'Individualism, Communitarianism, and the Rights of Ethnic Minorities' (1992) 67 *Notre Dame Law Review* 615, 638. See also L-A Thio, *Managing Babel: The International Legal Protection of Minorities in the Twentieth Century* (Leiden, Martinus Nijhoff Publishers, 2005).

arguably been resistance to group rights based on perceptions that collective rights manifested preferences of non-Western states during the Cold War.[21] And there have even been suggestions that other political agendas have affected discourse on collective rights in certain politicised contexts; for instance, some in Canada see reluctance to recognise collective aboriginal rights as partly motivated by a wish to sustain denials of collective rights to the Québecois.[22] Analogously, some have suggested that generalised protections for minority rights were left out of the League of Nations system in significant part because Australia and New Zealand wished to avoid international scrutiny of their treatment of their indigenous populations.[23] States have sometimes, conversely, supported particular group rights provisions in the hopes of causing problems for other states.[24] This book, however, is a project of moral argument rather than such crass *realpolitik*. Moreover, it is not a project in intellectual history, so I am not concerned with analysing various possible historical explanatory propositions here, although issues about collective rights warrant the sort of interdisciplinary attention they are just starting to receive in meaningful form.[25] My questions pertain, rather, to what can truthfully be said from a theoretical perspective about collective moral rights.

There can be no doubting the importance of such an endeavour. Issues about collective rights pose challenging, important questions about how to run a community. To the extent theoretical analysis of collective rights remains underdeveloped, our answers to important political questions remain similarly underdeveloped.[26] Even some theorists who accept collective moral rights in principle have suggested caution with collective legal rights in the absence of a solid account of and argument for the existence of collective moral rights.[27] At the same time, claims about 'collective rights' are continuously raised in political debates, and courts engage in morally impregnated reasoning that similarly raises issues of collective rights.

I will return later in the book to some domestic law examples, but notably, developments in international law over recent decades have witnessed the emergence of significant new protections of collective rights.[28] Some such develop-

[21] SJ Anaya, 'Superpower Attitudes Toward Indigenous Peoples and Group Rights' (1999) 93 *American Society of International Law Proceedings* 251, 256–57.

[22] *Cf* Paul Chartrand 'On Further Thought: Reflections on the Last Two Decades in Canada' (keynote at the Centre of Canadian Studies conference, Edinburgh 6 May 2005).

[23] Thio, (n 20) 59.

[24] A Erueti, 'The International Labour Organisation and the Internationalisation of the Concept of Indigenous Peoples', in S Allen and A Xanthaki (eds), *Reflections on the UN Declaration on the Rights of Indigenous Peoples* (Oxford, Hart Publishing, 2011).

[25] See eg de Feyter and Pavlakos (n 5).

[26] *Cf* N Miscevic *Nationalism and Beyond: Introducing Moral Debate About Values* (Budapest, Central European University Press, 2001) 278.

[27] For example, J Waldron, 'Taking Group Rights Carefully' in G Huscroft and P Rishworth, *Litigating Rights: Perspectives from Domestic and International Law* (Oxford, Hart Publishing, 2002) 206.

[28] A Xanthaki, 'Multiculturalism and International Law: Discussing Universal Standards' (2010) 32 *Human Rights Quarterly* 21; Xanthaki, *Indigenous Rights and United Nations Standards* (n 11).

ments have been in regional human rights contexts.[29] At the broader international level, the recent United Nations Declaration on the Rights of Indigenous Peoples[30] explicitly refers to collective rights.[31] It is in this dimension that the Declaration especially marks a significant break from past approaches that continued to see rights as held only by individuals.[32] As Alexandra Xanthaki put it, 'the whole essence of the draft Declaration is the recognition of indigenous collective rights'.[33] There were some collective rights provisions removed in reaching the final approved Declaration,[34] and there arise now complex issues from the recognition of collective rights of indigenous communities but not of other minority communities.[35] But the Declaration nonetheless marks a clear move in international law to a recognition of collective rights actually held by groups.

Kymlicka's moral argument for 'group-differentiated' rights held by individuals rather than collective moral rights held by groups has both been consistent with much policy thinking and had a real impact on policy thinking. It is not entirely coincidental that many protections of minority rights through even recent times have not identified groups as rights-holders but continued to adhere to the recognition of rights held by individuals as members of groups.[36] However, collective rights have in fact attained recognition in international law, and claims by some states otherwise are demonstrably false.[37]

At the same time, leading theoretical writing, at least of a certain school of thought, continues to reject the possibility of collective moral rights. James Griffin's recent book on rights rejects the possibility outright, reiterating the claim that collective rights must be reducible to individual rights if they are to be of any value.[38] Pavlos Eleftheriadis, in mentioning the Human Rights Council resolutions

[29] Apart from the more obvious Banjul Charter (African Charter on Human and Peoples' Rights, adopted 27 June 1981, OAU Doc CAB/LEG/67/3 rev 5, 21 (1982) *International Legal Materials* 58), consider even regional developments in Europe: R O'Connell, 'Let's Talk: Dealing with Difference in Human Rights Law' in K de Feyter and G Pavlakos (eds) (n 5) 131, 143ff.

[30] Declaration on the Rights of Indigenous Peoples, GA Res 61/295, UN Doc A/RES/47/1 (2007).

[31] For a wonderfully rich and insight-laden collection on the Declaration, see Allen and Xanthaki (eds) (n 24). For my previous discussion of state concerns with the prospect of entrenching collective rights in the Declaration, see DG Newman, 'Theorizing Collective Indigenous Rights' (2007) 31 *American Indian Law Review* 273.

[32] R Stavenhagen, 'Making the Declaration Work: The Challenge Ahead' in Allen and Xanthaki (eds) (n 24); A Carmen, 'International Indian Treaty Council Report from the Battle Field – the Struggle for the Declaration' in C Charters and R Stavenhagen (eds) *Making the Declaration Work: The United Nations Declaration on the Rights of Indigenous Peoples* (Copenhagen, Indigenous Work Group for Indigenous Affairs, 2009) 86, 86 and 93.

[33] Xanthaki, *Indigenous Rights and United Nations Standards* (n 11) 107.

[34] On these negotiations, see eg ibid, 107–109; DG Newman, 'Africa and the United Nations Declaration on the Rights of Indigenous Peoples' in S Dersso (ed) *Perspectives on Minority and Indigenous Peoples' Rights in Africa* (Pretoria, Pretoria University Law Press, 2010).

[35] See eg Kymlicka, *Multicultural Odysseys* (n 13) 274–91; W Kymlicka, 'Beyond the Indigenous/Minority Dichotomy?' in Allen and Xanthaki (eds) (n 24); K Knop, *Diversity and Self-Determination in International Law* (Cambridge, Cambridge University Press, 2002) 246.

[36] See generally Thio (n 20) 120–75. See also Xanthaki, *Indigenous Rights and United Nations Standards* (n 11) 22ff; Xanthaki 'Multiculturalism and International Law' (n 28).

[37] See Xanthaki, *Indigenous Rights and United Nations Standards* (n 11) 107.

[38] J Griffin, *On Human Rights* (Oxford, Oxford University Press, 2008) 256.

of recent years supporting rights by religious groups not to be defamed, suggests that it is 'hard to understand what they [the advocates of such resolutions] are saying.'[39] The latter claim of not even being able to understand why such protections would be sought is striking in the context of a long history of defamation of particular religious figures so as to demonise particular religions.[40] A fully developed theory of collective rights has the potential to enhance understandings about dimensions of political morality that some schools of theory currently find hard even to comprehend.

Collective rights demand our attention. Because issues about collective rights are challenging and complex, however, the aspiration within the book is explicitly limited to addressing a set of theoretical issues – without claiming to demonstrate a complete application to specific political problems calling into play many complex empirical factors. In doing so, the hope is to provide a framework for detailed work addressing specific political and legal problems that I invite readers to pursue further.

In the fifth section of this chapter, I will set out the full structure of the book. However, before doing so, it is worth establishing some boundaries on the task and defending the approach against Kymlicka's rival claims, which have been tremendously influential with policymakers,[41] and for which Kymlicka once attempted to claim an 'emerging consensus'.[42] The third section of the chapter defines the main boundaries and assumptions of the book. Although Kymlicka will not exit our stage in the first scenes of this chapter, I will nonetheless offer in the fourth section of the chapter initial reasons to doubt the adequacy of his theoretical approach and to prefer an approach more like the one that I shall develop.

III. BOUNDARIES AND ASSUMPTIONS

If it is to be manageable, the task at hand must be specific and limited. It is therefore necessary to set certain boundaries and to set out the key assumptions behind the argument. These boundaries and assumptions pertain to the general nature of rights and the basis of moral concern.

In order to concentrate efforts where they are most needed, one can exclude any general exploration of the nature of rights; I will instead assume Joseph Raz's widely utilised interest theory of rights. As Raz describes it, a right exists when an interest is sufficient to ground a duty.[43] On this conception, '[r]ights ground

[39] P Eleftheriadis, 'Human Rights as Legal Rights' (2010) 1 *Transnational Legal Theory* 371, 389.

[40] *Cf* Modood (n 7) 120.

[41] See eg United Nations Development Programme *Human Development Report 2004: Cultural Liberty in Today's Diverse World* (New York, UNDP, 2004) iii; DG Newman 'Liberal Multiculturalism and Will Kymlicka's Uneasy Relation with Religious Pluralism' (2003) 64 *Bijdragen* 265, 266–67.

[42] Kymlicka *Politics in the Vernacular* (n 11) 39.

[43] J Raz, *The Morality of Freedom* (Oxford, Clarendon, 1986) 166. A parallel argument could be structured within a 'will theory', but I will not analyse that argument at length in this book.

requirements for action in the interest of other beings',[44] thus making assertions of rights 'typically intermediate conclusions in arguments from ultimate values to duties'.[45] Although I will later modify Raz's description of rights slightly, I will not alter the main substance of Raz's theory of rights as based on interests. That said, while I employ Raz's definition of rights and draw further on his work, I will differ from him on the argument for collective rights, the use of the term 'collective rights', and the conclusions on what collective rights exist. No reader should understand the book as merely expositing particular theorists' views; it is, rather, an original argument for collective moral rights.

Inherent in this definition of rights is their special importance. Rights are not ordinary interests but those that, because of their particular weight, ground a duty. In other words, they have a special force distinct from ordinary interests. To argue for the existence of collective rights is to argue that at least some collective claims share this special force. Ronald Dworkin would presumably describe them as 'trumps',[46] although even within Dworkin's conception, trumps need only rule out some other reasons, not all, so there can nonetheless be limits on rights.[47] I will turn in Part II of the book to analyse conflicts of rights.

My argument is an explicitly moral one. A *moral right* is an entitlement or justified claim whose justification does not depend on whether any legal or political system recognises the right.[48] A *legal right* is an entitlement or justified claim that a legal system recognises according to the correct interpretation of its own rules and principles,[49] though a legal system, or actors within it, may fail to recognise a legal right in particular circumstances. Analogously, a *political right* is an entitlement or justified claim that other governmental systems recognise according to the correct interpretation of the rules and principles governing them (for example, conventions followed in legislative deliberations).

The present argument is for *collective moral rights*. While collective moral rights might form part of an argument for certain collective legal rights, the relationship between the two concepts is not straightforward. As Peter Jones notes, some collective moral rights could find expression in individual legal rights: the moral rights of an indigenous collectivity to fish certain waters may be expressed in individuals' legal rights to fish.[50] Of course, collective legal rights may also have

[44] Ibid, 180.

[45] Ibid, 181. This nature of rights makes possible that they will enable a common culture 'around shared intermediate conclusions, in spite of a great degree of haziness and disagreement concerning ultimate values'.

[46] In Ronald Dworkin's alluring metaphor, they trump other interests: Dworkin, *Taking Rights Seriously* (n 4) xi. Raz denies that this element of Dworkin's account is compatible with his (*Morality of Freedom* (n 43) 166n). We need not resolve the interpretive questions here.

[47] For example, Dworkin *Taking Rights Seriously* (n 4) 191–92.

[48] This usage is aligned with Finnis's conception of a natural right: J Finnis, *Natural Law and Natural Rights* (Oxford, Clarendon, 1980) 198–99.

[49] Legal rights are those following from a correct interpretation of the legal system. Accounts differ on whether this correct interpretation inherently has a moral element. The definition accommodates both sides of that vexed debate.

[50] P Jones 'Group Rights and Group Oppression' (1999) 7 *Journal of Political Philosophy* 353, 355.

other justifications altogether, whether to promote equality or to promote diversity in certain spheres of endeavour.[51] Though collective legal rights serve as interesting examples throughout, this book seeks primarily to develop the conditions under which collective moral rights exist. It does not seek to determine the appropriate legal expression of these rights in every circumstance, although Part III turns to certain principled issues concerning the translation of collective moral rights into legal rights. Given the present focus, unless the context dictates otherwise, use of the term 'rights' without an adjective will refer to *moral rights*.

I will also employ another thesis well-articulated by, though not unique to, Raz. This is what Raz calls the *humanistic principle*, which says simply that it is individual well-being that is of 'ultimate concern'.[52] The 'ultimate concern' at issue, of course, is that within the realm of what can be understood through philosophical means and bears no anti-theistic implications.[53] Other theorists presume similar principles, such as in Philip Pettit's 'personalist assumption' that 'the relevant constituency for judging the normative adequacy of political institutions is human beings'[54] or John Broome's 'principle of personal good' that 'one alternative cannot be better than another unless it is better for someone'.[55] Such a principle is not uncontested, for it is at odds with a claim that equality is of intrinsic value even if this implies that there is something better about a world where all are equal but worse off – a claim that some theorists do maintain.[56] But my argument will nonetheless proceed based on the humanistic principle, endeavouring to show how this narrow grounding can support a substantial theory of collective rights.

Other theorists, notably Kymlicka, have theorised on related matters based on a broader set of assumptions of the sort sometimes categorised within *liberalism*, a broad body of thought with specific value placed on individual autonomy and equality.[57] They have done so even when some of the groups whose rights they purport to advance claim not to share fully liberal values. Reacting to the possibility some Canadian aboriginal groups would disagree with the manner in which he advances their claims, Kymlicka suggests any argument not firmly in the liberal camp is risky. He disparages the actual arguments of aboriginal groups as 'not very strong *politically*, for they do not confront liberal fears about minority rights'[58] and rapidly defers to a characterisation of the *realpolitik* in which '[f]or better or worse, it

[51] Parekh, *Rethinking Multiculturalism* (n 8) 263.

[52] *Cf* Raz, *Morality of Freedom* (n 43) 194.

[53] *Cf* Finnis *Natural Law and Natural Rights* (n 48) 371–410 (discussing relations of human understanding and common good to Eternal Law and God).

[54] P Pettit, *The Common Mind: An Essay on Psychology, Society and Politics* (Oxford, Oxford University Press, 1993) 287.

[55] J Broome, *Weighing Goods: Equality, Uncertainty and Time* (Oxford, Basil Blackwell, 1991) 131. *Cf* also J Finnis, 'The Priority of Persons' in J Horder (ed) *Oxford Essays on Jurisprudence*, 4th series (Oxford, Oxford University Press, 2000) 1.

[56] For example, L Temkin 'Equality, Priority, and the Levelling Down Objection' in M Clayton and A Williams (eds) *The Ideal of Equality* (London, MacMillan, 2000) 126, 155.

[57] W Kymlicka, *Contemporary Political Philosophy: An Introduction*, 2nd edn (Oxford, Oxford University Press, 2002) 53ff.

[58] Kymlicka, *Liberalism, Community and Culture* (n 10) 153.

is predominantly non-aboriginal judges and politicians who have the ultimate power to protect and enforce aboriginal rights, and so it is important to find a justification of them that such people can recognize and understand'.[59] This approach does not always constrain his conclusions. For example, although he refuses to advance the substantive claims of some aboriginal theorists that aboriginal governments should not be subject to the *Canadian Charter of Rights*,[60] he nonetheless recognises an argument that the national judicial system has a history that makes it ill-suited to decide aboriginal claims, which may alter appropriate jurisdiction without departing from his general principles.[61]

My analysis will not prefer the alleged theoretical position of those presently holding power. My concern will be with what stands up to reason in the hopes that reason can speak to power. My argument does not deny the value of autonomy, although it also recognises the value of other human interests. While not opposed to liberalism, its arguments are thus not beholden to any liberal litmus test but build simply from the narrower foundation of the humanistic principle. One important result is an escape from liberalism's common problems with religious groups. Parekh accurately notes that '[l]iberals in general, and European liberals in particular, have long been troubled by religion'[62] and either disregarded it or treated it as a solely individual matter.[63] Indeed, liberal-oriented theories of group rights have often either excluded religious groups from having rights claims[64] or simply declined to understand religious claims.[65] Another significant result, perhaps even a broader implication, is an accessibility of the premises of the argument to a less restricted set of those concerned with rights questions, hopefully even including some of those beginning from non-Western perspectives on rights.[66] A theoretical account not taking on all the baggage of liberalism thus has important promise. I turn now to critique explicitly Kymlicka's use of principles going beyond the humanistic principle.

IV. INADEQUACY OF KYMLICKA'S THEORY OF GROUP-DIFFERENTIATED RIGHTS

Kymlicka's main development of the theoretical bases for his approach avoids talk of 'collective rights', preferring to employ the concept of 'group-differentiated

[59] Ibid, 154.

[60] Kymlicka, *Multicultural Citizenship* (n 10) 38–39.

[61] Ibid, 39–40.

[62] B Parekh, *A New Politics of Identity: Political Principles for an Interdependent World* (London, Palgrave Macmillan, 2008) 113.

[63] Parekh, *Rethinking Multiculturalism* (n 8) 168.

[64] See eg Seymour, *De la Tolérance à la Reconnaissance* (n 16) 487ff.

[65] *Cf* Modood (n 7) 141, 150; Newman 'Will Kymlicka's Uneasy Relation with Religious Pluralism' (n 41).

[66] For a particularly pointed recent comment on the dangers of parochialism in human rights discourse, see Daniel A Bell, *Beyond Liberal Democracy: Political Thinking for an East Asian Context* (Princeton, Princeton University Press, 2006).

rights' as rights held by members of groups on account of their group membership.[67] He then argues for such group-differentiated rights on grounds of equality: 'certain collective rights can be defended as appropriate measures for the rectification of an inequality in circumstances which affects aboriginal people collectively',[68] with the argument obviously also potentially applying to other non-aboriginal cultural groups. Such statements, of course, are arguments for legal rights that advance a particular goal, since a moral right is not a 'measure'. Kymlicka's arguments, then, are essentially for legal rights based on a desire to avoid adverse impacts on the situation of some individuals who are in different cultural groups.

My approach differs from Kymlicka's in two principal ways. First, Kymlicka, despite his famed treatment of 'group-differentiated rights', specifically questions the development of any general theory of collective rights, whereas later chapters in this book seek to develop just such a general theory. The scope of the theory matters because, just to cite one instance, Kymlicka's theory is minority-focused and not able to recognise the rights of majorities, as a full-fledged theory of collective rights can.[69] Secondly, Kymlicka ultimately narrows the object of equality behind the rights he advocates to an object concerned solely with individual autonomy, whereas later chapters in this book will use the broader humanistic principle. Although Kymlicka's arguments will recur elsewhere, it is possible even at this stage to tentatively reject the constraints his theory would impose. Specifically, there are strong reasons to reject his suggestion that 'collective rights' are not an examinable category and his claim to have identified the applicable normative distinction for analysing groups' claims.

First, Kymlicka has objected to study of collective rights in any integrated form, stating that collective rights constitute a 'large and heterogeneous' category and that such rights 'have little in common, and it is important not to lump the idea of group-differentiated citizenship with the myriad of other issues that arise under the heading of "collective rights".'[70] There are, of course, variations amongst different collective rights that might require more contextual arguments.[71] But this fact does not vitiate all general argument on collective rights. Opponents reject collective rights *en masse* on conceptual grounds,[72] so a defence against these charges is appropriate and warranted. Kymlicka's decision not to deal with collective rights renders his account unequipped to deal with such objections.

[67] See eg Kymlicka, *Multicultural Citizenship* (n 10) 35.

[68] Kymlicka, *Liberalism, Community and Culture* (n 10) 194.

[69] *Cf* M Seymour, 'Collective Rights in Multi-nation States: From Ethical Individualism to the Law of Peoples' in M Seymour (ed) *The Fate of the Nation-State* (Kingston and Montreal, McGill-Queen's University Press, 2004) 105 at 112.

[70] Ibid, 35; Kymlicka 'Individual and Community Rights' (n 10) 18.

[71] *Cf* J Spinner-Halev 'Land, Culture and Justice: A Framework for Group Rights and Recognition' (2000) 8 *Journal of Political Philosophy* 319 (recognizing the contextual role of historical agreements and other considerations).

[72] For example, J Narveson 'Collective Rights?' (1991) 4 *Canadian Journal of Law and Jurisprudence* 329, 345; M Hartney 'Some Confusions Concerning Collective Rights' (1991) 4 *Canadian Journal of Law and Jurisprudence* 293, 312.

Kymlicka has made a strategic decision to take a different tack, and his so-called objection is actually an explanation of why he argues for certain kinds of rights without using the concept of collective rights.

If one takes the statement as more, as a challenge to the concept of collective rights, then arguments emerge against the challenge. At the very least, the statement would prejudge, without justification, the issue of whether it is possible to develop a theory of collective rights that shows their common foundation, when some of the opposition itself implies common issues at stake. In answering such opponents through a theory of collective rights, the common issues are apparent. The problems at the outset of this chapter raised common issues about whether collectivities hold rights and on what basis, and, if so, what principles determine which groups hold which rights. Although Kymlicka would discourage the endeavour at the outset, any evaluation of these claims depends ultimately on elaborating a more developed theory of collective moral rights that faces up to the generalised criticisms. To the extent that such rights are heterogenous, they are no more so than individual rights, and much writing has sought to analyse the justifications of individual rights. Collective rights deserve no less.

Kymlicka has articulated a concept of 'group-differentiated rights' – certain forms of special rights for minority cultures,[73] or, more specifically, certain rights held by individuals because they are members of a cultural group[74] – as meeting the challenges at issue and offering appropriate normative guidelines. There are, however, reasons to doubt the adequacy of his approach and conclude that our analysis must go in the direction Kymlicka has resisted. To see this, it is worth focusing on his important distinction between 'external protections' and 'internal restrictions'. Kymlicka rejects general talk of collective rights partly because such talk seems to support claims to internal restrictions,[75] so the distinction is closely interlinked with his approach generally.

In Kymlicka's approach, *external protections* are 'the claim[s] of a group against the larger society', whereas *internal restrictions* are 'the claim[s] of a group against its own members'.[76] Sometimes, these descriptions of the concepts lapse casually into internal restrictions as concerned with preserving the 'cultural purity' of the group against those seeking to revise elements of its traditions[77] or slightly polemical descriptions of protections 'intended to protect the group from *external decisions*' as opposed to restrictions 'intended to protect the group from the destabilizing impact of *internal dissent*'.[78] But this lapsing leaves unexplained why these particular intentions are necessary to the characterisation of a particular protection/restriction. Given that the polemical categories cease to be jointly exhaustive (and may not be mutually exclusive), they become less helpful, meaning that they

[73] Kymlicka, *Multicultural Citizenship* (n 10) 6.
[74] For example, ibid, 34–36; Kymlicka, *Liberalism, Community and Culture* (n 10) 139–40.
[75] Kymlicka, *Multicultural Citizenship* (n 10) 46–47.
[76] Ibid, 35.
[77] Kymlicka, *Politics in the Vernacular* (n 11) 60.
[78] Kymlicka, *Multicultural Citizenship* (n 10) 35 (emphasis in original).

might be good politics but are problematic theorizing. We thus ought to take something close to the non-polemical original statement as the key distinction.

Let us endeavour to be clear as to the alleged meaning of the distinction. Kymlicka claims that the distinction has both empirically descriptive and normatively prescriptive dimensions. He maintains, first, that groups generally do not seek legal powers to impose internal restrictions. Although he mentions some counterexamples, he says that '[m]ost of the demands for group-specific rights made by ethnic and national groups in Western democracies are for external protections' and that other sorts of claims have been rejected.[79] So, the distinction is partly an empirical claim as to what sorts of claims groups make, a characterisation of what is theoretically at issue. One of Kymlicka's acknowledged counterexamples is that of claims by the British Muslim community to apply Islamic family law. Exactly this sort of group claim has been recognised in various jurisdictions[80] and is under significant current debate.[81] Moreover, group claims to some measure of jurisdictional authority are a significant issue in many contexts, with many examples of recognition of some jurisdiction for a different legal tradition in some measure so that a particular minority community may maintain its identity.[82] One might have some uncertainty from the outset about the empirical use of the distinction, but I will return to this point in a different way after explicating the normative sense of the distinction.

Kymlicka maintains, secondly, that this distinction maps onto the normative acceptability of group decisions. The distinction between external protections and internal restrictions derives fundamentally from Kymlicka's conception of legal rights held by groups being justified by the group's role in providing a cultural context of choice grounding members' autonomy.[83] His theory grounds protections for groups in a certain form of equalisation payment for members of groups that face obstacles in providing culturally-based freedom. Indeed, he refers explicitly to 'certain collective rights' as 'appropriate measures for the rectification of an inequality in circumstances which affects aboriginal people collectively'.[84] Note that he is discussing legal rights held by groups; moral rights could not be described as 'measures'.

As a result, Kymlicka accepts only cultural protections consistent with the advancement of individual freedom. As he puts it, 'the very reasons we have to

[79] Ibid, 42.

[80] See eg JL-C Neo, 'The Protection of Minorities and the Constitution: A Judicious Balance?' in L-A Thio and KYL Tan, *Evolution of a Revolution: Forty Years of the Singapore Constitution* (London, Routledge-Cavendish, 2009) 234, 254–57 (discussing the protection given to Islamic family law in Singapore); G Mahajan, 'Indian Exceptionalism or Indian Model: Negotiating Cultural Diversity and Minority Rights in a Democratic Nation-State' in W Kymlicka and B He, *Multiculturalism in Asia* (Oxford, Oxford University Press, 2005) 288; R Bhargava, 'The Majority-minority Syndrome and Muslim Personal Law in India' in Seymour (ed) (n 69) 327, 334ff..

[81] See eg R Ahdar and N Aroney (eds) *Shari'a in the West* (Oxford, Oxford University Press, 2010).

[82] One historical example would be the British decision to allow Lower Canada (Quebec) to maintain its French civil law tradition.

[83] Kymlicka, *Liberalism, Community and Culture* (n 10) 166ff.

[84] Ibid, 194.

support external protections are also reasons to oppose internal restrictions'.[85] Kymlicka initially drew the distinction between 'external protections' and 'internal restrictions' in *Liberalism, Community and Culture* while discussing what he termed 'theocratic American Indian bands'.[86] There, he was prepared to acknowledge 'difficult questions' about the acceptability of internal restrictions where (on his account, in rare cases) a particular community 'really would disintegrate without restricting religious liberty'.[87] He also referred, unusually, to acceptable temporary internal restrictions in an Indonesian tribe whose children jumped off a cliff after viewing newly-introduced television programmes.[88]

However, Kymlicka's main later theoretical works have arguably taken a harder line. He has now repeatedly asserted that internal restrictions are unjustified and that instances where they could be justified do not arise.[89] In one sense, then, one might read him as having sharpened the distinction. At the same time, Kymlicka has also arguably blurred the distinction differently. Now implying that no internal restrictions could be acceptable, he also states that external protections 'become illegitimate if, rather than reducing a minority's vulnerability to the power of the larger society, they instead enable a minority to exercise economic or political dominance over some other group',[90] although this latter blurring was always inherent in his basic rationales.[91] Kymlicka thus maintains that 'liberals can and should endorse certain external protections, where they promote fairness between groups, but should reject internal restrictions which limit the right of group members to question and revise traditional authorities and practices'.[92] In this statement, he uses the more polemical description of internal restrictions, so we might take it as either describing all internal restrictions as objectionable or as distinguishing between different kinds of restrictions, again manifesting how the polemical description can be rhetorically powerful but less clear.

Kymlicka offers a rich spectrum of thought whose facets go beyond this liberal egalitarian argument for group-differentiated rights. In writing about what might enable the adoption of his preferred policies at a broader international level, he

[85] Kymlicka, *Multicultural Citizenship* (n 10) 44.

[86] Kymlicka, *Liberalism, Community and Culture* (n 10) 195–96.

[87] Ibid, 198.

[88] Ibid, 170.

[89] Kymlicka, *Multicultural Citizenship* (n 10) 42–44; W Kymlicka *Finding Our Way: Rethinking Ethnocultural Relations in Canada* (Oxford, Oxford University Press, 1998) 62. For other examples, see DG Newman 'Putting Kymlicka in Perspective: Canadian Diversity and Collective Rights' in S Tierney (ed) *Accommodating Cultural Diversity: Contemporary Issues in Theory and Practice* (Aldershot, Ashgate, 2007).

[90] W Kymlicka 'Western Political Theory and Ethnic Relations in Eastern Europe' in W Kymlicka and M Opalski (eds) *Can Liberal Pluralism Be Exported? Western Political Theory and Ethnic Relations in Eastern Europe* (Oxford, Oxford University Press, 2001) 28.

[91] Kymlicka, *Liberalism, Community and Culture* (n 10) 245–52. One complicating factor on the interpretation that he has hardened the distinction, though, is his nuanced discussion of the success of the Quebec language law (Kymlicka, *Politics in the Vernacular* (n 11) 286–88), which we will discuss below. He seems to permit that as an exception to his general theory: Newman, 'Putting Kymlicka in Perspective' (n 89).

[92] Kymlicka, *Multicultural Citizenship* (n 10) 37.

has departed from this main argument and allowed for internal restrictions in some communitarian societies,[93] but this departure does not reflect any general abandonment of the argument that these internal restrictions are morally objectionable.[94] He has been ready to try to defend group legal rights even on purely pragmatic grounds of forestalling violence in contexts where this argument has application.[95] Similarly, some of his more recent writing on related themes now questions the likelihood of broad adoption of his preferred policies,[96] but this work is just good political science and not a reversal of his theoretical argument or the key distinction between external protections and internal restrictions.

We may thus endeavour to bring additional clarity to the distinction to get at what Kymlicka might reasonably have meant by it, or what provides a reasonable interpretation. Obviously, Kymlicka cannot have meant literally that every internally-directed decision is problematic. That a group exercising some powers of governance establishes reasonable traffic rules, say, surely does not impose unacceptable internal restrictions, or the distinction would be untenable and recognise a somewhat amputated vision of group rights that precludes a fostering of shared identities.[97] And some of Kymlicka's language might give rise to a stronger interpretation. For instance, he describes the concern about internal restrictions as arising 'where the basic civil and political liberties of group members are being restricted'.[98] One might adopt an interpretation where 'internal restrictions' include only those restrictions actually infringing individual rights.

However, there are two problems with this approach. First, it is not fully consistent with Kymlicka's text, as several pages after that seemingly helpful description, he refers to all internal taxes (which presumably do not automatically infringe individual rights) as being internal restrictions in his sense.[99] Reading Kymlicka generously, we might, of course, read out that particular statement for the sake of discerning a stronger position. But a second problem arises in that the interpretation under consideration would arguably be circular. A major objective of the distinction is to delineate circumstances in which individual rights, all-things-considered, differ from those one might have envisioned without Kymlicka's insights. After all, external protections similarly reshape individual rights. However, internal restrictions cannot be defined in terms of that which they are meant to help delineate.

This conclusion leaves some uncertainty as to the meaning of the distinction. Can we interpret it based on the references to external protections or internal

[93] W Kymlicka, 'Universal Minority Rights? The Prospects for Consensus' in M Yasutomo, I Fumihiko and S Tetsu (eds), *Universal Minority Rights? A Transnational Approach* (Stuttgart, Franz Steiner Verlag, 2004) 13, 17–18.

[94] W Kymlicka, 'Reply to Commentaries' in Yasutomo, Fumihiko and Testu (eds) (ibid) 105, 114–15.

[95] W Kymlicka, 'Rights to Culture, Autonomy and Participation: The Evolving Basis of Minority Rights in Europe' in OA Payrow Shabani (ed) *Multiculturalism and Law: A Critical Debate* (Cardiff, University of Wales Press, 2007) 235.

[96] Kymlicka, *Multicultural Odysseys* (n 13) 254ff.

[97] *Cf* Michel Seymour, 'Collective Rights in Multi-nation States' (n 69) 112–13, 117–18.

[98] Kymlicka, *Multicultural Citizenship* (n 10) 36.

[99] Ibid, 42.

restrictions as flowing from a 'claim' as against the larger society or against group members?[100] On this phrasing, one might get the sense of a protection or restriction going beyond those that would reasonably exist without the particular justifications giving rise to these claims. In other words, one might interpret internal restrictions and external protections specifically as those group claims going beyond what would be permitted in the absence of justifications developed specifically for internal restrictions or external protections. This reading may still seem somewhat circular, but there is perhaps visible a non-circular conception behind it – that both concern limits on rights, not all-things-considered but as-considered-without-analysis-of-groups. So reading Kymlicka, he claims that there is a fundamental normative schism between external protections that limit ordinary liberal rights as they would be analysed without reference to these considerations and internal restrictions that limit ordinary liberal rights as they would be analysed without reference to these considerations. This interpretation, in some ways, renders the distinction into one speaking to political theory rather than a political theory distinction applicable to political reality. But one might nonetheless proceed and apply it as if offered as a claim concerning reality and see how it fares.

Some theorists, of course, have questioned the precision of the distinction between internal restrictions and external protections. Kymlicka himself admits that measures designed as external protections often have internal implications – if nothing else, in requiring taxation where the protections have a monetary cost.[101] Ayelet Shachar has highlighted other challenges on the distinction's precision, reincarnating the issues raised by Kymlicka's reference in the course of his first enunciation of the distinction to *Santa Clara Pueblo v Martinez*.[102] In that case, the United States Supreme Court upheld the Pueblos' autonomy over membership rules as against challenges that these membership rules discriminated based on sex. Shachar expresses concerns that internal discrimination is rendered into an external protection and thus protected under Kymlicka's distinction,[103] drawing the conclusion that 'the external aspects of multicultural accommodation are not so easily distinguished from the policy's internal impact'.[104]

The distinction, however, must face a yet more problematic critique. It actually cannot deal meaningfully with many of the cases Kymlicka himself touches upon as examples, cases that deal precisely with who is and is not a member, and thus with *what is external or internal*. Cases like *Santa Clara Pueblo v Martinez* are thus significant in ways beyond those Shachar identified. Kymlicka's distinction presupposes a previously defined boundary between external and internal, when

[100] Ibid, 35.

[101] Ibid, 42. *Cf* Garet (n 1) 1030 ('a power against the "outside" is a power against the "inside" '); J Levy, *The Multiculturalism of Fear* (Oxford, Oxford University Press, 2000) 118 (noting restrictions on outsiders often entail restrictions on insiders).

[102] *Santa Clara Pueblo v Martinez*, 436 US 49 (1978); Kymlicka, *Liberalism, Community and Culture* (n 10) 197.

[103] A Shachar, *Multicultural Jurisdictions: Cultural Differences and Women's Rights* (Cambridge, Cambridge University Press, 2001) 18–20.

[104] Ibid, 30.

it is often this very boundary to which the rule would need to apply. One cannot know in advance if the practice of the Pueblos concerning membership is an internal restriction or external practice, because asking such a question presumes one knows whether those affected are internal or external to the Pueblos, when that is what the membership practice addresses. These critiques raise important concerns about the distinction, but they are just the beginning of its problems.

Both the empirical and normative accuracy of the distinction are subject to some questions. Although the scope of the argument in this book is wider than Canada, it is nonetheless worth framing the initial challenge against Kymlicka in the Canadian context from which his theory grew before making use of examples from elsewhere in later chapters.

Kymlicka does not claim his distinction applies empirically in every case. Rich as his theorising is, he appropriately qualifies it as describing the claims only of 'most' groups.[105] One could take this as a statistical claim, to which an appropriate response might be an amassing of quantitative data concerning how many groups claim which kinds of rights. But this would not seem the most helpful interpretation (nor the most likely), and there is an alternative way of approaching matters. The distinction's helpfulness as an empirical generalisation is limited, rather, because there are *qualitatively important* exceptions. If the distinction does not cope with approaches taken by policymakers on central issues, then it is not the empirical tool it was claimed to be.

This problem is evident in an area illustrating a sort of internal implication to which Kymlicka referred. Religious school rights are established in the constitutional arrangements under which a number of Canadian provinces, including Saskatchewan, entered Confederation, typically providing for the right of the Catholic or Protestant minority in a given district to establish a separate school board. These religious school rights often lead to some internal restrictions, including taxation of individuals by the relevant religious group in ways other than they might choose to be taxed. This point is neatly illustrated by a pertinent case of the Saskatchewan Court of Appeal.[106] The appellants in the case sought to be separate school supporters, but the public school division appealed to the Board of Revision to claim that the appellants were not members of the minority religious faith as required. Justice Lane, writing for the Court, and dealing with some complex points concerning legislative interpretation, ultimately held that the legislative framework left a taxpayer's claimed religion subject to challenge. A taxpayer is required to support the school system actually according with his or her religious faith. In the Canadian polity, certain religious groups having the right to establish school boards thus also have a right to internally restrict members by subjecting them to taxation and by preventing them from redirecting this taxation. Individuals are subject to taxation by their religious group for purposes of religious schooling. This point, notably, is not a singular conclusion of

[105] Kymlicka, *Multicultural Citizenship* (n 10) 42.

[106] *Buhs v Board of Education of Humboldt Rural School Division No 47*, 2002 SKCA 41, 217 Sask R 222.

Saskatchewan's Court of Appeal but is rather a generalisation applicable to much education legislation across Canada.

Although taxation for the provision of schooling systems might not seem like the most dramatic internal restriction, and some would characterise it as a merely incidental exception to a general norm against internal restrictions, the example surely says something more. Internal restrictions on rights as they would otherwise exist are accepted in actual Canadian political practice, thus beginning to undermine Kymlicka's empirical claim. The example points immediately to the reality that the categories must be more complex and the possibility that internal restrictions cannot be categorically dismissed.

Language policy is another part of the Canadian approach to pluralism where qualitatively important policies cross from external protections into internal restrictions. Notably, the collective aspiration of the Québecois for *la survivance* (which Charles Taylor rightly describes as involving a desire to see future Québecois continue to speak French)[107] has led to Quebec language policy that involves restrictions on members of the very community this policy seeks to protect and perpetuate. Under Bill 101, also known as the *Quebec Charter of the French Language*, language policy developed that went so far as to limit access to English-language schooling and to prohibit non-French-language commercial signage. This latter aspect in particular led the Supreme Court of Canada to strike down the law in *Ford v Quebec* because a less restrictive law requiring French as the dominant language of signage would have met the law's objectives.[108] The Quebec government retained the law by using the 'notwithstanding clause' (the provision in the Canadian constitution allowing temporary democratic override of judicial interpretations of certain constitutional clauses).[109] Upon the impending expiration of the override and in a politically pressured situation after the United Nations Human Rights Committee ruled against the legislation, a later Quebec government accepted the Supreme Court's reasoning and amended the legislation to require only French predominance in signage.[110] More recently, the courts have accepted the continuing constitutionality of these amended provisions. Following a 1999 trial decision declaring inoperative the signage provisions absent evidence showing that they remained justified limitations on constitutional rights,[111] a question arose concerning whether the portions of the Supreme Court reasoning allowing for the less strict law had continuing currency in the absence of new evidence. The higher courts accepted that they did, thereby tacitly accepting the modified legislation as constitutional.[112]

[107] C Taylor, 'The Politics of Recognition' in A Gutmann (ed) *Multiculturalism: Examining the Politics of Recognition* (Princeton, Princeton University Press, 1994).

[108] *Ford v Quebec (Attorney General)* [1988] 2 SCR 712, 780.

[109] SQ 1988 c 54.

[110] SQ 1993 c 40.

[111] *R c WFH Enterprises ltée* [1999] JQ no 4586 (CQ pén).

[112] *R c WFH Enterprises ltée* [2000] JQ no 1165 (Que SC), *R c WFH Enterprises ltée*, [2001] JQ no 5021 (Que CA), leave to appeal to SCC refused: [2001] SCCA No 625.

This legislation includes substantial internal restrictions. First, and less constitutionally contentious, sections 72–73 of the legislation limit children attending publicly-funded schools to French-language schooling unless their parents had English-language schooling.[113] The law thus restricts francophone parents from sending their children to English-language schooling to gain, say, economic benefits from learning English. Secondly, and most contentiously, section 58 of the legislation restricts expression by limiting the medium of expression in commercial signage by requiring French-language predominance, thus restricting individuals from expressing themselves as they might choose. These restrictions seem to be internal restrictions of the sort Kymlicka's theory would try to rule out. Someone might claim that these restrictions do not restrict ordinary liberal rights, such as by arguing that there is no right to send a child to school in any language chosen. Indeed, I will offer an argument below for the normative acceptability of similar restrictions in the appropriate circumstances. But that is precisely the point: the circumstances of a group's collective life affect the appropriate response to these restrictions. Absent such circumstances, nobody would defend restrictions on the language of expression in commercial signage; they are clearly restrictive of ordinary rights as they would exist in a world without groups. Absent the circumstances of collective life at hand, nobody would suppose that a group of parents could not at least propose whatever language they wished for their children's education. The Quebec legislation rules out *ab initio* a request for education in a particular language that might offer certain individual economic benefits. The provisions surely amount to internal restrictions.

Although they have been controversial, these internal restrictions have ultimately been accepted (and, I will argue, for good reason, subject to some qualifications) as a delicate compromise protecting the language of the Québecois. They are a qualitatively important instance of a minority group using internal restrictions to protect its language and culture in a collective effort at *la survivance* and, indeed, an instance of *la survivance* giving a minority group reasons to impose internal restrictions not accommodated in Kymlicka's theory.

Some will object to the last sentence, claiming that the francophone community is not the relevant 'minority group' and that any attention to a minority ought to be to the anglophone and allophone[114] minorities within Quebec. This is a manifestation of the phenomenon sometimes labelled a 'Russian doll problem': as one peels off layers, the majority and minority groups keep changing. I will return implicitly to this issue later, but we can note for now that this 'Russian doll problem' poses particular challenges for Kymlicka: his argument faces problems on both the main argument and on this objection to the main argument. Kymlicka's choice to distinguish between external protections versus a majority and internal restrictions within a minority, aside from the other presuppositions it

[113] Note, though, that it has been read down somewhat: *Solski (Tutor of) v Quebec*, 2005 SCC 14. But see also the more recent and controversial decision in *Quebec (Education, Recreation, and Sports) v Nguyen*, 2009 SCC 47, [2009] 3 SCR 208.

[114] Allophones are those with a first language other than French or English.

makes, presupposes an identification of the majority and the minority. It makes strong assumptions here, beyond those needed by a theory that did not depend on the same distinctions between internal and external.

Some might also object to the claims against Kymlicka here, noting that Kymlicka has more recently explicitly noted possible justifications for Quebec's sign law.[115] However, he did not discuss the Quebec sign law as giving rise to amendments to the 'internal restrictions'/'external protections' dichotomy but simply as an ad hoc policy helping Quebec to move toward a post-ethnic conception of nationalism. In one sense, then, he admits limits to the application of his distinction, himself eroding the claim initially at stake. In another, he reiterates the distinction, implying that the internally restrictive aspects of the law make it 'illiberal'[116] but accepting the occasional use of an illiberal policy for the greater good. An alternative interpretation, and one to be pursued further in the normative discussion, is that the presence of an internally restrictive aspect is not the basis on which to accept or reject a policy. For the moment, however, the empirical usefulness of the distinction is in some decay.

Consider now a third area posing qualitatively important challenges to Kymlicka's distinction: self-government agreements for indigenous peoples being reached with Canada's Aboriginal First Nations. Although the Supreme Court of Canada remains due to pronounce more definitively on the matter, the Canadian federal government has explicitly recognised an inherent right of aboriginal self-government as protected by section 35 of the Constitution Act, 1982, although its document endeavours to prescribe certain features of self-government.[117] The Canadian government has subsequently entered into negotiations of self-government agreements, and some important clauses from self-government agreements can bear on the present issue.

Someone might argue, though, that Kymlicka's account can explain claims for self-government. After all, self-government is an issue he explicitly addresses.[118] Kymlicka is, of course, right to alert readers to the fact that a group claiming what it calls 'collective rights' might be claiming group-differentiated rights that are not necessarily collective.[119] And the monumental achievement of Kymlicka's writings right from *Liberalism, Community and Culture* is his persuasive argument that some group-differentiated rights can be accepted and advocated within an entirely liberal framework.

However, self-government is sometimes considered a species of internal self-determination, which in the international legal arena is the pre-eminent right giving rise to extended discussions on collective rights differing from traditional

[115] Kymlicka, *Politics in the Vernacular* (n 11) 286–89.

[116] Ibid, 286.

[117] Canada Department of Indian Affairs and Northern Development, *Aboriginal Self-Government: Federal Policy Guide* (Ottawa, Minister of Public Works and Government Services, 1995).

[118] Kymlicka, *Multicultural Citizenship* (n 10) 38–40.

[119] Kymlicka, *Politics in the Vernacular* (n 11) 70.

liberal rights.[120] And just as any nation's self-government presupposes the possibility that it might limit individual rights in certain contexts, so, too, aboriginal First Nations exercising self-government might do so. Other nation-building projects have involved internal restrictions. In saying that, of course, one does not say that nations or First Nations ought to be able to infringe individual rights in every way imaginable. Some restrictions have been and are inappropriate, but the point is that their inappropriateness does not derive directly from their being internal restrictions. Other principles can govern which right takes priority over which, and individual rights will often be vitally important. Any broad assumption against internal restrictions is overly sweeping. Such a requirement would rob self-government of a substantial part of its meaning and render aboriginal self-government into a poor second cousin of self-government more broadly.

The self-government agreements being negotiated with Canada's Aboriginal First Nations arguably recognise the possibility of self-government leading to restrictions on members, as is evident in very different ways from two prominent examples of such agreements. The Nisga'a Final Agreement, concluded in May 1999, thus took pains to require that the Nisga'a government respect the Canadian Charter, though with intriguing additional language: 'The *Canadian Charter of Rights and Freedoms* applies to Nisga'a Government in respect of all matters within its authority, bearing in mind the free and democratic nature of Nisga'a Government as set out in this Agreement.'[121] Though there might conceivably be other meanings intended by the language as well, the latter clause must arguably be taken as textually suggesting an expectation that many Nisga'a government actions would qualify for justification under section 1 of the Charter as limits on rights 'necessary in a free and democratic society'.

The more recent Tlicho Self-Government Agreement, concluded in August 2003, contains yet more intriguing provisions. Although the Tlicho government is explicitly subject to the Canadian *Charter* on matters within its authority,[122] the Agreement also provides for a Tlicho Constitution, subject to a requirement, amongst others, that it provide 'protections for Tlicho citizens and for other persons to whom Tlicho laws apply, by way of rights and freedoms *no less than* those set out in the *Canadian Charter of Rights and Freedoms*'.[123] The drafting is beyond opaque. The language clearly contemplates variation, or it would refer simply to 'the rights set out in the *Charter*' rather than rights 'no less than' those in the *Charter*. Yet any variation implies the possibility that some rights will indeed be given a more limited extent, since a different interpretation on some rights will end up implicitly constraining others. This latter point arises particularly when the terminology stands together with companion provisions on Tlicho government powers

[120] For example, J Crawford (ed) *The Rights of Peoples* (Oxford, Clarendon, 1988); *cf* Xanthaki, 'Multiculturalism and International Law' (n 28).
[121] Nisga'a Final Agreement (25 August 2003) ch 2 art 9.
[122] Tlicho Agreement (4 September 2002) art 2.15.1.
[123] Ibid, art 7.1.2 (emphasis added).

like that to enact laws for the 'protection of spiritual and cultural beliefs and practices of Tlicho Citizens and protection and promotion of the Tlicho language and of the culture of the Tlicho First Nation'.[124] The Agreement arguably implies a Tlicho power to protect the Tlicho 'distinct society', even where this may require limits on certain rights not normally permitted by the Canadian Charter and liberal jurisprudence.

Such variations are contemplated in the Charter. Notably, section 25 of the Charter mandates that '[t]he guarantee in this Charter of certain rights and freedoms shall not be construed so as to abrogate or derogate from any aboriginal, treaty or other rights or freedoms that pertain to the aboriginal peoples of Canada'. The legally correct interpretation of section 25 is, of course, debated. Some take it as a general interpretive prism,[125] others suggest it may provide some interpretive shield for aboriginal governments (even though these authors claim the section did not contemplate the idea),[126] and yet others identify a wide range of possible protections it might provide for aboriginal self-government.[127] There have thus far been few mentions of the section in case law,[128] likely because there have not been many challenges against decisions of aboriginal governments. At the very least, however, section 25 must be read as having some protective effect for aboriginal practices such that they can diverge from elements of the rest of the Charter in some ways, allowing First Nations communities to protect some practices even where doing so involves variations on the usual set of Canadian citizenship rights.

Although reading an 'external protections'/'internal restrictions' rule into the interpretation of aboriginal self-government provisions might not be inherently impossible, such a reading would be neither the most natural nor one corresponding structurally to the concept of self-government. Although Kymlicka himself has anticipated, and enriched, some of the debates on whether the Charter should apply to Aboriginal First Nations, and argued for the possibility of different mechanisms for enforcement of individual rights in the self-government context,[129] the provisions actually included in self-government agreements go farther than his claims. These self-government agreements arguably accept a very real possibility of some internal restrictions being legitimate means of pursuing collective purposes connected with maintaining First Nations communities. Again, rights to impose internal restrictions are more widely claimed than Kymlicka would have

[124] Ibid, art 7.4.4.

[125] W Pentley 'The Interpretive Prism of Section 25' (1988) 25 *University of British Columbia Law Review* 22.

[126] PW Hogg and ME Turpel 'Implementing Aboriginal Self-Government: Constitutional and Jurisdictional Issues' (1995) 74 *Canadian Bar Review* 214.

[127] JM Arbour 'The Protection of Aboriginal Rights Within a Human Rights Regime: In Search of an Analytical Framework for Section 25 of the Canadian Charter of Rights and Freedoms' (2003) 21 *Supreme Court Law Review* (2d) 3.

[128] Ibid, 15ff. The majority of the Court refrained from addressing issues concerning s 25 in a recent opportunity to do so in *R v Kapp*, [2008] SCC 41, [2008] 2 SCR 483. The Court preferred to leave these issues to be addressed on a later day, with only Bastarache J choosing to engage in extensive discussion of s 25.

[129] For example, Kymlicka, *Politics in the Vernacular* (n 11) 86–88.

had us believe and, indeed, are actually accepted within the delicate compromises of Canadian federation.

Qualitatively important examples go beyond the empirical claims of Kymlicka's theory. It is thus questionable whether Kymlicka's key distinction is as empirically accurate as claimed, and there is a need to develop new distinctions in the area of group rights that better describe the actual claims of groups, as well as the actual policy of states like Canada in their responses to diversity.

There are also reasons to doubt whether Kymlicka's distinction is as normatively useful as claimed to be. These issues will return, but it is apparent from the outset that Kymlicka's approach, regrettably, cannot accommodate even appropriate solutions to standard coordination problems concerned with public goods. Consider again the example of a cultural-linguistic community with political power over matters such as the educational system to which its members are subject. Suppose this community seeks to promote its culture through steps to preserve its language. To do so, it enacts legislation – call it Bill ABC – requiring its members to attend educational institutions in the community's language. It does so because some individuals otherwise have individual incentives to attend school in a dominant language of the broader region to attain individual economic benefits. On one interpretation, Bill ABC thus harms individual members who are now denied a choice about their education.[130] On another, however, by enacting Bill ABC, the community simply protects the public good individual members would otherwise have had distorting incentives to work against. That is, the legislation corrects the incentive individuals would otherwise have to focus only on their individual non-membership interests. It actually benefits members by protecting a flourishing of the community that contributes to the flourishing of their individual lives. Indeed, the legislation could conceivably go even farther on the same basis, even restricting public signage in the dominant language that threatens to supplant the linguistic-cultural community. What might have initially seemed to some to have no possible basis except as an act of tyranny now begins to seem like a plausible policy to protect a collective interest that actually benefits members.[131]

This example, admittedly, is both abstracted and idealised. It has, to a degree, implicitly assumed a homogeneous community in which protection of that community's culture is of benefit to everyone within that community. In the real world, of course, any such situation is inherently more complex because communities are non-homogeneous. The promotion of a public good will work neutrally or

[130] *Cf* eg, B Barry, *Culture and Equality: An Egalitarian Critique of Multiculturalism* (Cambridge MA, Harvard University Press, 2001) 106–107 (claiming that requiring children in Wales to learn Welsh denies them the chance to learn a more widely spoken foreign language); JT Levy 'Language Rights, Literacy, and the Modern State' in W Kymlicka and A Patten (eds) *Language Rights and Political Theory* (Oxford, Oxford University Press, 2003) (claiming that there are dangers of using children as a means to prop up unsustainable languages).

[131] *Cf* A Buchanan, 'Liberalism and Group Rights' in JL Coleman and A Buchanan (eds) *In Harm's Way: Essays in Honor of Joel Feinberg* (Cambridge, Cambridge University Press, 1994) 10; Levy *The Multiculturalism of Fear* (n 110) 115ff.

even harmfully, on balance, to some members. There will be some individuals for whom cultural membership is less valuable than the individual interests they might pursue outside the legislative framework. Of course, the same would be true of any public good problem. So long as the community still serves such members in other ways on balance and in a broad sense, however, the community does not automatically do them an injustice (unless this particular step simply goes too far as against a particularly weighty individual interest, considering it in light of the competing individual aims and collective interests). As long as it is not inherently unjustifiable to promote public good, the point gives no grounds for rejecting the conclusion from the idealised example that Kymlicka's theory fails in a standard public good problem. This conclusion may or may not mean it fails to give the right answer on particular facts, but it diminishes its normative force.

Kymlicka's distinction is thus not the morally relevant distinction it purports to be. As with Bill ABC, an internal restriction may actually be to the benefit of most – or even all – members. An internal restriction can contribute to individuals' lives by promoting the flourishing of a community which in turn contributes to their lives. The initial restriction of their pursuit of other individual non-membership interests may be necessary to the fulfillment of more weighty interests as members. The morally relevant distinction is thus not on Kymlicka's line but between compliance and non-compliance with other moral requirements. Such requirements will emerge from the humanistic principle in Part II of the book.

It is understandable why Kymlicka's distinction originally had an intuitive appeal. It expresses a serious concern – that individuals and subcommunities should not suffer perpetually under their community's restrictions. But we can develop such a concern as an adjunct to the requirements in Part II, which will include a requirement that a community serve its members. A strict distinction between 'external protections' and 'internal restrictions' surely does not figure as prominently, or have the moral determinacy, as expressed in Kymlicka's account.

Kymlicka's distinction is thus less normatively applicable than originally claimed and even has some potential to work normative harm. Given the empirical and normative problems apparent, it is time to try to theorise collective rights in a manner going beyond Kymlicka's framework that has had so much influence on many authors in the field.[132]

[132] We reach this conclusion without even exploring a further potential problem concerning Kymlicka's treatment of historically-rooted claims. Kymlicka seems to accept the notion of abiding by historic promises made to certain groups (Kymlicka, *Politics in the Vernacular* (n 11) 306), although with certain implications that any historically-rooted claims must yield to equality-based claims (Kymlicka, *Multicultural Citizenship* (n 10) 120). It is not clear how the sorts of claims for compensation for historic injustices we described at the outset could survive any significant countervailing considerations on Kymlicka's theory (other than perhaps on a utilitarian type of rationale concerning the ongoing availability of believable government promises: Magnet (n 1) 195), although they can do so clearly on a theory recognizing collective moral rights: Posner and Vermeule (n 19) 707. However, we will not explore every complexity of claims for historic injustices, since they raise many temporal issues not relevant to collective rights more generally.

V. APPROACH AND STRUCTURE

Rather than taking group-differentiated rights and those defined by Kymlicka's distinction as operative categories of analysis, this book works toward an account explaining the moral appropriateness of collective rights. Undertaking this project of integrated theory as begun earlier in the chapter, then, certain assumptions will structure the argument. The structure in the remainder of Part I flows from a conception of a right as a triadic relationship. A right is a right *to* something and a right *against* someone who is under a duty. In other words, a right is a justified entitlement of X to Y against Z.[133] A right is held by a subject to an object and imposes an obligation. The terminology, of course, should not cause confusion. A subject need not be a 'subject' in some vulgar sense, nor need an 'object' be some physical item (it might be something abstract or even an action). The exploration of this relation in the context of collectivities will lead us to different understandings of the concept of a right, but this basic structure helps frame the discussion, with the key emphasis being on the first two components since who owes the obligation will ultimately correspond to the nature of the specific right at issue in a fact-specific context.

Thus, chapter two's analysis concerns the issue of what kinds of collectivities, if any, have the capacity to hold collective rights – to be the subject in this triadic relation. It will challenge objections that collectivities cannot hold rights independently of their individual members. In particular, while certain forms of dependence of a collectivity on its members are true, these forms of dependence do not make the collectivity reducible to its members; nor are its responsibilities reducible to responsibilities of members. Then, by examining the relationship between having moral responsibilities and having the capacity for rights, an argument will follow that collectivities having moral responsibilities must have a capacity for moral rights.

The discussion in chapter three will focus on the object in the triadic relation, arguing for a particular, non-aggregative conception of a collective interest. Then, considering whether certain goods are inherently in a collective interest, it will consider the arguments of Joseph Raz, Denise Réaume and Jeremy Waldron. While these theorists illuminate some aspects of the question, there is a different argument to be made for certain interests being held inherently by collectivities rather than by individuals. Finally, to establish that at least some collective interests have the special force of rights, the argument will follow that the fulfillment of certain individual interests presupposes the fulfillment of certain collective interests. *If certain individual moral rights exist*, then, at least some collective moral rights exist.

133 *Cf* J Raz, 'Rights and Politics' in J Tasioulas (ed) *Law, Values, and Social Practices* (Aldershot, Dartmouth, 1997) 80; G MacCallum 'Negative and Positive Freedom' (1967) 76 *Philosophical Review* 312, 312 (if Y is a freedom, then this relation incorporates a freedom on MacCallum's account).

The structure in Part II (chapters four through seven) develops the moral requirements necessary to legitimate collective rights-holding. Chapter four begins by confronting a challenge put by some theorists who have claimed collective rights necessarily conflict with individual rights and/or with one another. I will argue that these objections have force only if conflicts of rights are pervasive (in a particular sense to be developed) and that pervasive conflicts are avoided by collectivities meeting appropriate moral conditions. The challenge of Part II is to flesh out these conditions, labelled the Community Conditions. Chapter five will develop the first of these, the Service Principle, a requirement that a collectivity serve its members in a broad sense. Chapter six will develop the Mutuality Principle, a requirement that a collectivity not act in a manner showing disregard for the equivalently weighty interests of non-members. Chapter seven will challenge claims that other rights, such as rights to exit and to democratic consultation, must follow, instead developing a theory recognising both individual and collective roles in membership control.

Part III of the book begins to lay foundations for how to institutionalise the theory of the previous chapters. Chapter eight will confront the issue of 'partial compliance', concerned with how the principles emerging from Part II apply to real communities in situations where already-constituted collectivities comply with the Community Conditions only imperfectly. I will argue that the Community Conditions are subject to a degree of approximation but also that those with political power may act rightly in helping collectivities to comply with the Community Conditions. Chapter nine will turn to an analysis of principled deference to and interference with collectivities, seek to develop an account of principled contestation within communities, and show how a reasonable policy for those with political power will often be to facilitate this principled contestation in a manner such that communities have the opportunity to bring themselves into compliance with the Community Conditions.

I will thus argue that at least some collectivities having the characteristic of community hold a form of *irreducibly collective moral rights*, that moral principles in the form of the Community Conditions can guide us on what communities hold which rights, and that this moral theory has important implications for our ordering of our various communities.

2

Collectivities as Moral Rights-Holders

> [C]ommunities also figure as agents among whom justice must be done, within the bounds of some wider association.[1] (Charles Taylor)

> Now if this is meant literally, I find it incoherent. Groups have no moral claim to well-being independently of their members – groups just aren't the right sort of beings to have moral status. They don't feel pain or pleasure. It is individual, sentient beings whose lives go better or worse, who suffer or flourish, and so it is their welfare that is the subject-matter of morality.[2] (Will Kymlicka)

I. INTRODUCTION

CONTEMPLATING THAT COLLECTIVITIES could hold rights – could have interests sufficient to ground duties – raises a preliminary question as to whether collectivities are the sort of entities that can have moral status and thus a capacity to hold rights. Despite the challenge this issue might present for theories of collective rights, it has been subjected to significantly less analysis than it warrants.[3] Although the above interchange between Taylor and Kymlicka manifests stark positions on the question, the matter ended there, and neither seems to have gone on to analyse this specific question at greater length.

In these quotations, Kymlicka's argument trades on a patchwork set of theoretical positions concerning moral status. Keith Graham has criticised Kymlicka for the alleged implication that holding moral rights requires sentience, arguing that any such premise conflicts with the reality of moral harms not involving sentience, amongst which Graham would include offence and deception.[4] But one need not cogitate over whether offence and deception involve

[1] C Taylor, 'Justice After Virtue' in J Horton and S Mendus (eds) *After MacIntyre: Critical Perspectives on the Work of Alasdair MacIntyre* (Cambridge, Polity, 1994) 16, 42.

[2] W Kymlicka, *Liberalism, Community and Culture* (Oxford, Clarendon, 1989) 241–42. Brian Barry in turn attacks Kymlicka for entitling another book '*The Rights of Minority Cultures*': 'Cultures are simply not the kind of entity to which rights can properly be ascribed' (B Barry *Culture and Equality: An Egalitarian Critique of Multiculturalism* (Cambridge MA, Harvard University Press, 2001) 67).

[3] Y Tamir, 'Against Collective Rights' in C Joppke and S Lukes (eds) *Multicultural Questions* (Oxford, Oxford University Press, 1999) 158, 165.

[4] K Graham, *Practical Reasoning in a Social World* (Cambridge, Cambridge University Press, 2002) 90.

sentience. Kymlicka's argument also refers to concerns, such as lives going better or worse and such as suffering or flourishing, that are not necessarily coterminous with sentience. One may more properly view Kymlicka's argument as endeavouring, if somewhat untidily, to encapsulate a number of different approaches to identifying what sorts of beings have moral status and to claim that collectivities do not meet the resulting tests, without needing to choose amongst the approaches. A quick answer like Graham's, that some of the relevant moral theories are mistaken, unfortunately does not fully respond because it presumes that only one of Kymlicka's arguments is relevant without offering an account of why the other arguments are not determinative.

In this chapter, I will develop reasons to favour Taylor's position on this point over Kymlicka's that depend solely on drawing several careful distinctions that permit, consistently with the humanistic principle assumed in chapter one, certain collectivities both to depend on their members and to have irreducible moral status. The position adopted will be a controversial one. Allen Buchanan, although analysing the matter only very briefly, has asserted that something much like the humanistic principle implies that groups cannot hold moral rights. Buchanan first defines what he calls 'justificatory individualism' in terms much like the humanistic principle:

> According to moral individualism in the justificatory sense, all justifications for ascriptions of moral and legal rights (and duties) must be grounded *ultimately* on consideration of the well-being and freedom of individuals.[5]

He then rapidly asserts that this principle is incompatible with moral rights being held by groups:

> But to assert that a collectivity, as opposed to an individual, is a possessor of a *moral*, as distinct from a legal, right is incompatible with justificatory individualism because regarding a collectivity as a possessor of moral rights assumes that collectivities are moral subjects, and hence the kinds of things that have interests that can serve as the ultimate ground for moral justifications.[6]

In this chapter, it will start to be clear how collectivities can have moral status even though only individuals are of ultimate value.

The reasons will not come from some deep-seated ontology. Some theorists have supposed that the existence of collective moral rights hinges on a primary ontological question of whether collectivities 'exist': they say so directly;[7] begin their arguments for collective responsibility or rights with long chapters on ontology;[8] or imply that ontological doubt about collectivities challenges collective

[5] A Buchanan, *Justice, Legitimacy, and Self-Determination: Moral Foundations for International Law* (Oxford, Oxford University Press, 2003) 255.

[6] Ibid, 256.

[7] For example, M Galenkamp, *Individualism versus Collectivism: The Concept of Collective Rights*, 2nd edn (Rotterdam, Gouda Quint, 1998) 87.

[8] For example, L May, *The Morality of Groups: Collective Responsibility, Group-Based Harm, and Corporate Rights* (Notre Dame, University of Notre Dame Press, 1987); P French, *Collective and Corporate Responsibility* (New York, Columbia University Press, 1984). For an argument for collective rights based substantially

rights.[9] Without undertaking a long digression into what it means for something to 'exist' or, rather, the various senses in which something can 'exist' – thereby leaving decisions on important political questions held hostage to an apparently interminable metaphysical debate – a case can be made for the moral status of collectivities. To do so, it is sufficient to make more minimal ontological and moral claims.

Notably, the more minimal set of claims here are consistent with the reality of collectivities that undergo change over time. Anne Phillips has raised the concern that many discussions of cultural group rights seem to assume the presence of reified cultures, with preservation of a culture in some form typically amounting to preservation of some frozen form of the culture.[10] Courts tasked with interpreting legal entrenchments of rights held by cultural communities have fallen prey to this difficulty, as is evident in such contexts as the Australian and Canadian courts' interpretations of tests for aboriginal title and aboriginal rights, which have explicitly referred to instantiations of legal norms or practices from pre-contact times.[11] My argument will rest on specific collectivities having particular structures and central values, but it will also allow for change over time in these structures and values, and chapter nine will make especially clear the role of ongoing contestation within collectivities – something that has often been overlooked in theories of group rights.[12]

Both Bhikhu Parekh and Tariq Modood are alive to these concerns insofar as they seek to highlight the internal reformative resources within groups often stereotyped in frozen forms.[13] However, their highlighting of this point is actually in some degree of tension with their main argument for rights held by these groups. Their main argument is focused on the contribution of a diversity of cultures to humanity as a whole.[14] But focusing on the diversity of cultures is in tension with the possibility of cultural changes over time that bring groups closer together, as such changes would implicitly work against the diversity value at stake. A diversity-based argument for group rights, moreover, has a problematic feature in that it seems always to value *your* culture for the benefit it yields to *me*.

on ontology, see RR Garet, *The Existence of Groups: An Adjudicative Theory of Group Rights* (PhD thesis, Yale University, 1981).

[9] For example, J Narveson 'Collective Rights?' (1991) 4 *Canadian Journal of Law and Jurisprudence* 329; *cf* Kymlicka, *Liberalism, Community and Culture* (n 2) 242–44.

[10] A Phillips, *Multiculturalism without Culture* (Princeton, Princeton University Press, 2007) 21–25. See also J Griffin, *On Human Rights* (Oxford, Oxford University Press, 2008) 270.

[11] For discussions, see K McNeil, 'The Vulnerability of Indigenous Land Rights in Australia and Canada' (2004) 42 *Osgoode Hall Law Journal* 271; A Eisenberg, 'Reasoning About Identity: Canada's Distinctive Culture Test', in A Eisenberg (ed) *Diversity and Equality* (Vancouver, University of British Columbia Press, 2007).

[12] See S Song, *Justice, Gender, and the Politics of Multiculturalism* (Cambridge, Cambridge University Press, 2007) 31–33.

[13] B Parekh, *Rethinking Multiculturalism: Cultural Diversity and Political Theory* (London, Macmillan, 2000) 177–78; T Modood, *Multicultural Politics: Racism, Ethnicity and Muslims in Britain* (Minneapolis, University of Minnesota Press, 2005) 172.

[14] This is Parekh's argument in *Rethinking Multiculturalism* (n 13) and encapsulated well in the explication in Modood (n 13) 171–73.

The value of cultural diversity can help support a theory of collective rights, but there is important value in a broader theory of collective moral rights grounded in the interests of collectivities themselves.

Admitting that collectivities are subject to change and developing a theory in which there is room for ongoing contestation within collectivities, though, might evoke a different objection. Courtney Jung, in her normative argumentation on indigenous rights, argues that because groups are constructed rather than existing in some inherent, natural form, only Kymlicka-style group-differentiated rights make sense.[15] Derek Gillman, in his argument on cultural rights claims in respect of heritage objects, argues that heritage is a social construction, and suggests the implication that cultural claims to any specific objects are relatively weak.[16] However, these arguments do not follow. Even if collectivities are in some sense 'constructed' in that they are susceptible of processes of social change, there are two important replies. First, it is not an automatic assumption that every collectivity is constructed to the same degree.[17] Second, even a 'constructed' identity is not necessarily any less valuable as a result.[18] Although a very rapid construction of an identity might lead to some questions about claims arising, the fact that cultures have formed through social processes over the course of history does not undermine their importance in the lives of their members today.[19]

In the second section of this chapter, I make a prima facie case for the irreducibility of collectivities, collective actions, and collective blameworthiness. Although I do not develop the argument in precisely the same form as the likes of David Copp,[20] there is a parallelism in our argumentation. What differs about these arguments compared to some others is that they involve a relatively limited set of claims not needing to draw on the full body of recent work on collective action.[21] Fuller analysis of collective action would be necessary in an argument based on a 'will theory' of rights but is not essential in the context of an 'interest theory' of rights such as that

[15] C Jung, *The Moral Force of Indigenous Politics: Critical Liberalism and the Zapatistas* (Cambridge, Cambridge University Press, 2008) 282.

[16] D Gillman, *The Idea of Cultural Heritage* (New York, Cambridge University Press, 2010) 66ff.

[17] *Cf* Modood (n 13) 172.

[18] *Cf* A Eisenberg, *Reasons of Identity: A Normative Guide to the Political and Legal Assessment of Identity Claims* (Oxford, Oxford University Press, 2009) 30–31.

[19] *Cf* ibid.

[20] D Copp, 'The Collective Moral Autonomy Thesis' (2007) 38 *Journal of Social Philosophy* 369; D Copp, 'On the Agency of Certain Collective Entities: An Argument from "Normative Autonomy" ' in PA French and HK Wettstein (eds), *Shared Intentions and Collective Responsibility*, Midwest Studies in Philosophy 30 (Oxford, Blackwell Publishing, 2006) 194.

[21] Important monographs include: Graham, *Practical Reasoning* (n 4); M Bratman, *Intention, Plans, and Practical Reason* (Cambridge MA, Harvard University Press, 1987); M Bratman, *Structures of Agency* (Oxford, Oxford University Press, 2007); C McMahon, *Collective Rationality and Collective Reasoning* (Cambridge, Cambridge University Press, 2001); R Tuomela, *The Importance of Us: A Philosophyical Study of Basic Social Notions* (Stanford, Stanford University Press, 1995); R Tumoela, *The Philosophy of Social Practices: A Collective Acceptance View* (Cambridge, Cambridge University Press, 2002); R Tuomela, *The Philosophy of Sociality: The Shared Point of View* (Oxford, Oxford University Press, 2007). Two important collections of essays applying this work to issues of collective responsibility are French and Wettstein (eds) (n 20) and a special issue of the *Journal of Social Philosophy*, vol 38(3) in Fall 2007, edited by Larry May and Raimo Tuomela.

adopted in the present argument. Conceiving of rights grounded in a broader set of interests rather than conceiving of rights as grounded only in respect for the moral will and agency of rights-holders changes the capacity questions for what entities can hold rights. Will theories of rights perhaps more easily rule out collectivities – and, infamously, infants and persons with certain disabilities.[22] Within an interest theory of rights, not every interest relates to the autonomy of agents, so there can be rights held without the full set of preconditions on rights-bearers that apply within a will theory. That said, there are of course, entities that have interests but do not hold rights (certain plants, perhaps[23]), so it is still important to argue for a moral status of collectivities that permits them to hold rights.

I make the necessary case by responding to the claims of Anthony Ellis that the supervenience of collectivities on their members implies their reducibility to their members. *Supervenience* is a certain sort of relation between properties in which one set of properties does not vary without variation in another. I will explicate this concept further in the next section, where I will use it to show that although collectivities *supervene* on individuals in certain ways, this claim does not imply that they are reducible to individuals. This conclusion will make room for recent writing on collective action and collective intention revealing that the moral blameworthiness of a collective action does not depend (or at least does not solely depend, or supervene) on the moral blameworthiness of individual members' actions. Accordingly, the collectivity, although supervenient on its members in many respects, can be regarded as an irreducible agent, with its actions subject to independent moral analysis.

In the third section of this chapter, grounded in this prima facie case, I will bring some of these new distinctions to bear along with Ronald Dworkin's account of community to explicate how some collectivities have moral responsibilities. Thereafter, I will seek to show how we can generalise Dworkin's account so that it accommodates even communities with profound differences within them, so long as they meet certain requirements that emerge from the analysis.

In the final section, I will establish the significance of this argument for the question with which I began. This bearing of moral responsibilities entails, in turn, at least a capacity for moral rights-holding, thereby establishing some collectivities as full participants – responsibility-bearers and potential rights-holders – in the moral sphere.[24] This argument completes the narrow task of establishing that certain sorts of collectivities, those meeting the requirements of community, can have the capacity to hold rights. It thus sets the stage for an argument in the next chapter concerning collective interests that are objects of moral rights.

[22] James Griffin accepts this implication suggesting that any obligations to infants and those with certain disabilities are from non-rights-related parts of morality: Griffin (n 10) 95.

[23] The example originates from discussions with George Rainbolt.

[24] These arguments will not address fully the important concerns of JW Nickel, 'Group Agency and Group Rights' in I Shapiro and W Kymlicka (eds) *Ethnicity and Group Rights: Nomos 39* (New York, New York University Press, 1997) that attribution of rights to collectivities is problematic because of unclear membership and ineffective agency. I will face these issues in ch 8.

II. SUPERVENIENCE AND COLLECTIVITIES

I begin with a simple claim: A corporation might act wrongfully even though no officer or member of the corporation has acted wrongfully.[25] This might be the case, for instance, with a mistaken decision by a corporate board, leading to a gross wrong, when each member of the board reasonably expected the others to have information that they did not. Some will find this whole claim absurd. They will pull out of their trunks a standard argument against collectivities having moral status, a claim that they are in some way ultimately reducible to their members so cannot be of independent concern.[26] Yet the claim also musters support. Modern criminal law in many jurisdictions permits the prosecution of corporations such that even where no officer or member has committed a legal wrong, the corporation may be convicted for wrongs flowing from its corporate culture.[27] The point may be to deter certain forms of corporate culture through the resulting incentives (something evident in the frequent focus of the elements of offences for which corporations are prosecuted being concerned with the end result of the behaviour),[28] but it may also be to denounce wrongful acts.[29] The point is not that there should be prosecution of corporations in lieu of individuals generally,[30] but that circumstances arise in which every individual has acted rightly, yet a wrong has been committed through some collective wrong for which nobody can be individually blamed.[31] Prosecution of corporations can be not just popular politics, but a just holding to account of the blameworthy.

The claim is attractive because it holds out the promise of preventing everybody from claiming innocence on the grounds that nobody individually committed a wrong.[32] Any approach that would deny the possibility of collective responsibility where there is no individual responsibility could amount, in some instances, simply to denying responsibility even though the acts of a corporation have caused not a natural disaster (for it is an instrument of human agency[33]), but a grievous

[25] *Cf* R Dworkin, *Law's Empire* (London, Belknap, 1986) 169–71.

[26] For example, HD Lewis, 'Collective Responsibility' (1948) 23 *Philosophy* 3; A Ellis, 'Minority Rights and the Preservation of Languages' (2005) 80 *Philosophy* 199.

[27] See generally J Clough and C Mulhern, *The Prosecution of Corporations* (South Melbourne, Oxford University Press, 2002). See also discussions in Sally Simpson and Carole Gibbs (eds) *Corporate Crime* (Aldershot, Ashgate, 2007).

[28] *Cf* Clough and Mulhern (n 27) 5–8; B Fisse and J Braithwaite *Corporations, Crime and Accountability* (Cambridge, Cambridge University Press, 1993) 31–44.

[29] Clough and Mulhern (n 27) 5–7; Fisse and Braithwaite (n 28) 44–50.

[30] *Cf* Clough and Mulhern (n 27) 8–9 (warning of dangers that prosecution of corporations might be so misperceived).

[31] *Cf* Fisse and Braithwaite (n 28) 29–31.

[32] For an important set of objections to this style of argument, see K Ludwig, 'The Argument from Normative Autonomy for Collective Agents' (2007) 38 *Journal of Social Philosophy* 410. Ludwig suggests seeking more careful possibilities in terms of who might be blameworthy, arguing in part that those who created the situation may have a greater share of blame than is first perceived.

[33] *Cf* J Finnis, 'The Priority of Persons' in J Horder (ed) *Oxford Essays on Jurisprudence*, 4th series (Oxford, Oxford University Press, 2000) 1, 10–11.

wrong.[34] The claim may also have certain conceptual advantages. For instance, it may deal better with the problem of changing membership in the corporation.[35] An explanation attributing all the wrongs to individuals would become enmeshed in a tremendously complex task once one considered the effects of different members joining and leaving at various points in time during the continuous commission of a wrongful act. Again, we see the attractiveness of an understanding that refers to the collectivity. But is it true?

The example arguably plays on intuitions arising in the context of a collectivity having a well-specified institutional and legal form. Indeed, certain arguments on the responsibility of corporations have been based closely on the way in which the corporate structure can make a corporate intent identifiable.[36] The example also arguably toys with a certain ambiguity between legal and moral wrongs, given that one might think of a corporation initially in specifically legal terms. Corporations and unions are sometimes conceptualised as legal fictions or, at best, as associations of individuals acting through certain legal forms. Even such associations may have legal rights as demonstrated, for instance, in the controversial United States Supreme Court decision in *Citizens United v Federal Election Commission*,[37] in which the Court upheld political speech rights of corporations and unions. However, the attachment of a legal form to a collectivity does not undermine its status as a collectivity. Some Canadian freedom of association jurisprudence has been ready to recognise irreducibly collective rights held by unions, such as the right to engage in collective bargaining.[38] Thinking of a corporation or a union as a collectivity rather than just an association gives the possibility of different interpretations that make clearer how they could illustrate the issues. In any event, if a particular indigenous people took control of sacred artefacts not belonging to it but to another indigenous people,[39] its less transparent decision-making structure would not undermine the claim that the collectivity had acted wrongly. Again, there would be collective wrongdoing. But as against a claim that a collectivity ultimately exists only because of its members, how could one maintain that a collectivity has independent moral status?

[34] *Cf* J Patterson, 'A Maori Concept of Collective Responsibility' in G Oddie and R Perrett (eds) *Justice, Ethics and New Zealand Society* (Auckland, Oxford, Oxford University Press, 1992) 21; F Jackson, 'Group Morality' in P Pettit, R Sylvan and J Norman (eds) *Metaphysics and Morality: Essays in Honour of JJC Smart* (Oxford, Basil Blackwell, 1987) 100.

[35] *Cf* DE Cooper, 'Collective Responsibility' (1968) 43 *Philosophy* 258, 260.

[36] For example, P French, 'The Corporation as a Moral Person' (1979) 16 *American Philosophical Quarterly* 205; French, *Collective and Corporate Responsibility* (n 8). James Griffin harumphs against those arguing for the moral status of collectivities by, as he puts it, 'gestur[ing] at corporations' (Griffin (n 10) 323n) – my aim here is to use corporations only as a tangible example of a set of claims applying more broadly to a range of collectivities and, in any case, to more than gesture.

[37] *Citizens United v Federal Election Commission*, 130 SCt 876 (USSC 2010).

[38] This was ultimately the conclusion in *Health Services and Support – Facilities Subsector Bargaining Association v British Columbia*, 2007 SCC 27, [2007] 2 SCR 391. This decision marked a final overturning of earlier decisions against this conclusion.

[39] For example, MF Brown, *Who Owns Native Culture?* (Cambridge MA, Harvard University Press, 2003) 19–20.

In answering this challenge, I will use the concept of *supervenience*, a concept currently commonly employed in philosophy of mind but having potentially wider application.[40] As explicated in Jaegwon Kim's leading analysis, the concept refers to a relation wherein a thing cannot differ in respect of certain properties (its supervenient properties) without a difference in other properties (base properties).[41] The aesthetic qualities of a sculpture, for instance, seem to be supervenient properties that cannot vary without a variation in base properties, these being the physical qualities of the sculpture.[42] The aesthetic qualities, then, *supervene* on the physical qualities.

Someone maintaining that a collectivity is wholly reducible to its members might be tempted to claim that all properties of the collectivity, its existence foremost amongst them, supervene on properties of its members. Anthony Ellis's recent arguments verge on this view.[43] Ellis argues that although semantic reductions of statements about collectivities seem difficult, this observation implies only that reduction is complex. Ellis then goes on seemingly to equate supervenience with reduction: 'Though statements about a nation's right to a seat at the UN cannot be translated without circularity into statements about the rights of individuals, nonetheless the fact that a nation has that right *supervenes upon*, more basic individual rights and obligations; indeed, in my view, it simply *consists in them*'.[44] Ellis, then, would deny the existence of irreducible corporate responsibilities, maintaining, for instance, that a corporation's duty to implement procedures to deal with sexual harassment 'consists in the duties, and rights, of various particular employees'.[45] This latter implication sits ill at ease with an observation of possible ways in which a corporation could commit a wrong even though each individual member has acted rightly. But Ellis's argument is subject to more conceptual challenges as well.

First, any claim of supervenience depends on a complex set of assumptions. A collectivity's existence might be thought to supervene on its members' existence. If no members ever existed, no alleged collectivity would exist. But if some members have existed or do exist, the collectivity's existence will supervene on more than just their existence. It will supervene on the relationships amongst the members and their beliefs about these relationships;[46] for example, the existence of certain collectivities, such as a nation, supervenes on the beliefs and attitudes of

[40] *Cf* J Kim, 'Supervenience, Emergence, Realization, Reduction' in MJ Loux and DW Zimmerman (eds) *Oxford Handbook of Metaphysics* (Oxford, Oxford University Press, 2003) 556, 557. For a creative use of the concept to sharpen analysis of linguistic indeterminacy, see TAO Endicott, *Vagueness in Law* (Oxford, Oxford University Press, 2000) 104ff.

[41] Kim (ibid) 559 (equivalently describing it as the base properties determining the supervenient properties).

[42] Ibid, 558.

[43] Ellis (n 26).

[44] Ibid, 204 (emphasis in original).

[45] Ibid, 205.

[46] IM Young, *Justice and the Politics of Difference* (Princeton, Princeton University Press, 1990) 44 ('[g] roups are real not as substances, but as forms of social relations').

certain persons,[47] along with practices, actions, and conventions. So any claim of supervenience depends on a set of assumptions about what is given. Similarly, anyone advocating a reductionist view – and others besides[48] – will urge that an election result supervenes on the votes. Probing the claim further, however, one sees immediately that it is not unqualifiedly true. The election result supervenes on a combination of the votes and other matters, such as the rules specifying how votes are to be counted, the electoral system (proportional representation or first-past-the-post), and so forth. Obviously, in many contexts, one takes these other matters as givens, but drawing attention to this aspect calls into question any equation of supervenience and consistence or reduction.

Supervenience does not amount to consistence or reduction. Given that supervenience claims depend on a set of other factors taken as givens, the relation of supervenience is weaker than a relation of reduction. Supervenience is a relation, as stated, such that collective acts, states, or intents cannot change without changes in individual acts, states, or intents. This relation simply does not entail a relation of reducibility.[49] Supervenience is a variegated relation, and 'there is no single kind of dependence that underlies all cases in which supervenience holds'.[50]

It is difficult to argue in general terms for any greater dependence of collective properties on individual properties. Even where one identifies some sort of supervenience – consider again the election example – the collectivity will typically remain ineliminable (having an indispensable role, taken in practical terms, in an adequate description[51]) in our understanding of what is going on. If a people is participating in an election, one might try to reduce this act to a set of statements about individual members voting, but the reduction makes no sense of what they are really doing. Their individual votes make no sense apart from the larger process, a collective form. Each voter makes a choice on behalf of a people and contributes to the people's choice, so the individual vote cannot be adequately understood without a reference to the collectivity. My act of putting a marked piece of paper in a box is baffling in the absence of a reference to something beyond the individual. So, even if we were to find some form of supervenience of the collective act of electing particular candidates on individual acts and other considerations, the collective form of the people will be ineliminable to an understanding of both the meaning of the individual acts and the content of these other considerations.[52] So long as these sorts of ineliminabilities apply, reduction seems prima facie implausible.

[47] *Cf* D Miller, *On Nationality* (Oxford, Clarendon, 1995) 17.

[48] For example, Endicott (n 40) 105.

[49] *Cf* K Graham, 'Collective Responsibility' in T van den Beld (ed) *Moral Responsibility and Ontology* (Dordrecht, Kluwer, 2000) 59.

[50] Kim (n 40) 167.

[51] *Cf* Graham, *Practical Reasoning* (n 4) 83.

[52] *Cf* Graham 'Collective Responsibility' (n 49) 60.

John Finnis has written that '[s]ocial acts, though irreducible to the acts of people in the acting group, are constituted exclusively by those acts'.[53] We might reverse that: social acts, though constituted by (or, perhaps more precisely, supervening on) the acts of persons in the acting group, are not inherently reducible to those individual acts.[54] This point applies more generally to the relations between collective properties and individual properties. In the sort of collectivities of interest, those stipulated as the topic of study in chapter one, individual members of the collectivity identify themselves in some non-trivial way as members. The coming sections of this chapter will explore, based on the writings of Ronald Dworkin, how they can so identify fully only if the collectivity has the character of community. When it does, the collective form will interact with their actions and make the collectivity irreducible to its members.

Before turning to Dworkin's analysis, however, it is worth extending the prima facie claims to the irreducibility of collective moral obligations. Rejecting assumptions that supervenience relations between individuals and collectivities imply automatic reduction opens the door also to recent writing arguing that a collective action or intention need not be reducible to actions or intentions of its members and, more importantly, that the moral blameworthiness of a collective action is not reducible to the moral blameworthiness of the individual actions on which it supervenes. Where collectivities are ineliminable, then, certain collective intentions and acts may be objects of moral judgment.

In hypothesising an irreducibly collective act, dependent physically and even mentally on individual acts but nonetheless irreducibly collective, one must be ready to subject it to moral judgment other than via moral assessment of underlying individual acts.[55] Recent writing on collective action and collective intention can help make clear why. In particular, Pettit's account of collective intention and Graham's account of collective agency both support well such a claim, giving good reason to believe that some collectivities are ineliminable and subject to independent judgment.

First, then, consider Pettit's argument that one can distinguish a collective intention from individual intentions.[56] Pettit begins his discussion with the 'doctrinal paradox' discussed in recent theoretical literature on adjudication[57] (and analogous to what others call the 'discursive dilemma' if describing it in non-legal contexts[58]). The outcome of a case from a multi-member bench will differ based on whether

[53] Finnis, 'The Priority of Persons' (n 33) 11.

[54] *Cf* CC Gould, 'Group Rights and Social Ontology' (1995) 28 *Philosophical Forum* 73, 73 (groups 'come into being by virtue of actual relations among their constituent individual members, but are not reducible to the individuals distributively, taken apart from these relations').

[55] *Cf* Jackson (n 34) 91.

[56] P Pettit, 'Collective Persons and Powers' (2002) 8 *Legal Theory* 443, 456–60.

[57] For example, Lewis A Kornhauser and LG Sager, 'Unpacking the Court' (1986) 96 *Yale Law Journal* 82; B Chapman, 'Law, Incommensurability, and Conceptually Sequenced Argument' (1998) 146 *University of Pennsylvania Law Review* 1487; G Brennan, 'Collective Coherence?' (2001) 21 *International Review of Law and Economics* 197. See also ML Eber, 'When the Dissent Creates the Law: Cross-Cutting Majorities and the Prediction Model of Precedent' (2008) 58 *Emory Law Journal* 207.

[58] See eg Copp, 'On the Agency of Certain Collective Entities' (n 20) 196.

judges aggregate their conclusions on the individual issues in the case or on the conclusion in the case. This is a particular instance of a more general issue about how a group of individuals reasons together. Pettit argues that a collectivity displays the marks of a distinct intention when it meets the requirements of rationality in its collective behaviour and it does so if it 'collectivizes reason'[59] in its formation of judgments, in the sense that it brings together individual judgments in ways that may bring its judgment on some particular matters into disaccord with the judgment of the majority of its individual members.

This reasoning depends on the sort of distinctions developed earlier. Pettit admits that: 'The integrated collectivity will not be distinct from its individual members in the sense that it will not be capable of existing in the absence of such members. But it will be distinct in the sense of being a center for the formation of attitudes that are capable of being quite distinct from the attitudes of the members.'[60] In other words, by distinguishing between different sorts of dependence between individuals and collectivities, the possibility of collective intentions becomes clear.

Graham reasons that when one is dealing with situations involving collective actions distinct from individual actions, then those collective actions can be subject to moral analysis, as seen in practices of moral comment.[61] Even though each member of a university committee votes individually, it is their collective decision to close a department that attracts moral comment. Their individual votes may also be subject to moral comment, depending on what particular moral obligations each individual member was under, but the collective decision (aside from the individual votes) can be the subject of comment. There is an ineliminable reference to the collectivity in our moral commentary, and that is sufficient to make a prima facie case that the collectivity's actions can be morally analysed independently of the individual acts on which they supervene in some respects.

This argument does face a possible objection that it is setting up false alternatives in saying that either the individuals identified thus far in the scenario or the collectivity itself are the relevant actors to blame. For instance, might it be that someone else is to blame for creating the rules under which the scenario has emerged where everyone has acted rightly but the collectivity acted wrongly?[62] There might, of course, be situations in which some other actor does need to be identified and blamed. But one could construct more elaborate Pettit-style dilemmas in which one accounts for those acting under the rule and those creating the rule and the collectivity still commits a wrong that must be attributed to it.

Some would also challenge the argument on the basis that the collective decision is still under the control of individual agents and the collectivity is thus not a morally autonomous agent in the sense needed for moral responsibility to

[59] Pettit (n 56) 456.
[60] Ibid, 457.
[61] Graham, 'Collective Responsibility' (n 49) 53.
[62] Ludwig (n 32) 410ff. See also S Miller, 'Against the Collective Moral Autonomy Thesis' (2007) 38 *Journal of Social Philosophy* 389, 407.

attach.[63] But this amounts almost to a circular argument. If one starts from the assumption that collectivities are not morally autonomous and therefore cannot incur moral responsibility, one can try to override the facts that gave rise to their responsibility. But if one looks to those facts, there is as strong an argument for broadening the scope of responsibility giving rise to moral comment.

Even other recent theoretical work offering alternative accounts of individual reasoning in social contexts can be read consistently with this analysis.[64] To take the account seemingly most sceptical toward the ontological status of collectivities, Christopher McMahon argues for an account of collective reasoning as consisting of individual reasoning premised on mutual awareness of the reasoning of others and individual judgments premised in collective judgment on agreement with other individual judgments.[65] Such an account can be taken as ontologically sceptical in cohering with older claims that attributing judgments, intentions, and so on to groups is just shorthand for ascribing them aggregatively to individuals.[66] However, even McMahon's account is fully consistent with a claim that collective judgments can face moral comment in irreducible forms. Individual judgment of what individuals should do together is transformed precisely because individuals are thinking of themselves as members in something beyond their individual selves. We have already a situation in which we cannot describe matters fully without reference to the collectivity. As Graham puts it, 'an incredibly large portion of what we wish to describe would simply disappear if we denied ourselves the vocabulary of collectivities'.[67] A large portion of what we want to judge would disappear if we denied ourselves judgment on collectivities.[68]

Modern work on collective intention and collective action can thus support a prima facie case that reference to some collectivities in moral judgment is ineliminable. Returning to the corporation example, that powerful case is at play. The reference to the collectivity enables moral assessment where there could otherwise be none. And that moral assessment has further theoretical backing behind it, with a strong prima facie case for collectivities as in certain respects

[63] See P Mäkelä, 'Collective Agents and Moral Responsibility' (2007) 38 *Journal of Social Philosophy* 456, 458. See also Ludwig (n 32) 425; I Haji, 'On the Ultimate Responsibility of Collectivities' in French and Wettstein (eds) (n 20) 292, 293.

[64] Such work has thrived in recent years: eg M Gilbert *On Social Facts* (Princeton, Princeton University Press, 1989); R Tuomela, *The Importance of Us* (n 21); M Bratman 'Shared Intention' (1993) 104 *Ethics* 97.

[65] McMahon, *Collective Rationality and Collective Reasoning* (n 21).

[66] For a classic argument of this kind, see A Quinton, 'Social Objects' [1975] *Proceedings of the Aristotelian Society* 75.

[67] Graham, 'Collective Responsibility' (n 49) 55.

[68] Someone might try to claim that we should be concerned not with collective responsibility but with 'co-responsibility' of members, the complicity of members in a wrong, which we would analyse individually. (For a powerful account of complicity, see C Kutz, *Complicity: Ethics and Law for a Collective Age* (Cambridge, Cambridge University Press, 2000).) But if members accept 'co-responsibility' in a situation where no member has committed a wrong, it has to be because they belong to a collectivity which is itself guilty: D Cooper, 'Collective Responsibility, "Moral Luck," and Reconciliation' in A Jokic (ed) *War Crimes and Collective Wrongdoing: A Reader* (Oxford, Blackwell, 2001) 206. Otherwise, there is nothing with which to be complicit. Complicity may be relevant to some cases, but any claim that it could account for all would be mysterious.

irreducible, something to be developed further in the coming sections. But we can maintain prima facie that a corporation that commits a moral wrong, even though each individual officer avoids wrongdoing, must face judgment day.

III. DWORKIN'S ACCOUNT OF COMMUNITY

The corporation example, of course, comes from Ronald Dworkin, though he offered it only in passing.[69] Dworkin might initially appear a surprising theorist from whom to draw when defending collective rights. Popular readers take Dworkin to say that rights are held only by individuals.[70] Yet, in an undeveloped footnote, he writes 'I count legal persons as individuals, so that corporations may have rights; a political theory that counts special groups, like racial groups, as having some corporate standing within the community may therefore speak of group rights.'[71] Elsewhere, he seems indifferent as to whether groups might also hold rights. He defines arguments of principle as establishing 'some individual or group right' eight pages before he refers to only 'an individual right' in the same definition.[72] He says that anti-discrimination protections manifest the principle that '*a minority* has a right to equal respect and concern'[73] and then later refers to the constitutional equality guarantee as manifesting an '*individual right* to equality'.[74] In some instances, then, he refers rather cavalierly to the possibility of group rights. As Kymlicka has noted, Dworkin never really discussed or developed his theory for situations like the special constitutional status of indigenous peoples, so perhaps such subjects have simply not been an area of attention.[75]

In this section, we can in any event draw on another Ronald Dworkin, the Dworkin who cares deeply about community, and see how he provides a conception of community consonant with and further encapsulating the distinctions we have developed. Then, I will turn to Dworkin's account of political community, arguing from it that obligations within a political community can be associated with the political community as a whole having responsibilities. Finally, I will explore the issue of generalising from Dworkin's account of political community, to other kinds of community, including those involving more substantial difference. Obligations within other collectivities, depending on their characteristics, can also provide an argument for collective responsibilities.

Dworkin responds to the notion of some philosophers and non-Western cultures that communities are the fundamental ontological being with various

[69] Dworkin, *Law's Empire* (n 25) 169–71.
[70] *Cf* C Wellman, 'Alternatives for a Theory of Group Rights' in C Sistare, L May and L Francis (eds) *Groups and Group Rights* (Lawrence, University Press of Kansas, 2001) 20–21.
[71] R Dworkin, *Taking Rights Seriously* (London, Duckworth, 1978) 91n.
[72] Ibid, 82, 90.
[73] Ibid, 82 (emphasis added).
[74] Ibid, 226 (emphasis added). *Cf* ibid, 365.
[75] Kymlicka, *Liberalism, Community, and Culture* (n 2) 137.

epithets.[76] He also casts doubt on some collective acts or forms, such as the intention of a legislature, that are unproblematic for others.[77] Nevertheless, he provides an account of community in which the community can be a moral agent and not just shorthand for its members, describing his community as a 'deep personification'.[78] Dworkin begins, both in *Law's Empire* and in an article entitled 'Liberal Community', by offering examples of this 'deep personification': he refers to the corporation example discussed earlier[79] and to how Germans born well after 1945 feel guilt for Nazi atrocities.[80] In a further example borrowed from Rawls (who borrowed from Marx), he writes: 'A healthy orchestra is itself a unit of agency. . . It is the orchestra that succeeds or fails, and the success or failure of that community is the success or failure of each of its members.'[81]

Dworkin develops 'deep personification' only briefly. But he explicates it somewhat as 'a complex, two-stage way of reasoning about the responsibilities of officials and citizens that finds a natural expression in the personification of community and cannot be reproduced by a reductive translation into claims about officials and citizens one by one'.[82] We can understand such a metaphor in light of the previously drawn distinctions that awaken us to the possibility of an entity that is both supervenient on yet irreducible to individuals. A personification is a sort of analytical separation of a community from its members that allows us to reason about the properties of a community, which we could not reason about reductively. At the same time, it treats the community as an agent, since its acts and wrongs exist only through the set of relationships constituting the community. A personification, in one sense, stands in the place of the individuals; it would not exist without its individual members. But it is at the same time no mere placeholder, for one can attribute to such a personification intentions and actions, responsibilities and rights. A deep personification mediates for its individual members in irreducible ways.

The orchestra example, for Dworkin, also illustrates the limits on community life. The orchestra, says Dworkin, has no sex life: '[The first violinist's] moral integrity is not compromised by the drummer's adultery.'[83] This example, of course, might fail simply as an example. The appropriate judgment might differ had Dworkin written that the first violinist's moral integrity was unaffected by the drummer's life as a child molester. In this case, one might think the orchestra morally compromised unless it expelled its drummer. But, issues with the example apart, we can accept the intuition behind it: there are some limits on a community's communal life. We must explore this intuition further and seek a fuller account of community.

[76] For example, Dworkin, *Law's Empire* (n 25) 63 ('mysterious'), 64 ('difficult ontology'), and 168 (rejecting 'some spooky, all-embracing mind that is more real than flesh-and-blood people'.)

[77] Ibid, 318–19; *cf* French, *Collective and Corporate Responsibility* (n 8) 39ff (on corporate internal decision structures).

[78] Dworkin, *Law's Empire* (n 25) 166, 171.

[79] Ibid, 169–71.

[80] Ibid, 172–73; R Dworkin, 'Liberal Community' (1989) 77 *California Law Review* 479, 493.

[81] Dworkin, 'Liberal Community' (ibid).

[82] Dworkin, *Law's Empire* (n 25) 168–69.

[83] Dworkin, 'Liberal Community' (n 80) 496.

Dworkin, of course, did not stop with glib references to community but offered an account of 'associative obligations' in *Law's Empire*. He describes 'fraternal obligations' as existing where these obligations are recognised as being: (1) special (applying to those within the group); (2) personal (running to each other member and not just to the group); (3) showing concern for the well-being of others in the group; and (4) showing equal concern for all members.[84] For Dworkin, a 'true' community must be a 'bare' community (as defined by conventions about genetics, geography, history, and so on) that meets these four requirements of members' obligations.[85]

Although Dworkin describes fraternal obligations as having four characteristics, these narrow to two central elements. A community has what we might be termed a *structure* and what might be termed *central values*. First, the *central values*, which can be understood in a rough sense as the aims of the community or the common good around which it is oriented, are factors rendering the continued collaboration of the members viable and reasonable.[86] Dworkin's political community is based on certain values, those of characteristics (2), (3) and (4). These values describe a particular liberal egalitarian model of a political community oriented toward the equal well-being of members (in 3 and 4) and the role of the individual (2). Not every political community will have this same combination of values. In this sense, a community's values are particular rather than universal. However, this characteristic of the values does not make them subjective whims. As those around which the community is oriented, they are objective to the particular community (though not necessarily unchanging).

The *structure* is the definition of the community isolating it from other communities sharing similar values. In other words, it is that which gives rise to the possibility of characteristic (1), the presence of special obligations to members of the community. Dworkin explains the structure in terms of a 'bare community' and conventions about genetics, geography, history and the like.

The structure is a vital element in the definition of a community. As Jacob Levy argues, many nations' values are so similar that we could not distinguish between nations based on their values alone, so we need other distinguishing features.[87] Dworkin does not explore the morality of the structure, which excludes non-members in particular ways,[88] but neither need we at this stage. It suffices for the present argument that the community is set off from other communities. Again, different communities could have structures based on different conventions.

Dworkin's account describes a particular conception of political community. In the next section, I will seek to show that we need not accept this conception for all communities and that other kinds of collectivities may differ in some ways. In this

[84] Dworkin, *Law's Empire* (n 25) 199–201.

[85] Ibid, 201–202.

[86] *Cf* J Finnis, *Natural Law and Natural Rights* (Oxford, Oxford University Press, 1982) 154 (defining a 'common good').

[87] J Levy, *The Multiculturalism of Fear* (Oxford, Oxford University Press, 2000) 85–86.

[88] This example has been criticised by the likes of Denise Réaume: D Réaume, 'Is Integrity a Virtue? Dworkin's Theory of Legal Obligation' (1989) 39 *University of Toronto Law Journal* 380.

section, however, we can focus on the claim that Dworkin's account of obligations within a collectivity, if we accepted it, would justify us in saying that the collectivity as a whole has responsibilities.

Dworkin's associative obligations are intimately connected with the central value of his political community. The obligations he describes, by definition, must show equal concern for all members. They are thus tied to his central value of equal concern and respect. One of Dworkin's (in)famous examples illustrates the centrality of this value. In a complex situation mixing culture and political community, Dworkin discusses whether a woman can have special responsibilities to defer to parental choice in marriage. He suggests that a woman can have such responsibilities within a community of equal concern and respect *if* the rule requiring such deference reflects the community's genuine manifestation of equal respect and concern.[89] The example is intuitively unappealing because many will question whether such a rule can reflect equal respect and concern. However, supposing that it could, then the example illuminates something very important. Whether members have obligations as members is contingent on these obligations being in line with the central political value in Dworkin's theory. The central political value simultaneously defines the responsibilities of the community. In this instance, the community must manifest equal respect and concern towards its members, which leads ultimately to Dworkin's development of his concept of individual rights.

But consider the prior stages more closely. Why does the presence of associative obligations within the community mean that the community itself has responsibilities? Obligations oriented around a certain value attach to the members of a community with that central value. Indeed, one can properly say that the obligations attach by virtue of the membership. But the obligations exist only where the community itself, by mediating such obligations, acts according to the central values. In other words, the community itself has obligations to conform to the central values. The community has a responsibility to show equal respect and concern. The community fails its responsibilities to someone living in dire poverty because her plight manifests a failure to display equal respect and concern for this member. If members have responsibilities as members, the community itself also has responsibilities.

Here, of course, Dworkin's account might mistakenly lead to thinking that the responsibilities of a collectivity are simply internal. In reality, of course, a collectivity will also have external obligations, determined not by the internal conventions, structure, or values of the members, but based on the requirements of morality. Some of the more minimal of these requirements will be matters for attention in chapter six.

A degree of concern for all members is essential in any community. Were the central values entirely demeaning of individual members or of certain denigrated groups of members (both would arise in certain fascist collectivities), those

[89] Dworkin, *Law's Empire* (n 25) 204–205.

members would cease to be able to identify with the collectivity even minimally, leading to either their exclusion from the collectivity or the breakdown of the collectivity. Values and structure are, in that sense, not inseparable. That being said, one cannot automatically rule out every community that has different values, including values diverging from Dworkin's particular interpretation of equal respect and concern.

Nevertheless, Dworkin's account explains how a collectivity can have responsibilities. Taking this explanation in general terms, it is a good explanation. It identifies responsibilities of members and of the community oriented around central values. Notably, this explanation also produces coherent theory that is interlaced with Dworkin's notion that my life goes better when our life goes better: it fundamentally connects my life and the community life.[90] Responsibilities are both individual and simultaneously located within a community unit of agency. Dworkin's explanation makes sense of the notion that I have responsibilities as part of the community, and that the community has responsibilities as a whole.

IV. EXTENDING DWORKIN'S DEEP PERSONIFICATION

Different conceptions of community oriented around different values can still fit within Dworkin's basic framework, thereby revealing its power. Indeed, his framework plausibly applies in other contexts. The power of Dworkin's framework comes across in another account of community that can be read as constructed along Dworkinian lines. In the early chapters of *Punishment, Communication, and Community*,[91] Anthony Duff, rather than using the family to develop 'fraternal obligations', constructs a general account from the academic community. But the two key elements to which Duff refers are a shared commitment to defined values and a regard for one another as members structured by these defining values. These elements effectively abstract from Dworkin's fraternal obligations the element of *central value*, with a hint also at the need for a definition of membership or *structure*. Dworkin's basic framework plausibly applies in other contexts.

In the orchestra analogy, of course, the values at play would be quite different than in Dworkin's political community. The orchestra has united on an artistic mission, to make a statement to the world. The trombonist's poor timing clearly violates this mission; his negligent interruption of the flutist's solo is not just unfortunate, but a transgression of the communal values. Whether the drummer's moral misconduct is a similar blemish depends, in the first instance, on the precise conception of the orchestra's artistic statement and to what degree its mission has a moral element. Secondly, and no doubt partly explaining intuitions about the drummer, it depends on the fact that a real orchestra will probably not be united

[90] R Dworkin, 'Foundations of Liberal Equality' in GB Peterson (ed) *The Tanner Lectures on Human Values XI* (Salt Lake City, University of Utah Press, 1990) 47–52; R Dworkin *Sovereign Virtue: The Theory and Practice of Equality* (Cambridge MA, Harvard University Press, 2000) 223–29.

[91] RA Duff, *Punishment, Communication, and Community* (Oxford, Oxford University Press, 2001) 43–50.

solely around an artistic mission but around values of friendship as well. Any collective responsibilities the orchestra had would be defined in relation to these defining values. The answers in the orchestra case are not ultimately significant; it was an analogy for a limited purpose. But it illustrates the challenges that need to be addressed across the range of conceptions of political community and range of collectivities other than political communities.

Abstracting from Dworkin's conception of political community to give an account of community within other collectivities awakens additional challenges. One issue left unexplored in the earlier discussion of Dworkin's community concerns individuals within a community who do not agree with the community's central values. Such persons may still be part of the community by virtue of its structure. Within Dworkin's political community, one might have pretended that all members would share the central values. But actual political communities are, of course, inhabited by various dissenters. Particularly when we consider other collectivities, we can no longer ignore such challenges and must touch on the impact of disagreement on both the collective responsibilities and the responsibilities of the dissenting members.

As noted, the values of a community are objective but particular. They are the common thread that makes the specific community's existence worthwhile. However, as we will examine further in chapter three, even where a particular central value is not shared by every member, it may still be a common good or collective interest. Dissenters who can still identify with the community, though not sharing its every value, do not undermine the community's existence. However, one might imagine that if the dissenters were sufficient in number, their refusal to endorse the value in question might begin to raise questions about whether it was a value that was objectively sustaining viable and reasonable cooperation. Then, the community would need to reconsider its interpretation of that value or begin to risk breakdown as cooperation was gradually undermined. Similarly, discourse within a community could eventually exclude some from membership if it assumed forms that affected structure. However, mere disagreement by some with some values does not undermine the life of a community. Indeed, suffice it to say that this challenge is actually a major motive for discussing collective rights, for such a theory of collective rights is concerned with the rights of subcommunities within a community, just as with those of the community itself.

This last point highlights another challenge that arises when abstracting from one single account of political community. Individuals seem to be simultaneously members of various collectivities (for example, Inram is a Muslim Pakistani Londoner), and indeed some collectivities may seem to include other collectivities as members (for example, Jean, as a Montrealer, may also automatically be a Québecois and a Canadian, depending whom you ask).[92] In other words, individuals are likely to be members of overlapping and intersecting collectivities.

[92] For my related critique of Dworkin in my younger days, see D Newman 'Subnational, National, and International Identity: A Critique of Dworkin's Conception of Community' (1999) 17 *Windsor Yearbook of Access to Justice* 86.

However, individuals are often subject to a variety of responsibilities based on various roles. This fact says only that life is complex. Individuals who are members of overlapping collectivities may sometimes feel a tension between their competing collectivities, but these tensions do not undermine the existence of community. They are subject to the same analysis as dissent within a community.

One might wonder about alternative ways of identifying a community. Some political scientists have implied that the existence of a community may be defined in terms of the frequency of interaction between individuals.[93] But we do not make sense of such interactions if we do not ask what their point is.[94] After all, the counter in a fast-food restaurant is a place of frequent interactions but without significance to community. Even if we accepted accounts wherein persons sharing a common location can establish a social network and develop common values over time,[95] mere spatial location could not explain individuals' responsibility to the community or its responsibility to them, nor could pure frequency of action, until we identify some purpose and values. So we cannot give a moral account of community in such terms.

Some might put more stress on the structure of a community and less on its values. As David Ingram has suggested: 'New Englanders coexist more or less happily with southerners not because they share values but because they share an identity: they are all Americans.'[96] And there is no doubt that structure is *important.* But it cannot define a community in the absence of values, as the presence of values is essential to the existence of obligations amongst members. Mere shared identity with no purposes would be a different mode of existence, one not giving rise to special responsibilities.

Finally, there might be a challenge that this approach to community risks reifying collectivities, essentialising them in certain ways, when they are actually fluid. As Iris Marion Young puts her vision: 'Groups are real not as substances, but as forms of social relations'.[97] I will actually agree with this claim throughout the book. But Young claims that '[t]hose who reduce group difference to identity implicitly use a logic of substance to conceptualize groups. Under this logic, a group is defined by a set of essential attributes that constitute its identity as a group.'[98] Young argues instead that '[a]ny group consists in a collective of individuals who stand in determinate relations with one another because of the actions and interactions of both those associated with the group and those outside or at the margins of the group'.[99] However, nothing about these claims contradicts an

[93] For example, DB Truman *The Governmental Process: Political Interests and Public Opinion* (New York, Knopf, 1951) 23–24.

[94] *Cf* Finnis's critique of the behaviourist approach: Finnis, *Natural Law and Natural Rights* (n 86) 150–53.

[95] For example, M Hechter, *Containing Nationalism* (Oxford, Oxford University Press, 2000) 97–100.

[96] W Norman, 'The Ideology of Shared Values: A Myopic Vision of Unity in the Multi-Nation State' in JH Carens (ed) *Is Quebec Nationalism Just? Perspectives from Anglophone Canada* (Montreal, McGill-Queen's University Press, 1995) 142.

[97] Young, *Justice and the Politics of Difference* (n 46) 44.

[98] IM Young, *Inclusion and Democracy* (Oxford, Oxford University Press, 2000) 87.

[99] Ibid, 89.

approach of analysing collectivities in terms of their structure and values; they call only for the possibility of analysing structure and values in light of social context. I do not essentialise collectivities but specifically envision their ongoing development.

Thus, an account of community that draws from Dworkin's account of political community the key elements of structure and central values can apply in other contexts. Dworkin's account can potentially describe various kinds of communities more appropriately than alternatives and can explain how communities can have responsibilities. It is time, then, to generalise Dworkin's arguments to other conceptions of political community and to other kinds of communities. Both the *structure* of a community and its *central values* will affect the extent of collective responsibilities. However, collective responsibilities are robust in that they can exist in (a wide range of) collectivities differing from Dworkin's.

We can begin with the central values aspect, later turning to the structure's important effects. Dworkin has described his political community as what might be termed a relatively 'shallow' community. He perceives the scope of a political community's life, the domains of life in which one is accountable to the political community, as limited to those in which we contribute to the community's efforts to attain equal respect and concern without ourselves giving up the equal respect and concern the community owes us. A 'deeper' community might exhibit a fuller accountability of members to the political community across more areas of life. What form our political community should take is certainly an important question of political philosophy. There may well be decisive arguments for or against shallower or deeper forms of community. However, a theory of collective rights need not decide this if it can indicate the implications for collective rights of either kind of community.

Indeed, the central values of many communities will be contested. This reality does not prevent us from seeing that the values around which a collectivity is oriented, determining its shallowness or depth, fundamentally affect the nature of the obligations within it and thus the collective responsibilities. Let us consider, again, the example of a corporation.[100] On one theory, the central value of any corporation is to maximise profits for the shareholders while acting consistently with legal requirements. We might reason that the responsibilities mediated by the corporate collectivity are minimal – simply those associated with the end of profit maximisation and the requirement of legality. Employees would owe their contractual responsibilities and expect their contractual rights, but would not expect the corporation to be especially kind to them at Christmastime (except as a motivational tool to boost profits, or in compliance with legal holidays). The obligations of the corporation are limited but not absent. Indeed, if some combination of decisions resulted in a planned corporate act that would undermine profit maximisation, upset shareholders could rightly object that the corporation was violating its responsibilities to them. Of course, substantial

[100] The seminal treatment of corporations in this manner is found in French, *Collective and Corporate Responsibility* (n 8).

literature challenges this simple theory of corporations, asserting that corporations have more substantial external responsibilities, and that there is a corporate social responsibility (CSR). If so, then a corporation has other responsibilities, either because of general moral requirements or because social values are ingrained upon it. Such issues, though, remain contested. Even if they were resolved, questions would remain about the values of particular corporations.

A community need not be tremendously deep to ground collective responsibilities. Dworkin's account of political community is not as deep as some. Profit-maximisation by a corporation is yet shallower. Marlies Galenkamp's important book on conceptualising collective rights has assumed the contrary position at this juncture.[101] Galenkamp suggests that the minimum community depth required for the possibility of collective rights is a fully constitutive community, one in which the individual's identity is determined primarily by the community. This assumption underpins her main conclusion that collective rights are inherently theoretically dissonant with traditional individual rights.[102] Reaching a different conclusion here, then, undermines her pessimistic analysis of collective rights. Given this dramatic result, it is appropriate to take a moment to re-examine her argument.

Galenkamp argues that a conception of what she calls solidarity and community 'as prerequisite background variables, in the loose sense, for the realisation of collective rights'[103] does not sufficiently distinguish collective rights from individual rights. She notes arguments that individual human rights are based on a loose solidarity among all humanity and suggests that a loose community thus cannot ground collective rights distinctly from individual rights. Galenkamp's argument rests on a presupposition that collective rights and individual rights must be radically different in their foundation. However, similarities in their foundation would actually seem to be an argument *for* collective rights rather than an argument against them. So long as collective rights are distinct in some other way, such as being held by a collectivity, the fact that they share some foundations with individual rights does not make them indistinct. Galenkamp's work is an important effort, but the presuppositions at this juncture seem to send it astray. The central values of a collectivity need not create a 'deep' community in order to ground collective responsibilities and, as argued in the next section, collective rights. The central values affect the scope of the responsibilities mediated by the collectivity, but there can be responsibilities even with relatively minimal central values.

Consider, then, the other element, the structure of the collectivity. The structure influences collective responsibilities through both *subjective* and *objective* elements. In the subjective element, voluntariness of membership in a collectivity may increase the stringency of whatever responsibilities apply to that community. Though voluntary associations will often have narrowly circumscribed central values (a book club may be oriented only around reading books, with varying

[101] Galenkamp (n 7) 65–69.
[102] Ibid, 174–76.
[103] Ibid, 66.

degrees of friendship), these values will ground responsibilities firmly if members have voluntarily agreed to them. The volunteer fire brigade's responsibilities are, in a moral sense, grounded more firmly than those of an involuntary army to the extent that consensual promises have greater weight than involuntarily imposed obligations.

There remains, of course, some, albeit lesser, degree of voluntariness in a collectivity that persons did not join but are free to leave. Similarly, where persons can otherwise meaningfully dissociate themselves from a collectivity, their failure to do so may implicate them in some voluntariness. Of course, we could not expect visible dissent from everyone opposed to a collectivity where dissent is punished severely, though there might be another means of dissociation. In the absence of dissent, if some agreement can be implied, the collective responsibility can likewise be more stringent.

Young has advanced two claims that we might interpret as objections to this analysis. She has said: (1) 'A person joins an association, and even if membership in it fundamentally affects one's life, one does not take that membership to define one's very identity, in the way, for example, being Navaho might';[104] and (2) associative models of collectivities mistakenly conceive of individuals as prior to collectivities, when in fact groups constitute individuals.[105] The first actually accords with the prior argument in that voluntary associations often have circumscribed central values. Where this is not the case, however, any such objection fails. If Cassius Clay converts to Islam, changes his name to Muhammad Ali, and presumably also changes his conception of his own identity, his voluntarily adopted association defines his identity as fully as being Navaho would.

On Young's second point, the relation between individuals and collectivities is more complex than the objection makes out. David Miller has argued that conceiving of an individual as a 'radical chooser' who always chooses the collectivities of which he or she is a member makes little sense, as it assumes that abstract reasoning alone can tell us which collectivities to join.[106] The rejection of a 'radical chooser' conception also follows from the paradox that if everyone at some point in time were a radical chooser, there would be no collectivities from which to choose, so such a model is actually incoherent. Individuals cannot make choices about collectivities in this sense. But the fact remains that individuals do change between collectivities, and *some* collectivities are voluntary associations. So, one cannot deny the possibility of individual choices. Young seems to go too far in negating individual choice, perhaps in the process of fighting against trends in the other direction, but too far nonetheless. Subjective voluntariness of association can be a relevant factor that affects the nature and depth of the responsibilities mediated by a collectivity.

A second aspect of the structure of collectivities is objective and consists of reasonable expectations as to responsibilities in a particular collectivity – what

[104] Young, *Justice and the Politics of Difference* (n 46) 46.
[105] Ibid, 44–45.
[106] Miller, *On Nationality* (n 47) 44–45.

members are 'getting into'. These reasonable expectations are context-specific. For instance, expectations about familial membership and responsibilities might differ culturally. And certain contexts might cause sudden shifts in reasonable expectations. A set of passengers on a plane might be suddenly constituted into a collectivity and made morally responsible to act when one passenger begins strangling another,[107] or when hijackers start taking over the cockpit. The collectivity's responsibilities, as typical of a collectivity concerned only with circumstances of urgency,[108] will be oriented around very narrow values, and there will be no disgrace in cooperating temporarily with Jack the Ripper if he will work with the other passengers to help avert disaster. Of course, these reasonable expectations open the door to a whole host of other moral considerations where appropriate. The origins of a collectivity may give moral reasons for why responsibilities are shattered within that collectivity, such as in a newly annexed nation that owes no moral responsibilities to its conquerors. As touched upon when expounding Dworkin's account, the morality of membership rules and structure is relevant to responsibilities. The structure of a collectivity can clearly have important implications for the nature and extent of the responsibilities mediated by the collectivity.

It is thus possible to account for collective responsibilities in different kinds of collectivities by abstracting the two key elements from Dworkin's account and applying these elements to the particular circumstances of different collectivities. Both the central values of the collectivity and the structure of the collectivity have important implications. Of course, there would be interminable lists of different collectivities, but a few examples suffice. Collectivities meeting the conditions of community have moral responsibilities based on the central values and structure, as well as those mandated by external moral requirements.

V. COLLECTIVE RESPONSIBILITIES AND COLLECTIVE RIGHTS

Someone might think the fact that some collectivities have responsibilities immediately implies that these collectivities have the capacity for rights because they have moral status.[109] Indeed, I will argue that collective responsibilities imply capacities for moral rights. However, 'moral status' is variegated and bears closer examination.[110]

An agent may have different relationships to a right. For instance, Michael McDonald writes, 'being a claimant or an obligant assumes the possession of certain intellectual and practical capabilities . . . Being a beneficiary requires a

[107] V Held, 'Can a Random Collection of Individuals Be Morally Responsible?' (1970) 68 *Journal of Philosophy* 471.

[108] *Cf* J Moravcsik, 'Communal Ties' (1988) 62 (Supp) *American Psychological Association Proceedings* 211, 214.

[109] *Cf* CH Wellman, 'Liberalism, Communitarianism, and Group Rights' (1999) 18 *Law and Philosophy* 13, 26; L Green 'Two Views of Collective Rights' (1991) 4 *Canadian Journal of Law and Jurisprudence* 315, 315; French, *Collective and Corporate Responsibility* (n 8) vii.

[110] Galenkamp (n 7) 94.

relevant capacity for enjoyment.'[111] The status of having moral responsibilities and the status of having a capacity for moral rights are not precisely equivalent. The distinction between them is obvious when one considers the status of persons with certain severe disabilities that might rob them of the capacity to make moral decisions without meaning that they cease to have rights.[112]

We can draw on a distinction as to the meaning of 'having responsibilities'. *Moral responsibility* is a state of being subject to praise or blame for conduct, which implies a liability to an ascription of fault.[113] *Outcome responsibility*, in Tony Honoré's words, 'means being responsible for the good and the harm we bring about',[114] which implies a duty to compensate for harms. We need not resolve the controversy over which of these senses of responsibility is more basic, or in which domains each might be more relevant.[115] While some theorists would seem ready to apply only outcome responsibility to collectivities,[116] the account of community developed here enables us to see collectivities meeting the requirements of community as subject to moral responsibility as well. So we are interested in both senses of responsibility.

Moreover, having responsibilities in either sense actually presupposes a capacity for rights as a necessary precondition. Moral responsibilities are perhaps initially the clearer case. To be subject to *blame* requires a capacity to have acted otherwise than one actually did. We cannot *blame* someone for having done wrong unless that someone had other options than the wrongdoing.[117]

This requirement, of course, is more complicated than it might seem at first glance. We actually do want to blame people for acts to which they, in some sense, had no alternative. The individual who becomes intoxicated to the point of automatism and commits a wrongful act, even if not having a real alternative at the time of committing the act, is often considered morally blameworthy because he or she had an alternative to becoming intoxicated to that degree. There is thus some duration and generality to the capacity we require.[118] This interpretation of the principle, however, does not undermine it. In the general case, we do not blame someone who had no alternative.

[111] M McDonald, 'Collective Rights and Tyranny' in G Lafrance (ed) *Pouvoir et tyrannie* (Ottawa, Éditions de l'Université d'Ottawa, 1986) 119.

[112] In offering this counterexample, of course, I reject extreme 'claim' theories of rights, under which we get statements like: 'The having of interests is a necessary, though not sufficient condition for speaking of rights. The existence of rights presupposes *an agent, someone who is capable of making a claim*.' (Galenkamp (n 7) 49). On Raz's definition of rights, which we have assumed, while the existence of a right presupposes a subject, someone whose right it is, this subject need not be *capable of claiming* the right.

[113] *Cf* J Feinberg, *Doing and Deserving: Essays in the Theory of Responsibility* (Princeton, Princeton University Press, 1970) 136–37, 222; P Cane, *Responsibility in Law and Morality* (Oxford, Hart Publishing, 2002) 63.

[114] T Honoré, 'Responsibility and Luck: The Moral Basis of Strict Liability' (1988) 104 *Law Quarterly Review* 530, 530.

[115] *Cf* ibid, 541 and P Cane, 'Responsibility and Fault: A Relational and Functional Approach to Responsibility' in P Cane and J Gardner (eds) *Relating to Responsibility: Essays for Tony Honoré on His Eightieth Birthday* (Oxford, Hart Publishing, 2001) 81–82.

[116] For example, D Miller, 'Holding Nations Responsible' (2004) 114 *Ethics* 240.

[117] Honoré, 'Responsibility and Luck' (n 114) 533–34.

[118] *Cf* ibid, 548–50.

A relevant alternative for the purposes of this requirement obviously must also have been morally preferable, or at least not morally worse, than the course of action actually followed. Someone who does something that would otherwise be wrongful to avoid a far greater evil often deserves praise rather than blame. Understanding this aspect, however, highlights the possible impact on responsibility of having rights. The possession of a moral right will sometimes affect the moral acceptability of a particular course of action.

Raz is, of course, correct to note that having a right to do something is different from it being the right thing to do.[119] Waldron derives from the proposition that one can have a right to do something wrongful a conclusion that having a moral right cannot provide any justification at all for acting in accordance with it.[120] He offers an example to illustrate his reasoning, which may actually help refine his statement. He says that the fact that one has the right to marry someone manifestly unsuitable would not make it right to marry that person.[121] But it is apparent, at once, that whether one has the right to marry someone *affects the rightness* of marrying that person. Comparing two situations, in one of which one has a right to marry the beloved and in the other of which one does not, it is clear that the example actually points to the possibility that having a right can make a difference. Whether one has a right to do something *can affect* whether it is the right thing to do. We condemn more harshly someone who has not only married the wrong person but has done so without a right to do so. Having a moral right could then be essential to having a moral responsibility because it might affect the moral availability of alternative courses of action.

This kind of principle applies in a number of situations involving plausible collective responsibilities. If a corporation has a responsibility to protect confidential information of employees, it needs a right to some degree of privacy to assert when a nosy neighbour comes knocking at its door requesting good gossip from payroll and other records. If a political community has a responsibility to ensure some form of equality, it needs rights to enact appropriate policies that will negatively affect some individuals, even affect their rights, for the sake of the common good. We could multiply the examples. In many relevant situations, having responsibilities presupposes a capacity to have certain kinds of rights in order for the collectivity to be able, consistently with morality, to fulfill the responsibility.[122]

These instances are just examples of possible collective rights to make this specific point. On fuller analysis, they might or might not stand. Most importantly,

[119] J Raz, *The Authority of Law: Essays on Law and Morality* (Oxford, Oxford University Press, 1979) 266–67.

[120] J Waldron, 'A Right to Do Wrong' in *Liberal Rights: Collected Papers, 1981–1991* (Cambridge, Cambridge University Press, 1993) 73.

[121] Ibid.

[122] *Cf* B Slattery, 'Aboriginal Sovereignty and Imperial Claims' (1991) 29 *Osgoode Hall Law Journal* 681, 698 (arguing that a social group must have moral capacity to advance the interests of its members); C Beitz, 'Rawls's Law of Peoples' (2000) 110 *Ethics* 669, 682 (arguing peoples should be treated as having ethical significance because their flourishing affects their institutional ability to benefit members).

describing these potential rights is not meant to set out the limits of what collective rights there are. Making use of accepted individual rights is one way of demonstrating that we should accept the existence of collective moral rights, but collective rights will exist in broader contexts in which collective interests are sufficient to ground duties.

Moreover, although these examples make the general claim plausible, the argument need not rest on examples alone. To rest it there would invite an induction to a general principle that having responsibilities entails having a capacity for rights. But there is also available a more deductive argument on the relation between these states, and this argument can helpfully apply to both moral responsibility and outcome responsibility.

Having responsibility itself calls for certain forms of respect. To have responsibility, whether moral responsibility or outcome responsibility, is to have a moral status demanding respect as an agent capable of responsibility. So, for instance, we see that in criminal law, certain classes of defendants, choosing between different defences, have argued defences that affirm their responsibility for some act rather than deny it.[123] To adopt such an argument is to affirm one's status as an agent having responsibilities and, in turn, to demand respect as such an agent. In other words, it is to claim a status that includes rights to certain kinds of respect. Having responsibilities is a status that includes within it a basic capacity to be both an object of respect and a subject holding rights.

This reasoning addresses a major objection. Having the capacity for rights is sometimes explained in terms of a requirement of having value, and value of a particular kind. To help make this claim clear, there is an important distinction to draw. For something to be of ultimate value is for it to have value that does not derive from its contribution to something else; for something to be of instrumental value is for it to have value that derives from the value of its real or potential consequences.[124] On a line of argument grounded in Raz and Haksar, one could object that the condition of a subject having rights is that of having 'ultimate value', which amounts to being 'non-replaceable'.[125] The requirement is that the purported subject be 'non-replaceable' in the sense not of something that *could not* be replaced (for example, a unique painting) but in the sense of something that *must not* be replaced (for example, a human infant). One could claim that even if collectivities have intrinsic value,[126] they do not have ultimate value, as one may legitimately replace them, so the mere conclusion that they have responsibilities does not imply they have a capacity for rights.

The account in this chapter responds to this objection. If we say that only entities of ultimate value have rights, we forget a statement from Raz that could

[123] *Cf* J Gardner, 'The Mark of Responsibility' (2003) 23 *Oxford Journal of Legal Studies* 157, 160–61.

[124] J Raz, *The Morality of Freedom* (Oxford, Clarendon, 1986) 177.

[125] Ibid, 166; V Haksar, 'Collective Rights and the Value of Groups' (1998) 41 *Inquiry* 21, 21–25.

[126] For example, AW Musschenga, 'Intrinsic Value as a Reason for the Preservation of Minority Cultures' (1998) 1 *Ethical Theory and Moral Practice* 201; R Dworkin, *Life's Dominion: An Argument About Abortion and Euthanasia* (London, HarperCollins, 1993) 72.

seem puzzling in the absence of an account such as that just explored. Raz writes: 'An individual is capable of having rights if and only if either his well-being is of ultimate value or he is an artificial person (eg a corporation).'[127] The capacity of an artificial person for rights in this statement could seem like a bizarre tag-on. However, once we realise that a collectivity, a corporation or other, can act as a deep personification, mediating for persons of ultimate value, we see that a collectivity's capacity for rights makes sense. The collectivity mediates for agents of ultimate value, its rights indirectly protecting them. As Raz notes elsewhere, even interests of instrumental value can ground rights, such as with the moral right held by a journalist not to reveal her sources.[128] The capacity of collectivities to hold rights is not problematic.

In the next chapter, I will turn to how collectivities can have interests that ground rights. But note for the moment that the scope of a collectivity's responsibilities interacts with the scope of its rights, because it needs to have a capacity for rights at least in domains appropriate to its responsibilities. In general terms, though, where collectivities meet the previously discussed conditions of having responsibilities, we can further conclude that the communities in question have the necessary moral status that includes the capacity to hold a moral right. Collectivities are not outside the sphere of potential rights-holders. This point is a narrow one, not one defining the scope of collective rights, but one laying the groundwork for the interesting work to follow.

[127] Raz, *The Morality of Freedom* (n 124) 166.
[128] Ibid, 179.

3

Collective Interests and Collective Rights

I. INTRODUCTION

THIS CHAPTER DEVELOPS the argument for the existence of collective moral rights, showing that if certain individual rights exist, then at least some groups have rights. The argument draws substantially on John Finnis's argument for a particular conception of the common good, adopting something much along the lines of Finnis's 'common good' conception as the most appropriate description of a collective interest.

I will state the argument for the preferability of this conception in only a brief form here, with those readers wishing to examine the full technical application of Arrow's Impossibility Theorem able to turn to my past publications on this issue.[1] Although I will introduce that argument in the second section of this chapter so as to offer some justification for a non-aggregative conception of a collective interest, the main object of this chapter is to put the argument that there are non-reducible collective interests, some of which ground rights. Thus, the second section introduces the concept of a collective interest and briefly references the technical arguments that support a non-aggregative conception of a collective interest to give some idea of their tenor.

The third section then argues that Finnis's account of the common good can apply analogously as an account of collective interests. The fourth section uses this conception to argue that there are certain kinds of goods in which collectivities typically have interests, collective interests that are non-reducible to individual interests. Finally, the fifth section draws together the strands from the previous sections to argue that some collective interests ground rights if certain individual rights exist (using examples that include a religious group's collective right, necessary if there is a right to freedom of religion), thus making out a claim to the existence of collective rights.

[1] The full technical argument appears in DG Newman, 'Collective Interests and Collective Rights' (2004) 49 *American Journal of Jurisprudence* 127, which has also been reprinted in the collection of leading essays on group rights in P Jones (ed) *Group Rights* (Aldershot, Ashgate, 2008).

II. INTERESTS AND COLLECTIVITIES

An *interest* is a normative relation that holds when something (an *object*, being a description of a feature or possible feature of the state of the world[2]) makes someone's life (the *subject's*) go better overall. Interests, then, are not subjective preferences but objective relations between a subject and an object describing what objects make the subject's life go better overall. Calvin's receiving an education makes his life better overall, and he has an interest in going to school, no matter how much he would prefer not to go. A subject has an interest in an object if and only if that object makes that subject's life go better overall. On this usage, other than for the loss of linguistic fluidity when we go on to make more complicated arguments, we might equally say that the object is in the subject's interest.

Some would prefer this latter means of speaking, then retaining the term 'interest' for something that makes one's life go better in some aspect.[3] There are two reasons for my adoption of the overall-interest approach, neither of which would interfere with an alternative exposition of the theory based on the aspect-interest approach. First, it makes the exposition clearer as it summarises the range of individual interests at stake. Second, our principal moral engagement is not with the protection of objects that make someone's life go better in some aspect but worse overall (if such a description is coherent in the aggregation it implicitly requires), as we are not principally engaged with various rights to be harmed. Rather, our reason for concern with any aspect of one's life is its contribution to the individual's life overall, so I will retain a focus here on overall-interests. If someone nonetheless wished to maintain the alternative usage, however, it would be possible to do so, at the expense of further complexity in what will already be complex arguments. I can proceed without worry to discuss as the central concern interests that make lives go better overall.

The concept of an *individual interest* thus seems to follow straightforwardly: an individual has an interest in an object if and only if that object makes that individual's life go better. This implication follows 'straightforwardly', of course, in only an attenuated sense. First, the good life remains contested. So, obviously, the content that fits within the formula would be contested. Secondly, and perhaps most importantly for the formula itself, it seemingly contains a fundamental ambiguity. Surely, what makes one's life go better depends on the present conditions and circumstances of one's life. Annette's owning a heavy copy of the *Aeneid* makes her life go better if she is engaged in a programme of reading Roman literature but not if she is a Saharan nomad unable to read Latin and harmed by carrying it. This implication does not undermine the formula itself, as it simply defines interests for each set of circumstances. Later, however, we will return to this point,

[2] The term 'object' obviously does not apply in a physical sense, though an individual may have an interest in the possession of a certain physical object.

[3] *Cf* eg J Raz, *The Morality of Freedom* (Oxford, Clarendon, 1986) 180 (discussing rights that make someone's life better in some respect but worse overall).

for the fact that the fulfillment of some interests is necessary to the very existence of others helps demonstrate the existence of collective rights.

Before I turn to those matters, I must introduce a concept that seems even less straightforward. The concept of a *collective interest*, referring to the interest of a collectivity, seems more problematic than the concept of an individual interest. I argued above that collectivities do have an irreducible identity, so we cannot be reluctant to conceptualise a collective 'life' that could go better or worse.

That said, some might object from the outset that any collective 'life' is metaphorical in a way that an individual life is not, perhaps arguing, for instance, that sentience is necessary to having an interest.[4] Any such restriction would actually risk undermining the claim of some individuals to the holding of interests, a possibly unacceptable result that tells against the theory.[5] However, in any event, my claim for rights based on collective interests is not based on an argument that collective interests are the same as individual interests but on the argument made later in this chapter that collective rights must be recognised if certain individual rights are. I established the claim that collectivities can hold rights in chapter two and rest on that argument.

Nonetheless, a collectivity itself has individual members, and its collective life is connected with their individual lives, so we might wonder if there is some relation between their individual interests and the collective interest. Does this complication disrupt the notion of a collective interest? There are two fundamentally different ways of conceiving of collective interests. One might conceive of collective interests as, in some fashion, *aggregative*: aggregative of the interests of individual members, or what we might describe more broadly as being functions of the individual interests of the members.[6] Or one might conceive of collective interests as *non-aggregative*, at least potentially independent of the individual interests of the members. I will consider first the possibility of aggregative conceptions of a collective interest, arguing that these conceptions do not work, before turning in the next section to a non-aggregative conception.

An aggregate interest has, from the outset, an odd feature in that it is non-neutral with respect to potentially trivial changes in a collectivity's membership.[7] An aggregate interest will vary based on both changes in the interests of continuing members and changes in membership. Even a very minor change in a collectivity's membership could change the aggregate interest if, for instance, a new member's interests diverged in the appropriate way. This feature is problematic

[4] See G Rainbolt, *The Concept of Rights* (Dordrecht, Springer, 2006).

[5] Griffin pursues the logical but devastating conclusion that infants and those with certain disabilities have no rights: J Griffin, *On Human Rights* (Oxford, Oxford University Press, 2008) 95.

[6] A *function* is a mapping of an element of one set (here, the set of vectors of interests of individuals) to an element of another set (here, the set of aggregate interests).

[7] David Miller offers a variation of this argument in his criticism of Raz's approach. Miller claims that on Raz's aggregation-based view, a trivial interest could turn into a right if held by enough persons: D Miller, 'Group Rights, Human Rights and Citizenship' (2002) 10 *European Journal of Philosophy* 178, 184–85. Miller's argument, however, does not present a convincing objection because it does not explain why one could not have a prior qualitative requirement on the interests that could ground rights.

in a collectivity, for a *collectivity* (as opposed to a *set*) remains the same collectivity even with changed membership. This latter requirement is in tension with the possibility of interests that are highly volatile with respect to changes in membership. While the interests of a collectivity obviously do not solely determine its identity, neither are they unrelated to it. We would need to analyse further the relationship between character and identity to say more, but we can nonetheless perceive that dramatic changes in a collectivity's interests could be tantamount to changes in its identity.

An aggregate interest's susceptibility to this problem, however, depends on the functional form of the aggregation. Some, such as those looking for a unanimity of interests, would be highly vulnerable to a change in membership, since it depends on a sort of identity amongst the members' interests. The addition of one member having different interests destroys the shared interest. Other functional forms of aggregation are less sensitive to a change in membership. Thus, one might conclude only that this odd feature restricts the kind of functions that could be used to relate individual interests to the aggregate interest.

More troubling yet would be any argument that calls into question the very principle of aggregation. That emerges when one considers that aggregation must have some *point*, must *tell us something* more about what matters to a collectivity than we knew before we began. If it fails to do so, it fails to *be* an *aggregation*, but becomes a sort of verbal trickery (in the way an arithmetical aggregation of three plus three would be unsatisfactory if it were reported back as 'the sum of three and three'), a mere *pretence*.

An aggregation of individual interests into an aggregated collective interest, I have argued,[8] cannot tell us something more about the collectivity. If it is even possible to aggregate interests – and I examine also a possible argument where interests are considered incommensurable – then their aggregation is subject to Arrow's Impossibility Theorem, which ends up having the implication that the aggregated collective interest function will not provide a logically consistent (transitive) ordered list of the collectivity's interest in different states of affairs.[9] The implication is that aggregative conceptions of a collective interest are very problematic.

III. NON-AGGREGATIVE COLLECTIVE INTERESTS

An alternative to the approaches outlined thus far is to describe a collective interest analogously to the way in which we would describe an individual interest. Given that an interest is something that makes someone's life go better, then, a collective interest is something that makes a collectivity's life go better. That life, consisting of the collectivity's flourishing as it contributes to the lives of its members and their purposes in coming together in the collectivity, can guide us toward

[8] See generally Newman, 'Collective Interests and Collective Rights' (n 1).

[9] For the full technical argument, see ibid.

a concept of collective interest. One may, on this conception, then take a *collective interest* to be a factor that contributes toward the continued collaboration of the members of a community as viable and reasonable, along the lines of Finnis's conception of the 'common good'.[10] It is something that makes a community thrive and flourish. This section develops this concept and argues that it offers a good account of the notion at issue.

What does it mean to speak of a factor that contributes toward the continued collaboration of the members of a community as viable and reasonable? As Finnis describes it, the common good is the

> factor or set of factors (whether a value, a concrete operational objective, or the conditions for realizing a value or attaining an objective), which, as considerations in someone's practical reasoning, would make sense of or give reason for his collaboration with others and would likewise, from their point of view, give reason for their collaboration with each other and with him.[11]

The collective interests of a particular collectivity are those factors corresponding to its common good. They are not unrelated to members' individual interests, for the collectivity's moral existence depends on its ability to provide a collective interest that improves the lives of its individual members. At the same time, the collective interest is not simply reducible to, or even an aggregative function of, its members' individual interests. It is, rather, a set of factors facilitating the fulfillment of the individual interests of diverse members at the same time.

An example helps make these abstract words clearer. Consider a union (as a collectivity, irrespective of whether it has legal recognition). It has structure consisting of membership rules and values concerned with representation of workers (and, perhaps, advancement of social justice). The union will flourish in being better able to advance these values if legal rules allow it to strike and require workers in a particular workplace to be members of the union. The union thus has a collective interest in the existence of these legal rules. This collective interest clearly may not correspond to the interests of each individual member. Some individuals would be better off negotiating their own contracts outside union membership, and it may be in some individuals' interests never to strike. Nonetheless, the union's collective interests will be attuned to the interests of its members in general terms because it represents them and serves them.

This example illustrates that although the collective interest is a different concept and is non-aggregative in its nature, individual interests are not irrelevant to it. The collective interest must respond in certain ways to the interests of individual members. A community will serve its members, making the two concepts of collective interest and individual interests inextricably bound together.

[10] *Cf* J Finnis, *Natural Law and Natural Rights* (Oxford, Clarendon, 1980) 154 (defining a 'common good'); J Moravcsik, 'Communal Ties' (1988) 62(Supp) *American Psychological Association Proceedings* 211, 214 (defining 'communal ties').

[11] Finnis (n 10) 154.

Some will properly raise the question of the relation to the collective interest of particular individuals and sub-collectivities whose interests differ from those of the collectivity as a whole. There are two distinct issues implicit in this question. First, it might call into question whether there is a collective interest at all. Second, it might suggest that there are other interests that conflict with the collective interest.

First, in some circumstances, one must be very careful about suggesting the existence of a particular collective interest. For instance, David Ingram has noted the dangers of stereotyping groups as having particular interests that are shared by all members of the group. He suggests that this danger has been at play when certain racial groups have been grouped in electoral districts for the purposes of representation on an assumption that they have interests in common, and some judges have shared these concerns.[12] Ingram writes: 'Unlike members of the American Cattle Breeders Association, who share a unique interest in furthering the breeding of cattle, members of the group racially designated as African Americans share no unique interest that distinguishes them from other groups.'[13]

Although Ingram's claim might apply to the special context of electoral representation, we do not generally need a unique collective interest to distinguish a collectivity from other collectivities. For instance, as Ingram recognises, a collectivity will also be distinguished based on various social, historical, and customary rules.[14] Indeed, were one to insist upon a unique collective interest, one would recognise very few collectivities. So, that part of the statement has limited applications.

Nonetheless, Ingram's statement raises an important point. One would act wrongly to stereotype diverse groups and somehow impose upon them non-genuine collective interests. But diversity within a collectivity does not mean that a particular collectivity has no collective interests. Ingram does not say what he means by a 'shared interest'. Even cattle breeders may have very limited 'shared interests' in any pertinent sense; larger and smaller cattle operations will prefer very different kinds of economic policies to support cattle breeding. So, his statements must refer to the sort of collective interest that the cattle breeders' collectivity will have. But then so could the African American community have such an interest. Even though members of the African American community are diverse in many ways, if they constituted a collectivity and a community, they would surely have collective interests that would include, though not necessarily be limited to, the prevention of group harms directed against their community. So, there is a need for caution, but the account does not cease to apply.

This discussion leads to the second issue: the possibility of conflicting interests and whether this possibility raises questions about collective interests. Where individuals or other collectivities within a collectivity are diverse and have interests differing from the collective interest, their interests can provide moral reasons against fulfillment of the collective interest. In some circumstances, the collective

[12] D Ingram, *Group Rights: Reconciling Equality and Difference* (Lawrence, University Press of Kansas, 2001) 51–52, citing O'Connor J in *Shaw v Reno*, 509 US 630, 647 (1993).

[13] Ingram (n 12) 56.

[14] *Cf* ibid, 53, 57, 67.

interest will ultimately be sufficient to outweigh them. In others, it will not, particularly where the minority interests are sufficient to ground a duty, and thus amount to rights. But, clearly, conflicts between different interests are a pervasive feature of life, and their existence does not challenge the initial existence and importance of collective interests.

A frequent complaint against collective rights is that they are a redundant concept, which must ultimately be reducible to some set of individual rights.[15] Michael Hartney has specifically questioned references to a 'collective interest' as being anything other than an aggregate interest. He has offered this test: 'If a collective interest is to be more than a mere aggregate interest, it must be possible, in principle, for it to conflict with the interests of *most* of the members of the group.'[16] However, this test is misstated. An aggregate interest, at least if based on a function considering weightiness of interests rather than simply a majority vote, could obviously conflict with the interests of most members where the interests of a minority of members in some object simply happened to be especially weighty and the contrary interests were relatively trivial. The test Hartney ought to have posed is that a non-redundant collective interest must conceptually be able to conflict with enough sufficiently important interests of individual members so as to be distinguishable from an aggregation of individual interests.

A trivial case can establish the distinguishability on this test of a collective interest from an aggregate interest. Consider a collectivity that has temporarily ceased to have any current members. This is permissible on the definition of collectivity with which we began, for it refers to a collection of persons in a non-time-dependent way and specifically refers to the possibility of all members of the collectivity simultaneously changing without the identity of the collectivity changing. Obviously, this is a non-standard case, but it illustrates an important principle. There could not be any aggregate interest, since there are no current members. But there could still be collective interests rendering the collaboration inherent in the community of the collectivity reasonable and viable.

This conclusion may not seem terribly satisfactory. Several objections could be made. First, someone could claim that this arrives at an immoral account, one that is now putting moral weight on personifications rather than on real persons. But the account does not do that. It does put moral weight on collectivities as well as on individuals, so perhaps the objection is to that. To wit, someone might try to assert an intuition that the moral interests and rights of a collectivity must be aggregative and based on the interests of persons. For example, the objector might suggest that the moral interests or rights of some church in governmental non-interference in its liturgy derive from its members' moral claims. After all, the objector might ask us to agree, if 'a church were suddenly abandoned by all its

[15] For example, C Wellman, *Real Rights* (Oxford, Oxford University Press, 1995) 167–69; V Haksar, 'Collective Rights and the Value of Groups' (1998) 41 *Inquiry* 21, 31–35.

[16] M Hartney, 'Some Confusions Concerning Collective Rights' (1991) 4 *Canadian Journal of Law and Jurisprudence* 293, 300.

members[,] [t]hen it would not, as a collective entity, retain a residual right to freedom of religion'.[17]

But such an intuition, like intuitions generally, gets us nowhere since someone could easily assert the contrary intuition. On this version, if a church did lose all of its members, one would not properly say that the church as a collectivity immediately lost any moral interests it held. The government could not come in and begin rewriting all of the church's doctrines and appropriate its name for a government youth club without causing harm. On the contrary, the church would retain residual interests or rights on a temporary basis in accordance with the structure and values of the collectivity and the factors that contributed to its continued collaboration as reasonable and viable. Of course, after a temporary period, if the church gained no adherents, perhaps no factors could any longer render its community reasonable and viable. If a community will never exist again, it cannot continue to have rights.[18] But this would not be an immediate and instantaneous result at the same moment that the members left.[19]

Someone could, however, object that this argument has not escaped the horns of logical redundancy. An objection could run that one could account for this case with an aggregate interest reductive to individual interests simply by devising a means of counting the interests of future persons, suggesting that we maintain the church because other persons will join it again in future and we are concerned for their interests. This objection, however, oddly assumes that one can impute group membership to individuals who do not yet exist and do not yet have identities, which verges on the unintelligible.[20]

This concept of collective interests thus escapes the problems faced by other conceptions of a collectivity's interest and is non-redundant. Whether such interests are of value is a question for the next sections. For the moment, however, there are good reasons to prefer it to the aggregative conception.

Notably, this account is better at explaining the normal mode of reasoning about self-determination. On an aggregative account of collective rights, 'though the existence of the interest does not depend on the size of the group, the existence of the right and its strength does'.[21] In other words, the logical implication is that the existence of a right like self-determination, since it depends on whether the cumulative interest is sufficient to ground a duty, depends directly on the number of members in the collectivity claiming self-determination. Were this conception correct, however, we might expect politicians, or at least political the-

[17] M Galenkamp, *Individualism versus Collectivism: The Concept of Collective Rights*, 2nd edn (Rotterdam, Gouda Quint, 1998) 193. This objection also draws inspiration from comments in an unpublished paper presented by Professor Elizabeth Kiss at the 1995 Amerian Political Science Association meeting.

[18] See M Seymour, *De la Tolérance à la Reconnaissance: Une théorie libérale des droits collectifs* (Montréal, Boréal, 2008) 31–32 (need for sufficient number and duration of membership).

[19] Indeed, in a case to be discussed later in this chapter, there were claims that a church that had ceased to exist in communist Moldova for some five decades had been revived under canon law: *Case of Metropolitan Church of Bessarabia v Moldova* app no 45701/99 (2002) 35 EHRR 13 (ECHR) [10].

[20] *Cf* P Jones, 'Group Rights and Group Oppression' (1999) 7 *Journal of Political Philosophy* 353, 367.

[21] Ibid.

orists, to make arguments such as 'Quebec has seven million people. Therefore, when we add up everyone's interests, Quebec has a right to self-determination.' But arguments for self-determination are usually couched in terms of claims about the presence of a distinct culture, a distinct identity, and so on. One might say that some of these considerations simply hide a numbers requirement. A distinct culture, for instance, presupposes some minimal number of people[22] – Robinson Crusoe cannot alone constitute a distinct culture, but simply manifests another culture conjoined with personal idiosyncrasies. However, here, the argument rests on something else, which depends on numbers only implicitly. The dependence on numbers is indirect.

Allen Buchanan has done a great service in his pioneering work on the morality of secession, which included a statement of the arguments for and against secession in ordinary moral reasoning.[23] The arguments for secession include arguments based on liberty, consensual political association, enhancing efficiency, ending exploitation, rectifying past injustices, self-determination and cultural preservation. Although Buchanan specifically suggests that the latter arguments must be considered as based on individual interests,[24] he simultaneously accepts that reduction of secession to individual acts is problematic: it is impossible to define the content of the decision in which an individual voting in a referendum to secede is participating without reference to a group, and the exercise requires collective action.[25] The arguments against secession are also relevant. They include: the prevention of anarchy; distributive justice and the prevention of wrongful taking; the minimisation of strategic bargaining; the preservation of legitimate expectations; and the self-determination and democratic governance of the larger community.[26] What is noteworthy in both lists is that the arguments in the latter part of the lists are inextricably tied to collectivities.

For example, the rectification of past injustices through the treatment of a modern group depends on a connection between the modern group and the historic group, which might best be realised through the existence of a collectivity having the same identity. Similarly, self-determination is necessarily an interest of a collectivity – the word as applied to an individual refers to a different concept. Our moral reasoning about secession or a right to self-determination properly includes references to collective interests such as a collectivity's interest in being self-determining (for example, a people determining its own political, economic, and cultural path).

The aggregative account that would reduce an interest in self-determination to a summation of individual interests fails for the reasons argued in these last two sections. Our ordinary moral discourse on secession and self-determination makes

[22] *Cf* Seymour (n 18) (who makes this a significant precondition to a collective right).

[23] A Buchanan, *Secession: The Morality of Political Divorce from Fort Sumter to Lithuania and Quebec* (Boulder, Westview, 1991).

[24] Ibid, 53.

[25] Ibid, 76. *Cf* also Jones (n 20) 353.

[26] He also discusses institutional considerations in A Buchanan, 'The International Institutional Dimension of Secession' in PB Lehning (ed) *Theories of Secession* (London, Routledge, 1998).

sense. But we cannot rest with mere intelligibility when the prospect of justifiability is before us. Let us now turn to the collective nature of certain interests and then to the necessity of certain collective rights.

IV. COLLECTIVE INTERESTS AND GOODS

Theorists who have touched on collective rights have sometimes argued for collective rights to certain kinds of goods. For instance, in describing collective rights, Raz states that one of the conditions of a collective right is that 'the interests in question are the interests of individuals as members of a group in a public good and the right is a right to that public good because it serves their interest as members of the group'.[27] A theoretical approach associating collective rights with interests in particular kinds of goods, of course, is not unique to Raz. This section discusses his account alongside the analyses of other writers such as Denise Réaume and Jeremy Waldron, all of whom suggest that rights to certain kinds of goods can be held only collectively, arguing for a sort of 'holding constraint'.[28]

I will argue, rather, that there are particular kinds of goods in which collectivities typically have interests. Some kinds of goods are obviously the objects of individual interests. Others might be the object of either individual interests or collective interests or both, and we can discuss briefly the significance of this point. Yet other kinds of goods, however, have a particular significance in being subject to a 'holding constraint' such that they can be the object in the fullest sense only of a collective interest.

First, however, it is useful to have certain terminology. *Goods*, in the relevant sense, are potential objects of interest that are of value. Goods in the category of *public goods* have been of particular interest to both economists and philosophers. A *public good* is, on the economists' definition, a good that is both non-exclusionary (meaning that if the good is provided to anyone, no member of society can be excluded from benefitting from it) and non-rival in consumption (meaning that more than one individual can simultaneously benefit from the good without preventing others from also consuming the good).[29] Raz has drawn a further distinction between inherent and contingent public goods. *Contingent public goods* are goods whose non-exclusionary nature is a contingent fact that results from the present state of technology; for instance, though we cannot do so today, with different technology, we might exclude some members of society from clean air, so clean air is a contingent public good. *Inherent public goods* (which Raz also calls 'collective goods', though I will not follow this usage) are '[g]eneral beneficial features of a society', diffuse in nature, from which we could not exclude individuals with

[27] Raz, *The Morality of Freedom* (n 3) 208.

[28] I believe the term in this context originates with James Morauta's critique of such a constraint: J Morauta, 'Rights and Participatory Goods' (2002) 22 *Oxford Journal of Legal Studies* 91.

[29] For example, JE Stiglitz, *Economics*, 2nd edn (New York, Norton, 1997) 157.

any technology.[30] Inherent public goods would include a tolerant society, an educated society, and so on.

Raz argues that inherent public goods are not objects of individual rights. He says that it is difficult to imagine an argument that the interest of one individual in an inherent public good could ground a duty:

> The maintenance of a collective good [inherent public good] affects the life and imposes constraints on the activities of the bulk of the population, in matters which deeply affect them. It is difficult to imagine a successful argument imposing a duty to provide a collective good on the ground that it will serve the interests of one individual.'[31]

Let us call this *Raz's inherent public good argument*, or *RIPGA*.

Later, Raz defines what he calls a 'collective right' (which we might call a 'Razian collective right' so as to distinguish this usage from our usage). A *Razian collective right* is defined thus:

> A collective right exists when the following three conditions are met. First, it exists because an aspect of the interest of human beings justifies holding some person(s) to be subject to a duty. Second, the interests in question are the interests of individuals as members of a group in a public good and the right is a right to that public good because it serves their interest as members of the group. Thirdly, the interest of no single member of that group in that public good is sufficient by itself to justify holding another person to be subject to a duty.[32]

Denise Réaume has posed important challenges to Raz's analysis, and her account merits attention. However, one might note first how one slip that she makes in describing Raz's argument can expose a particular feature of his argument. According to Réaume, 'Raz contends that valid individual rights to public goods are unlikely'.[33] However, Raz makes no such argument. As noted above, RIPGA does not argue against individual rights to public goods in general but against individual rights to inherent public goods. Razian collective rights, however, are defined in terms of public goods that serve the interests of individual members of a group 'as members of the group'. In other words, Razian collective rights are not defined as applying exclusively to inherent public goods. Although inherent public goods would presumably meet automatically the third condition of a Razian collective right, Réaume is right to question whether there might not be some other feature of certain goods more relevant to their status.

Réaume's argument makes use of a different distinction. She argues that individual rights 'can be claimed only with respect to goods or opportunities that can

[30] Raz, *The Morality of Freedom* (n 3) 199. Despite Denise Réaume's suggestion that Raz follows only half the economists' definition of public goods (D Réaume, 'Individuals, Groups, and Rights to Public Goods' (1988) 38 *University of Toronto Law Journal* 1, 3), Raz follows the economists' definition of public goods in general, though his mention of the non-rival feature is less noticeable (but present at *The Morality of Freedom* (n 3) 199). For a distinction similar to Raz's, *cf* L Green *The Authority of the State* (Oxford, Clarendon, 1990) 207–209.

[31] Raz, *The Morality of Freedom* (n 3) 203.

[32] Ibid, 208.

[33] Réaume (n 30) 3.

be individualized, that is, a good in which one's interest can be distinguished from, and possibly opposed to, that of others'.[34] She offers the concept of *participatory goods*, which are valuable because of the participation of many in their enjoyment and where 'the good *is* the participation'.[35] Examples include culture, friendship, and a hockey game, all of which require either certain or indeterminate numbers of participants, in any case more than one individual, if they are even to exist. According to Réaume, each exists only by virtue of joint participation in it, and there cannot be a distinguishable individual interest in such goods.[36]

However, this does not seem right. Participatory goods could seemingly be objects of some sorts of 'distinguishable' individual interests. Taking Réaume's description, there seems no reason why playing hockey could not be 'a good in which one's interest can be distinguished from, and possibly opposed to, that of others'. There would, after all, be nothing incoherent in saying that Bob is excited by a hockey game and it makes Bob's life better to play hockey, even though Carl, who has been coerced into playing against his better instincts to spend the time philosophising about rights, is made worse off by playing hockey. And Réaume would seemingly accept this point to a degree, since she accepts that 'many of these [participatory] goods may also be privately or individually enjoyed to a certain extent'.[37]

This example points toward a necessary reinterpretation. Suppose that Bob is part of a team, the Iglooville Icewizards, whose members want to play hockey. They eagerly await the freezing of the local pond, the only place they can play. Suppose also that Bob has no other use for the frozen pond except insofar as it gives the Iglooville Icewizards a place to play. In the circumstances, in the absence of the other team members, he would have nothing to do with a frozen pond but gaze at it plaintively and wish he had a team with whom to play hockey. Yet the Iglooville Icewizards, the collectivity composed of Bob and a number of others, does have a collective interest in having a frozen pond available, because the frozen pond's availability contributes toward the continued flourishing of this collectivity. We might then speak of Bob having an interest in the pond freezing, but we would have to do so only in a derivative sense. Bob has such an interest only insofar as it is mediated through the community of the hockey team; he has no such interest individually without the Iglooville Icewizards. In other words, the collective interest is primary.

An objector might try to claim that Bob has an individual interest in the pond freezing either (1) insofar as it provides one of the conditions for the existence of a

[34] Ibid, 8.

[35] Ibid, 10. This can be compared to several different concepts: Ronald Dworkin's 'social goods' in *A Matter of Principle* (Cambridge MA, Harvard University Press, 1985) 230; Leslie Green's 'shared goods' (Green (n 30) 208); and Jeremy Waldron's 'communal goods' in 'Can Communal Goods Be Human Rights?' in *Liberal Rights: Collected Papers, 1981–1991* (Cambridge, Cambridge University Press, 1993).

[36] Réaume (n 30) 9.

[37] Ibid, 10. See also G Rainbolt 'What are Group Rights?' in C Sistare, L May and L Francis (eds) *Groups and Group Rights* (Lawrence, University Press of Kansas, 2001) 77–78 (arguing a 'family's right to watch a baseball game' is plausibly simply the combination of each individual's right to watch the baseball game).

functioning hockey team, which is in his interest; or (2) because Bob has an interest in the frozen pond conditional on the availability of other individuals with whom to play hockey. Objection (1), however, merely restates that there is a derivative individual interest. On the terms on which the argument has proceeded, the conditions for the existence of a functioning hockey team are by definition collective interests, and Bob's individual interest, derivative from these conditions, is thus an individual interest derivative from a collective interest.

Objection (2) is perhaps more problematic, especially given that one can strengthen it further. James Morauta, writing in response to Réaume and Waldron, has made analogous arguments in the context of language rights. Morauta distinguishes between the satisfaction conditions of a right and the benefits that a right can have.[38] Applying this distinction in the present context, one might say that the freezing of the pond and the availability of other team members are simply both necessary satisfaction conditions for the fulfillment of an interest that ultimately benefits Bob as an individual.

This objection might seem compelling, but it is answerable. The two satisfaction conditions stated by the objector (the freezing of the pond and the availability of other team members) are conceptually different. The availability of other team members, while obviously not determinable by Bob, results from a reality of a collectivity or collective agent of which he is a member. This differs from a mere physical fact about the world, such as the freezing of a pond. The objection effectively blurs two conditions that have radically different connections to human agency. To change one condition, the freezing of the pond, would be to change a physical fact and not to coerce anyone; to change the other, to make a team available, would be to control the existence of a collectivity and thus to coerce human agency.

There is a difference between the two purported satisfaction conditions. This difference amounts to a realisation that one condition, the freezing of the pond, is simply a satisfaction condition. The other, the availability of the hockey team, is a statement about human agency and the existence of a collective agent that derivatively makes the beneficial good contribute to Bob's individual interest. Bob has no non-derivative individual interest in the freezing of the pond. Bob has an individual interest in the flourishing of the hockey team, and the flourishing hockey team has a collective interest in the availability of the ice rink. Again, Bob's individual interest in the frozen pond is derivative from the primary collective interest.

To say that the collective interest is primary does not claim that collectivities are the fundamental moral unit.[39] That Bob's interest is derivative from a primary interest does not mean that Bob is unimportant; persons might still be the fundamentally important unit and the hockey team might be important only instrumentally to its members. Bob's interest need not be derivative in the sense of

[38] Morauta (n 28) 102.

[39] Such a claim would have to face the challenges of A Sharp, 'What if Value and Rights Lie Foundationally in Groups? The Maori Case' (1999) 2 *Critical Review of International Social and Political Philosophy* 1.

'non-fundamental' in order to be 'non-primary'. The argument here makes a point about the non-reducibility of certain structures, not about their ultimate moral importance.

To speak of some interests as derivative from others in this sense might then seem a needless complication. Why, after all, could we not just say that Bob has an individual interest in the frozen pond, regardless of whether it is derivative? Why, when we could through various contortions refer to individual interests, should we affirm a sort of irreducibility to these collective interests? Three reasons present themselves. First, drawing the distinction offers more analytical precision, which is valuable in itself. To ascribe to Bob an individual interest in the frozen pond without saying more is to gloss over an essential element to his interest – the particular forms of human agency without which his interest ceases to exist – and thus to make a less precise statement. Second, this greater analytical precision allows us to understand better our various alternatives in the face of tough choices. If the collectivity can flourish in some other way, it becomes clear that there might be substitutes for the frozen pond – offering a clarity denied us if we adopted simply the reductionist account that Bob has an interest in the pond freezing. Third, this account can actually offer further explanation for somewhat fuzzy notions in the work of other theorists. In the last parts of this section, I will further develop the account, while simultaneously showing how it helps explain Raz's notion of interests of individuals 'as members', the notions of non-individualisable goods in Raz and Réaume, and Kymlicka's notion of 'group-differentiated rights'.

We can first make more sense of Raz's notion of interests of individuals 'as members of a group',[40] which is either unexplained or else explained in the scarcely clearer notion of an interest individuals have 'that arises out of the fact that they are members of the group'.[41] What makes one interest Catalina's interest as a Spaniard or as a Basque and another simply her interest? In an account based on an aggregation of individual interests, it is unclear what would differentiate an interest 'as a member' from any other interest. This concept is clearer in the context of the possibility of a collective interest. Just as the primary interest in a frozen pond resides in the team, the primary interest in self-determination resides in a collectivity. Self-determination enables a community to flourish. It impacts on individual lives only via their membership of that community. Individuals have an interest in self-determination as members. Individuals who have interests 'as members' have derivative interests, interests based on their membership of a collectivity whose flourishing would make their lives better.

One might begin to wonder if there are certain kinds of goods in which collectivities typically have interests. The range of different kinds of collectivities in human life may make it seem difficult to generalise. Nonetheless, there is an obvious implication that collectivities have interests in those goods that promote the flourishing of the collectivities. Nothing in this statement implies that collectivities

[40] Raz, *The Morality of Freedom* (n 3) 208.
[41] Ibid, 209.

do not have interests in non-public goods. A club will have a property interest in controlling its clubhouse, a union its office equipment, and a people its petroleum. But there is arguably a special relation between collectivities and some category such as inherent public goods or participatory goods, the arguments for which I have not yet directly addressed; after all, these categories purportedly refer to benefits of a sort that cannot be in individuals' direct interest as individuals. Might they be considered the paradigm senses of collective interests?

We must proceed cautiously, for more individual interests exist than we might initially consider. Obviously, many goods are in their primary sense individual interests – for example, Paul's ownership of a zippy sports car. (I say 'in their primary sense', for collectivities whose interests include interests in the well-being of their members may have a derivative collective interest in these objects.) In addition, some goods might be in both individual and collective interests. Thinking back to Bob and now stipulating that he will make use of an ice rink not just while playing on his hockey team but also to go skating alone, he would then have a distinct individual interest in its availability at the same time that his hockey team has a collective interest in it. If Seyla will improve her French language abilities in a francophone school, she has an individual interest in its operations at the same time that a francophone language community has a collective interest. Many contingent public goods will be of this sort.

This discussion raises a second notion which this account can help explain, the description of collective goods as in some way non-individualisable. Raz, Réaume and Waldron each offer different versions of this claim. On one reading of Raz, his RIPGA argument says that the right to a Razian collective good is non-individualisable (depending not only on the interests of an individual) because no individual interest alone is weighty enough to justify the right.[42] But it is mere conjecture that no individual interest alone is weighty enough to justify the good.[43] Indeed, one might as easily conjecture that some individual interests are weighty enough to justify Razian collective goods – even one individual's interest in life could justify measures to protect the person's life that would constitute a Razian collective good.

A slightly transformed reading of Raz would be that he claims some goods are non-individualisable (or not based solely on the interest of an individual) because they cannot economically be produced for one individual.[44] Réaume develops this reading, however, into a more refined form, suggesting that the nature of 'participatory goods' means that they cannot be produced *for* one individual, because they are produced *by* multiple individuals. A cultured society involves the participation of many in its creation, just as Waldron suggests 'conviviality' at a party requires collective production of the good.[45] Réaume then tries to draw a conclusion:

[42] Ibid, 186–90.
[43] Réaume (n 30) 3–6, 9.
[44] *Cf* Raz, *The Morality of Freedom* (n 3) 207–209; Réaume (n 30) 9.
[45] Réaume (n 30) 9–11; Waldron (n 35).

'An individual cannot have a right to such an activity [a cultured society] because it cannot be enjoyed as an individual. If it could be provided to a single person it would be worthless to him.'[46] On this argument, social participation in production and exercise of a right would mean that it was non-individualisable in a deeper sense.

However, social production of some good does not imply irreducibly social enjoyment of that good.[47] Moreover, social participation in the production or use of a good does not necessarily seem equivalent to social enjoyment either.[48] Neither argument fully makes the link to an irreducibly collective interest in certain objects. The present argument does. Réaume is right to point to social participation as important, but it is important because the individual has only a derivative interest in the collective good, based on the individual's interest in the flourishing of the collectivity that can produce and have an interest in the good. We can thus intelligibly discuss situations with a non-individualisable interest, those without, and those with both kinds of interest.

This last point can become more tangible yet. Each individual who comes into contact with the police discovers that he or she has a very important individual interest in the police not using torture because police torture will devastate that individual's life. At the same time, our political community has an important collective interest in the police not using torture because widespread use of police torture will, for instance, undermine democracy by repressing dissenting thought. Moral argument on torture, such as in the writings of Cesare Beccaria, thus refers both to the immorality of torture's devastation of individual human lives and to the irrational, counterproductive effects of torture in its failure to achieve its purported goals and consequent violations of collective interests as well.[49] The moral reasons affecting the decision to torture or not to torture Osama's henchman depend not only on his individual interests but also on collective interests that yield further important reasons against torture.

To say this much, of course, does not address every aspect of a complex issue. In today's world, some might argue that there are collective interests in torture for security purposes. The quick reply has traditionally been that the individual interest in not being tortured is sufficient to ground a duty not to torture.[50] This reply explains why an individual policeman is under a duty not to torture you, but it may or may not address the more diffuse actions actually inherent in ensuring an end to torture in societies in which it is perpetrated: laws to prosecute torturers; procedures to limit incommunicado detention; monitoring of security forces;

[46] Réaume (n 30) 11.

[47] *Cf* R Hardin, *One For All: The Logic of Group Conflict* (Princeton, Princeton University Press, 1995) 68.

[48] Morauta (n 28) 98. *Cf* C Taylor 'Irreducibly Social Goods' in G Brennan and C Walsh (eds) *Rationality, Individualism and Public Policy* (Centre for Research on Federal Financial Relations Canberra 1990). Those responding to Taylor on this issue argue that Taylor elided these distinctions: see the replies by RE Goodin, J Broome, and P Gärdenfors in Brennan and Walsh, ibid. See also Hardin (n 47) 69.

[49] C Beccaria, *On Crimes and Punishment and Other Writings* R Bellamy (ed) (Cambridge, Cambridge University Press, 1995) chs 2, 16.

[50] For example, Waldron (n 35) 350.

functioning complaints procedures; improved training in investigation skills; and a change in public consciousness.[51]

The whole political community needs to be engaged in these changed conditions; they cannot be actualised by one person alone. On Réaume's argument, that makes these conditions immediately non-individualisable goods. But she does not explain why one could not say that there is an individual interest in some of these changes, and an important one at that for the person in the police cells. These goods are simultaneously individualisable in that sense. The present argument allows one to identify both such an individual interest and an interest mediated through collective interests in the kind of society we are, a non-individualisable interest. In other words, the present account provides further explanation, while allowing us to turn to the questions that have actually wrenched our souls, questions about our fundamental societal values and deliberations upon the full array of policies needed to prevent torture.

While the individual interest against torture is actually compelling, there are other situations where individual interests have the same object as a collective interest but where, while the individual interest is not entirely derivative, the collective interest is clearly paramount. Marie-Eve might have an individual pecuniary interest in Quebec secession if she has found a bookie who took a ten-dollar bet on a referendum result. But such an interest strikes us as obviously morally secondary next to any collective interest in self-determination.

This conclusion does not change even if Marie-Eve has bet ten million dollars on the referendum result. In such circumstances, one must admit that there is an (important) individual interest in the result on which the bet was placed. But it would obviously be wrong for Marie-Eve to vote based on her bet. To do so would be to sell out democracy. Raz has suggested in an only slightly different context that the right to vote in an election is what he terms 'non-convertible': one can neither give it to another nor exercise it in a particular way for financial gain.[52] Raz suggests that this feature of the right is not based on an assumption that nothing could compensate the individual for its loss (for such an approach would involve extreme paternalism) but is based on the grounding of the right 'in the interests of the public at large alongside the interests of the right-holder.'[53]

This explanation might seem plausible to a degree. But its reference to the 'interests of the public at large' demands clarification. Jean-Pierre would not act rightly to consider in his electoral deliberations Marie-Eve's bet, which impacts on the interests of another member of 'the public at large'. The right must be grounded in the interests of citizens *as members of the community*, and, for the reasons

[51] *Cf* also J Waldron, 'Torture and Positive Law: Jurisprudence for the White House' (2005) 105 *Columbia Law Review* 1681. Waldron argues that a norm like the prohibition on torture occupies a larger place within the legal system, becoming what he calls an 'archetype'. For an important discussion of Waldron's piece, see M Plaxton, 'Reflections on Waldron's Archetypes' (2011) 30 *Law and Philosophy* 77.

[52] J Raz, 'Rights and Politics' in J Tasioulas (ed) *Law, Values and Social Practices* (Aldershot, Dartmouth, 1997) 83.

[53] Ibid.

identified earlier, non-aggregatively. Other citizens' interests, in this sense, have as their object a well-functioning democratic decision, a collective interest in the well-being of the collectivity. We must consider not just the individual interests of other citizens but the interests of the collectivities at issue.

We can then give a further explanation as to why Marie-Eve ought not to sell her vote, or act corruptly in analogous ways. Members of a political community voting in an election or a referendum do not act as individuals who may morally use it as a chance to maximise their wealth but as participants in a community decision-making process. As such, they ought to act in the interest of the community, at least as best they see it. Members' pecuniary welfare may matter to the community and thus be an indirect ground for a decision in some instances (for example, voters may consider the economic impact on Québec and the resulting effects on the community), but the paramount consideration must be the primary collective interest. National self-determination is a question about relationships of different collectivities, an inherently non-individualisable matter. The main grounds for the decision will be collective interests. The collective interests are paramount.

Having thus better explained the idea of non-individualisable interests and rights, finally, the reasoning in this section also reveals something very important about Will Kymlicka's theory of 'group-differentiated rights'. Consider the following example: an aboriginal First Nation may have a collective interest in hunting and fishing in its ancestral homeland, as its ability to do so affects profoundly the First Nation's desired maintenance of its cultural traditions and relationship with the land.[54] So as to protect such interests, constitutional provisions may protect the hunting and fishing rights of individual members of the aboriginal First Nation. Leroy, an individual member, may have a significant individual interest in his individual legally recognised hunting and fishing rights insofar as they provide him a source of subsistence, which is obviously important to him as an individual. But, following the reasoning here, we can say that his individual interests, while not wholly derivative from, are nonetheless secondary to the primary collective interest.

As his theory is structured, Kymlicka avoids talk of 'collective rights', preferring to employ the concept of 'group-differentiated rights' as rights held by members of groups on account of their group membership.[55] He then argues for such group-differentiated rights on grounds of equality: 'certain collective rights can be defended as appropriate measures for the rectification of an inequality in circumstances which affects aboriginal people collectively'.[56] Such statements, of course, are arguments for legal rights that advance a particular goal, since a moral right is not a 'measure'. Kymlicka's arguments, then, are essentially for legal rights based

[54] It may also be a form of collective compensation for historic wrongs and protection of continuing self-government, but let us leave those more complicated interests to the side for this example.

[55] For example, W Kymlicka, *Multicultural Citizenship* (Oxford, Oxford University Press, 1995) 35.

[56] W Kymlicka, *Liberalism, Community and Culture* (Oxford, Clarendon, 1989) 194.

on a desire to avoid adverse impacts on the situation of some individuals who are in different cultural groups.

But Kymlicka's arguments face difficulties when he faces the question of why we should not simply assimilate such individuals so that they do not face inequalities. He must resort to explaining why not in terms of what amount to practical difficulties with assimilation.[57] But these arguments can prevail only temporarily, and they fail to acknowledge moral reasons for preserving cultures over time. For instance, his argument would not actually resist a skilfully designed assimilation scheme that took account of maintaining a context of choice for each individual at each point in time while actually destroying various cultures over time[58] – a policy many minority and indigenous communities would unfortunately consider an all-too-real description of ways other communities have historically harmed them. Moreover, it is unclear how Kymlicka's arguments explain why substitutions responding to the inequalities with which he is concerned would not be permissible – why, for instance, is there a reason not to give Leroy some other different right of some equivalent value in place of his hunting and fishing rights as an alternative currency of compensation for the inequality that he faces? Kymlicka's attention to egalitarian justice concerns does not say as much as an approach concerned with collective rights.

Although the attempt to avoid adverse impacts on the situation of individuals in particular cultural groups can provide some relevant moral reasons, group-differentiated rights must actually be parasitic to a degree on unarticulated concepts of collective interests such as I have been exploring. Collective interests can clearly provide a moral reason for not substituting different legal rights which otherwise might be argued to give Leroy something just as valuable. Facts about what makes the cultural community flourish are determinative. In the example, only the hunting and fishing rights serve the collective interest and support the flourishing community in its ancestral traditions and relationship with the land. Collective interests can clearly provide moral reasons against assimilation policies that otherwise might be argued to give individuals opportunities just as valuable. Assimilation policies strike against a particular community. The group-differentiated rights which some say are held by individuals actually depend on deeper support from both individual interests and collective interests.

Before I turn to the argument that some collective interests are sufficient to ground duties and are thus collective rights, it is important to face the question toward which this section has alluded and been leading: are there objects in which only collectivities have interests and rights? I have said that there are objects in which the collective interest is primary, in which individual interests are derivative or secondary. I cannot pretend that we cannot make up some individual

[57] Ibid, 172–77; *cf* DG Newman 'Liberal Multiculturalism and Will Kymlicka's Uneasy Relation with Religious Pluralism' (2003) 64 *Bijdragen* 265 (criticising Kymlicka's refusal to protect religious practices). See also Griffin (n 5) 267 (discussing how all Kymlicka's theory effectively supports is the right to *a* culture, not necessarily one's own).

[58] See S Wall, 'Collective Rights and Individual Autonomy' (2007) 117 *Ethics* 234, 244.

interest even in these objects (think of the betting example), but we need not be deceived by such tomfoolery. Where an object contributes substantially to the flourishing of a community and is an object that is not easily individualisable, we rightfully speak of it as primarily in a collective interest.

A collective right exists when a particular collective interest is sufficient to ground a duty. We seek here a general theory of collective rights, not an elaboration of a particular collective right, though the subsequent argument will refer to certain examples of collective rights. We can, however, usefully ask a preliminary question as to whether we know that any such collective rights exist, and the next section seeks to show that at least some of these collective rights do exist if certain individual rights exist.

V. THE NECESSARY EXISTENCE OF COLLECTIVE RIGHTS

This section argues that the preceding arguments have an important implication. I will seek to show that these arguments yield the important hypothesis that if certain individual moral rights exist, then certain collective moral rights also exist. This conclusion does not specify which collectivities have which rights, but it is obviously sufficient to contribute to the discussion on the possibility and existence of collective moral rights and their ability to help explain the moral considerations at play in situations like those raised in chapter one.

There have been arguments with some parallels to the present argument. In *The Morality of Freedom*, Raz argues that certain collective goods are intrinsically valuable insofar as they constitute the options necessary for personal autonomy.[59] In other words, he uses fundamental individual interests to argue for the intrinsic value of certain collective goods. But this is a different argument from one concerned to establish the rights of collectivities to particular goods, a fundamentally different proposition from any advanced by Raz. Similarly, Kymlicka and others have referred to certain 'cultural structures' as conditions for individual development.[60] Here, too, there is some argument for the value of a collective condition as a necessary condition for flourishing individual lives. But this argument, too, stops short of arguing for any collectivity having a right. We could obviously develop many other sorts of arguments for various collective conditions as necessary to flourishing individual lives. However, there needs to be a more precise argument for collective rights.

This argument is that certain individual interests that ground duties are meaningful interests and can be fulfilled only on the precondition that certain collective interests are also rights. Bhikhu Parekh has made a similar claim that some collective rights are preconditions for individual rights but without developing the

[59] Raz, *The Morality of Freedom* (n 3) 205–206.

[60] Kymlicka, *Liberalism, Community and Culture* (n 56) 165–71; *cf* R Dworkin, *A Matter of Principle* (Cambridge MA, Harvard University Press, 1985) 230–33.

argument for the point,[61] as my account now does. We can put this statement in simplified terms: if we accept certain individual rights, we presuppose certain collective rights. In general terms, this proposition flows from two factors: (a) the primary interest of the collectivity in certain objects; and (b) the necessary dependence of certain individual interests on collective interests. I argued for (a) in the last section, which establishes the irreducibly collective nature of certain interests. So, if there are grounds for (b), then it follows that certain individual rights presuppose collective rights.

Someone might object to this reasoning. If an individual interest that is sufficient to ground duties presupposes certain societal conditions for the fulfillment of the interest, should we not simply say that the individual interest also grounds duties to create those societal conditions? But an interest sufficient to ground some duty, which is thus an individual right, need not, and indeed will not, ground every duty that would be helpful to the fulfillment of the interest. Someone might try to improve the objection and argue that some aggregation of individual interests grounds the duties to create the relevant societal conditions. On this objection, one would again argue directly from the individual interests to the relevant collective condition. But we saw earlier in this chapter that such aggregations are problematic.

If individual rights depend on objects in which a collectivity has a primary interest, then if we are to maintain the existence of these individual rights, we must also say that the collective interest is sufficient to amount to a right to those objects. To say that the collective interest itself is sufficient to ground duties is no mystery. It is the collectivity's interest that serves as an intermediary between individuals and non-individualisable goods. The collective interest grounds the duty, somewhat as an official's interests qua official ground rights from whose existence individuals benefit indirectly.[62]

So given that the argument will stand if (b) is established, we must be clear about what would establish (b). An individual interest *necessarily depends* on a collective interest if and only if the individual interest either does not meaningfully exist or cannot meaningfully be fulfilled in the absence of a collective interest being fulfilled. To establish that the existence of certain individual rights implies the existence of collective moral rights, then, we need only show that some individual interests are necessarily dependent on collective interests. We can do so via an example before touching on the more general structure of such instances.

To take up an example, freedom of religion must include protection of (at a minimal level, at least some degree of non-interference with) religious collectivities. Constitutional texts and interpretations on this issue vary across different states.[63]

[61] B Parekh, *Rethinking Multiculturalism: Cultural Diversity and Political Theory* (London, Macmillan, 2000) 216.

[62] Raz, *The Morality of Freedom* (n 3) 179; Raz 'Rights and Politics' (n 52) 80.

[63] The Constitution of Spain 1978 art 16(1) guarantees freedom of religion to 'individuals and communities': for discussion, see N López Calera *¿Hay derechos colectivos? Individualidad y socialidad en la teoría de los derechos* (Barcelona, Ariel, 2000) 47. The American Constitution, with exceptions, has generally been interpreted such that community manifestations of religion are protected only if also protected by

But any reasonable understanding of the moral right to freedom of religion must encompass its collective dimension. Freedom of religion 'is not the right of an individual to go into a closet and worship alone'.[64] Indeed, were we to consider religion to be a solely individual matter, we would effectively denigrate those religions in which more emphasis is placed on communal worship or other communal religious activities. Charles Taylor's book, *Varieties of Religion Today: William James Revisited*,[65] explores the inherently collective forms of many religious practices and experiences, providing a riposte to anyone presuming all religion to be individual. This variety of religious practices has an important implication. If freedom of religion is to extend beyond those who practise more individually-oriented religions and thus to be a meaningful *freedom of* religion, it must include some protection for religious communities.

Although we are concerned with moral rights, a recent case concerning legal rights to freedom of religion within the European human rights system further illustrates this point. In the case of *Bessarabian Church v Moldova*,[66] the European Court of Human Rights had to adjudicate on claims that Moldova had violated Convention rights to freedom of religion or freedom of association by refusing to recognise the Bessarabian Church. Under Moldovan law, religious denominations required state recognition to carry on their activities, to have legal guarantees of freedom from intolerance on denominational grounds, to maintain bank accounts and enforce legal rights, and generally to operate free from interference. Moldova refused to recognise the Bessarabian Church, claiming it was a schismatic group within the predominant Orthodox church within Moldova. However, the Court ruled that Moldova had violated Convention rights; in particular, the Court ruled that there was a violation of religious rights, meaning that it did not need to decide on association or other claims. The terms of its ruling are significant:

> [S]ince religious communities traditionally exist in the form of organised structures, Article 9 [freedom of religion] must be interpreted in the light of Article 11 [freedom of association] of the Convention, which safeguards associative life against unjustified State interference. Seen in that perspective, the right of believers to freedom of religion, which includes the right to manifest one's religion in community with others, encompasses the expectation that believers will be allowed to associate freely, without arbitrary State intervention. Indeed, the autonomous existence of religious communities is indispensable for pluralism in a democratic society and is thus an issue at the very heart of the protection which Article 9 affords.[67]

This adjudication on legal rights illustrates well the claim at issue on the moral right to freedom of religion. The moral right to freedom of religion presupposes

another constitutional guarantee: FM Gedicks 'Toward a Constitutional Jurisprudence of Religious Group Rights' [1989] *Wisconsin Law Review* 99, 121–22.

[64] V Van Dyke, 'Collective Entities and Moral Rights: Problems in Liberal-Democratic Thought' (1982) 44 *Journal of Politics* 21, 27.

[65] C Taylor, *Varieties of Religion Today: William James Revisited* (Cambridge MA, Harvard University Press, 2002).

[66] *Case of Metropolitan Church of Bessarabia v Moldova* app no 45701/99 (2002) 35 EHRR 13 (ECHR).

[67] Ibid, [118].

the protection of religious communities from acts that would damage them. In other words, the individual right to freedom of religion presupposes the fulfillment of certain collective interests of religious collectivities.[68]

This statement obviously does not mean that every interest of religious collectivities must be fulfilled; religious collectivities probably have no permanent right to certain forms of tax relief. However, at least some interests of some collectivities concerned with some fundamental aspects of their flourishing must be fulfilled, or else the individual right to freedom of religion becomes meaningless. The collective interest must also be sufficient to ground a duty if we are to recognise the individual interest in question as a right. If individuals have certain rights, then certain groups also have certain rights, and there are things nobody should do to them.[69]

Notably, the relevant interests are not solely those connected with advancing individual freedom, so any claim that such interests would be restricted to certain kinds of autonomy-promoting communities is not appropriate.[70] Moreover, the argument is obviously not restricted to freedom of religion. Indeed, a parallel argument obviously applies to other individual interests necessarily associated with collective interests.[71]

The individual right to property functions in many contexts in furthering individual autonomy and free enterprise economic values. However, where there is a different cultural relation to property, and a community relationship to at least certain land is part of a fundamental cultural framework, there has been a readiness to recognise that a collective right to that land is necessary to the fulfillment of individual interests protected by the right to property. The Inter-American Court of Human Rights was thus ready to recognise communal claims of indigenous communities as receiving protection via the right to property.[72]

In some contexts, the collective right at issue may even be meaningfully more specific than the individual rights affected. Thus, individuals have more general rights to maintain their culture in community with others. This right will not yield any individual right in relation to particular cultural heritage works. However, if the cultural community overall would be damaged by the loss of certain works and this loss would strike at its ability to serve its members' individual interests,

[68] See also *X v United Kingdom* app no 8160/78 (1981) (ECHR) (general discussion of rights to maintain religion in community with others as an essential part of freedom of religion); *Hasan and Chaush v Bulgaria* app no 30985/96 (26 November 2000) ECHR) app no 30985/96, (26 November 2000, Merits and Just satisfaction) (interference with organisation and leadership of religious community as violating religious freedom). See discussion in Z Machnyikova, 'Religious Rights' in M Weller (ed) *Universal Minority Rights: A Commentary on the Jurisprudence of International Courts and Treaty Bodies* (Oxford, Oxford University Press, 2007) 179, 188–91.

[69] Note that my argument also strikes against James Griffin's argument (n 5) that those considerations sometimes called 'group rights' can be moral considerations but are not rights; the denial of certain collective rights would mean the denial of certain individual rights we would presumably not want to deny.

[70] Contra Seymour (n 18) 487 (restricting collective rights to societal cultures).

[71] See also ibid, 512 (argument about language and individual identity).

[72] *The Mayagna (Sumo) Awas Tingni Community v Nicaragua* (Judgment of 31 August 2001) Inter-Am Ct HR (Ser C) No 79 (2001) [*Awas Tingni* decision].

then there does arise a collective right to maintain and have protected its overall body of cultural works as necessary toward this end.[73] The removal from a group's control of a key artwork or a prohibition on a certain form of artistic practice could well strike against the group in a manner that would violate its rights. The worldwide Buddhist community might reasonably have claimed a collective moral right against the Taliban's destruction of the Bamiyan Buddha sculptures in Afghanistan.[74] This statement, of course, leaves unaddressed many complex facets of cultural heritage policy in contexts where there is a need to balance cultural heritage preservation with economic realities[75] or where there are complex questions about restrictions on transactions with respect to certain national treasures or competing claims by a national community and a broader international community.[76] But there are a relevant set of collective rights in relation to cultural heritage property that are necessary to the fulfillment of individual interests to enjoy culture in community with others.[77]

There is of course a more general structure to such claims. Raz has referred to the concept of 'framing goods' – those collective goods whose existence 'is a precondition for the existence of an adequate range of other goods in the society in which they exist' – which he argues are widespread.[78] Certain goods that fulfill collective interests have a parallel structure in that they are preconditions for the fulfillment of individual interests: they are 'framing interests' that make certain individual interests meaningful and viable.

Certain individual rights thus cannot be separated from collective rights. Rights are interdependent: some interests cannot be rights without others also being rights. If certain individual rights exist, then there are also collective moral rights. Notably, this argument does not restrict the range of collective rights only to those necessary to particular individual rights. Chapter two identifies a range of collectivities as having the capacity to hold rights. Chapter three has set out how we can identify collective interests. Collective rights will exist when a collective interest is sufficient to ground a duty.[79] Some theorists have sometimes supposed that any collective rights

[73] *Cf* J Moustoukas, 'Group Rights in Cultural Property' (1989) 74 *Cornell Law Review* 1184.

[74] *Cf* D Gillman, *The Idea of Cultural Heritage* (New York, Cambridge University Press, 2010) 9ff.

[75] See *Kitkatla Band v British Columbia (Minister of Small Business, Tourism and Culture)* 2002 SCC 31, [2002] 2 SCR 146. The case considered complex legislation seeking to balance interests in the development of the forestry industry with protection of 'culturally modified trees' (CMTs) that were part of the cultural heritage of British Columbia aboriginal communities.

[76] See eg Gillman (n 74) 142ff.

[77] Contra ibid, 191–93. Gillman claims that there is no right in a cultural heritage object even to save a culture from dying but basing this too narrowly on a view that there would be such a right only if it contributed to democratic opportunities or basic individual liberties.

[78] Raz 'Rights and Politics' (n 52) 87; *cf* the analogous argument in Taylor 'Irreducibly Social Goods' (n 48) 54–55.

[79] This point is broad enough to support Finnis's intriguing claim that the 'general welfare' could in principle be expressed in terms of rights (Finnis, *Natural Law and Natural Rights* (n 10) 216, 218), although subject to the important realisation that rights must function at several levels – with individuals and various collectivities (which may overlap or interact, raising the important questions we will address in Parts II and III) all holding rights. For further discussion, see Newman 'Collective Interests and Collective Rights' (n 1) 162–63.

must be directly instrumental to the fulfillment of individual rights;[80] the present argument, though recognising and learning from interdependence between certain individual and collective rights, does not make this narrow link. The range of possible collective rights is subject to the further analysis of Part II.

Rob Edger has challenged these parts of my argument over recent years.[81] As he has most recently stated them, he has offered two challenges worthy of attention. First, he raises a concern as to an alleged inegalitarianism in the fact that individuals who are members of certain collectivities will implicitly acquire additional basic moral rights as members of those collectivities.[82] Kymlicka's egalitarian-based argument for group-differentiated rights, of course, simply avoids this concern. But one can also answer it simply in noting that not all rights are necessarily subject to simplistic independent egalitarian distribution. That a religious believer has certain needs because of freedom of religion does not mean that one then needs to engage in special efforts to extend some benefit of equal value to every other religious believer and secularist. If a religious group had a reasonable claim to a prayer room at the airport, the airport's decision to also build a television-viewing room would arise from its general policies on airport services and not from a special egalitarian claim of those preferring television to Torah.

The second notable objection from Edger is an argument that the mere fact one needs certain things for the exercise of some individual religious rights does not establish a free-standing community-held right; he goes so far as to say that the community in this instance is simply a tool or instrumentality for the exercise of the right, as the book one publishes might be a tool or instrumentality for exercising freedom of expression.[83] But this objection simply overlooks the social and moral status of the community developed in the argument in chapter two. Once the community has this social moral status, its collective interests are the sort of thing that can give rise to collective rights, in a way that takes them out of the category of tools and instrumentalities like books and pushpins.

A further objection might also arise. How can the argument as developed thus far suggest that any collective right is necessary when the collectivity itself is contingent? The arguments here have not specified what collectivity must hold the right. Religious believers might be members of different faiths and even change faiths at certain points in their lives; the fulfillment of their individual rights to freedom of religion appears not to depend on a particular collectivity's rights. Indeed, in referring to secession earlier, I arguably implicitly accepted the possibility of collectivities separating from one another, so I have clearly admitted contingency in collectivities.

[80] For example, M Nussbaum 'The Complexity of Groups' (2003) 29 *Philosophy and Social Criticism* 57, 66–67 (referring to, but not developing, a link between individual freedom of religion and rights for religious groups).

[81] See R Edger, 'Collective Rights' (2009) 72 *Saskatchewan Law Review* 1; DG Newman, 'Edger's Challenge to my Account of Collective Moral Rights: In Reply' (2009) 72 *Saskatchewan Law Review* 23.

[82] See R Edger, 'Mainstream Discrimination: A Consequentialist Examination of Restricting Discriminatory Publications in the Mainstream Media' (LLM thesis, Osgoode Hall Law School, 2010) 38.

[83] See ibid, 48–49.

This feature, however, is actually a strength of the account. There are no grounds for simply taking all de facto collectivities at face value. We can imagine better or worse communities, and better or worse interests. Communities are subject to normative evaluation.[84] The existence of some collectivities, such as certain violent criminal outfits, might even be wholly detrimental to the interests of persons, and there could be good grounds for getting rid of the relationships constituting such collectivities. Others, such as well-ordered communities, will contribute in vital ways to the individuals they serve. Part II turns to the task of distinguishing and evaluating communities' claims to hold rights.

Even recognising a contingency of collectivities, it is nonetheless the case that *some* collectivity necessarily has to have a collective right if we are to make sense of certain individual rights.[85] Unless we are prepared to abandon many individual moral rights, collective moral rights exist. This chapter has made that foundational point and has developed the argument for a conception of a collective interest along the lines of Finnis's common good over Raz's apparently more aggregative conceptions. Within Raz's theory of rights, some collectivities that one might not have initially contemplated as holding rights will in fact have interests that ground rights. We must now turn to the tasks of further analysing the conditions on which they do so.

[84] *Cf* Moravcsik (n 10) 212–13.

[85] Contra Miller (n 7) 186–90 (using indeterminacies on group rights claims to question the existence of group rights).

II

Moral Conditions for Collective Rights

4

Conflicting Rights

> [P1] The existence of rights against the Government would be jeopardized if the Government were able to defeat such a right by appealing to the right of a democratic majority to work its will. A right against the Government must be a right to do something even when the majority thinks it would be wrong to do it, and even when the majority would be worse off for having it done.[1]

> [P2] [Collective Rights] can rarely help to rebuild a community but can easily be used to strengthen dominant sub-groups, privilege conservative interpretations of culture over reforms, and disadvantage all those who wish to diverge from accepted social norms and question the traditional role of social institutions. Liberals should then be aware of the price embedded in bestowing rights on groups and be more cautious in their support of such rights.[2]

I. INTRODUCTION: THE SPECIFICATION PINCER

IN *P1*, RONALD Dworkin voices a common misgiving about collective rights. It is a masterly piece of rhetoric, with a majority 'working its will' and sending a fearsome alliterative shudder down one's spine. The worry has redounded with judges too, with Justice Deschênes once describing a Quebec government argument based on collective rights as inherently manifesting a 'conception totalitaire de la société'.[3]

In *P2*, Yael Tamir voices a more recent critique of collective rights, claiming that any collective rights that exist have undesirable ramifications for individual rights, particularly rights of systemically disadvantaged individuals. Amongst theorists with a similar take, collective rights are perceived as against the interests of individual women, as serving the interests of powerful and conservative group leaders, or as otherwise representing an illegitimate privileging of a collective interest over individual rights.[4]

[1] R Dworkin, *Taking Rights Seriously* (London, Belknap, 1978) 194.

[2] Y Tamir, 'Against Collective Rights' in C Joppke and S Lukes (eds) *Multicultural Questions* (Oxford, Oxford University Press, 1999) 160. Essentially the same essay appears in LH Meyer, SL Paulson and TW Pogge (eds) *Rights, Culture, and the Law: Themes from the Legal and Political Philosophy of Joseph Raz* (Oxford, Oxford University Press, 2003); citations here are to the earlier publication.

[3] *Québec Association of Protestant School Boards v Québec (Procureur Général)* 140 DLR (3d) 33, 64.

[4] *Cf* SM Okin, 'Is Multiculturalism Bad for Women?' in J Cohen, M Howard and MC Nussbaum (eds) *Is Multiculturalism Bad for Women?* (Princeton, Princeton University Press, 1999) 12, 22; M Deveaux

Similar claims come out in yet more pejorative forms. Russell Hardin tells us that '[d]efenders of communal "rights" are, implicitly, opponents of individuals' opportunities'.[5] Jin-Xue Fan tells us that 'Collective "rights" are usually little better than excuses for violating individual rights.'[6] Courtney Jung argues that the very language of collective rights 'allows ethnic activists to run roughshod over the rights of minorities within the community'.[7] In the context of this book's argument for the existence of collective rights, and this based on the existence of certain individual rights, there obviously arises a need for some further explanation.

These issues are of profound practical relevance. Opposition by states and others to the recognition of collective rights has often traded on precisely these arguments and was, for instance, an important means by which states long resisted the United Nations Declaration on the Rights of Indigenous Peoples.[8] One response by James Anaya has been that concerns of conflicts between individual and collective rights are a 'nonissue' because rights always need to be balanced 'against any competing right'.[9] But that response, well-intended as it is, does not escape any good faith worry, or any good or bad faith rhetoric, that collective rights will reduce the scope of individual rights.[10] Similarly, Alexandra Xanthaki's suggestions that conflicts between individual and collective rights in contexts like the Declaration can be resolved on an 'ad hoc' basis[11] reflect an intuition that the conflicts are not so serious as some worry but do little to calm those worries and, indeed, reflect the value of developing theoretical argument that speaks to addressing conflicts in a principled manner.

Such concerns will animate much of the remaining argument, as I seek to develop a model of collective rights consistent with the humanistic principle and the value it attaches to individual interests. In this chapter, specifically, I face objections that collective rights are inherently in conflict with individual rights

'Conflicting Equalities? Cultural Group Rights and Sex Equality' (2000) 48 *Political Studies* 522, 535–36; S Benhabib *The Claims of Culture: Equality and Diversity in the Global Era* (Princeton, Princteon University Press, 2002) 60.

[5] R Hardin, *One for All: The Logic of Group Conflict* (Princeton, Princeton University Press, 1995) 220.

[6] Jin-Xue Fan, 'On the Two Sides of Human Rights' (2003) 9 *International Legal Theory* 79, 82.

[7] C Jung, *The Moral Force of Indigenous Politics: Critical Liberalism and the Zapatistas* (Cambridge, Cambridge University Press, 2008) 290.

[8] See DG Newman, 'Theorizing Collective Indigenous Rights' (2007) 31 *American Indian Law Review* 273, 275–79.

[9] SJ Anaya, 'Superpower Attitudes Toward Indigenous Peoples and Group Rights' (1999) 93 *American Society of International Law Proceedings* 251, 257.

[10] The Canadian Human Rights Commission has struggled with what to do with a new legal provision calling for 'balancing' of individual and collective rights. Section 1.2 of the *Canadian Human Rights Act* now says that in the context of complaints made under the *Act* against a First Nation government, 'this Act shall be interpreted and applied in a manner that gives due regard to First Nations legal traditions and customary laws, particularly the balancing of individual rights and interests against collective rights and interests, to the extent that they are consistent with the principle of gender equality'. The Commission has had to engage in extensive research projects about the meaning of such a section: eg BW Morse, R Groves and D Vermette, 'Balancing Individual and Collective Rights: Implementation of section 1.2 of the *Canadian Human Rights Act*' (Canadian Human Rights Commission, 2010).

[11] A Xanthaki, *Indigenous Peoples and United Nations Standards: Self-determination, Culture and Land* (Cambridge, Cambridge University Press, 2007) 34, 36.

and that these objections in some way undermine our arguments for collective rights. Before I sketch the counterargument, however, I can flesh out further the argument that might be thought to arise against collective rights from alleged conflicts with individual rights.

Such a clarification is vital, for one might otherwise be inclined simply to dismiss the claims in *P1* and *P2* as having no application here. Tamir's challenges, for example, might seem to be of unclear meaning. Consider the last statement, Tamir's words of caution about 'bestowing rights on groups'.[12] One might naturally interpret such cautions as expressing concerns about the establishment of legal rights for groups, since only legal (or political) rights could be 'bestowed'. But Tamir earlier distinguished 'rights' from 'the political arrangements that ought to be put in place in order to defend and promote rights',[13] thus suggesting she used the word 'right' to refer to a moral right. Who, then, does she caution against 'bestowing' moral rights on groups, since moral rights are not 'bestowed' in any usual sense of the word?[14] Some of her argument draws on case studies in which collectivities have limited individual rights,[15] and she warns of a 'political danger' in collective rights,[16] so perhaps the concern is that recognising the rights collectivities have opens scope for abuse. But any such *in terrorem* argument cannot compete with the claims of justice. Tamir's argument seemingly provides reasons only to be clear about what is and is not justified in the name of collective rights, precisely what I seek to develop.

Dworkin's challenge might seem clearer. But it attacks a position nobody could reasonably maintain – even those most enamoured of collective rights would not claim a majority's right to 'work its will' heedless of what that was.[17] Moreover, Dworkin's claim in *P1* need not even be taken as expressing a concern with collective rights per se. Indeed, some collective rights are presumably rights of minority collectivities against the government and are not criticised, but implicitly approved of, by the passage.[18]

To best advance enquiry, however, we can seek to read these theorists' claims charitably. *P1* and *P2* do together point us toward a difficult dilemma. If whatever collective rights exist will conflict with individual rights, then either there must be a limited set or scope of collective rights, or else we have conflict between collective and individual rights. And conflict between collective and individual rights might seem to pose a challenge to the argument from the existence of individual rights to the existence of collective rights, conflict conceivably forming a sort of *reductio*. Although chapter three was clear that collective rights are not limited to those supported by the argument there, the status of those collective rights – those whose existence has been definitively established – remains significant. If conflicts

[12] Tamir (n 2) 160.
[13] Ibid, 158.
[14] *Cf* J Raz, 'Comments and Responses' in Meyer, Paulson and Pogge (eds) (n 2) 269–70.
[15] See eg Tamir (n 2) 164.
[16] Ibid, 159.
[17] *Cf* J Nickel, 'Dworkin on the Nature and Consequences of Rights' (1977) 11 *Georgia Law Review* 1115, 1137.
[18] *Cf* ch 1.I, above.

between individual and collective rights were pervasive such that the existence of those collective rights undermined the existence of the individual rights whose existence was crucial to the argument, then we would actually undermine the collective rights themselves. So, if conflicts between collective and individual rights are likely to arise, this possibility seems to pose an important challenge to the argument.

The possibility of such conflicts has been commonly presumed, with some authors asserting an 'enduring and pervasive irreconcilability' between individual and collective rights.[19] More generally, Jeremy Waldron has analysed the implications of an interest theory of rights for conflicts of rights generally: 'if rights are understood along the lines of the Interest Theory proposed by Joseph Raz, then conflicts of rights must be regarded as more or less inevitable'.[20] Waldron's argument, based on Raz's conception of rights, suggests that conflicts of rights in the real world are almost inevitable because interests conflict and because it is unlikely (what Waldron calls 'a massively improbable coincidence') that the set of interests 'associated with the special level of concern that rights indicate . . . just happened to be coextensive with [the set of interests perfectly compossible with one another]'.[21] If conflicts between individual and collective rights are inevitable and pervasive, the challenge to the argument developed in chapter three applies in full force. Does Waldron's claim about rights conflicts doom the argument?

Waldron's argument, although widely quoted, is probabilistic and not logically definitive. Strictly speaking, the set of interests associated with rights need not be coextensive with the set compossible with one another to avoid conflicts of rights: the former, for instance, could be a subset of the latter. Moreover, and yet more tellingly against Waldron's reasoning, it is unnecessary to have a set of interests perfectly compossible with one another for associated rights to avoid conflict; it is fully sufficient to have a set of interests such that special concern for each interest is reconcilable with special concern for each other interest. That is, there is nothing logically inconsistent in having conflicting interests but compatible rights. Further, even overlooking what were hopefully just missteps in Waldron's syntax, we can overcome his challenge, making a constructive argument for the pervasive compatibility of individual and collective rights.

To do so, I will adopt an argument exploring two branches of what can be called the *Specification Pincer*. In particular, I will show how the rest of the argument can stand on each of two concepts of a right – the Specificationist concept and the Non-Specificationist concept. Many theorists have made much of arguments between these two concepts; I will here suggest that each has its uses and that the main argument can stand on either concept.[22]

[19] A Petter and AC Hutchinson, 'Rights in Conflict: The Dilemma of Charter Legitimacy' (1989) 23 *University of British Columbia Law Review* 531, 542.

[20] J Waldron, *Liberal Rights: Collected Papers, 1981–1991* (Cambridge, Cambridge University Press, 1993) 203.

[21] Ibid, 205.

[22] *Cf* G Rainbolt, *The Concept of Rights* (Dordrecht, Springer, 2006) 157–94, 202–204 (showing how discussions of rights conflicts depend on the view adopted on specification of rights).

To make the two branches of the Specification Pincer clear, I must first state what I mean by conflicts of rights. Adopting Waldron's definition of a conflict of rights, '[w]hen we say rights conflict, what we really mean is that the duties they imply are not compossible'.[23] For reasons to be developed more fully later, the term 'compossible' here cannot mean simply 'logically consistent' but must mean 'can be both fufilled (in the appropriate manner and timeframes as demanded by the rights)'. That is, *rights conflict* if and only if the duties they imply are not both (or all) accomplishable, or if the rights cannot both (or all) be fulfilled. In an example I will call the *Financial Predicament,* both Popper's landlord and his credit card company have rights that he should pay them what he owes them. There is nothing logically impossible about his fulfilling both duties, but they may not be simultaneously feasible, depending on Popper's cash flow. And here the two branches of the Specification Pincer part ways.

A Specificationist will maintain that there is no conflict because a correct description of the rights encompasses a more limited content that does not bring about any inconsistency of duties. In the example, a Specificationist will say that the actual right of the landlord or the credit card company or both is limited so as to be a right to be paid to the extent possible subject to the priority of other creditors. In general, a Specificationist will hold to the view that a duty is, as Raz puts it, an exclusionary reason, one that gives reason 'to refrain from acting for some reason'.[24] If this is so, then inconsistency would seemingly follow if duties conflicted. So, the Specificationist says, rights cannot conflict but must be limited in their content, with correct description of the content avoiding conflicts.[25] As

[23] Ibid, 206. Some have claimed that a conflict of duties is not essential to a conflict of rights. I am indebted to Samantha Besson for bringing this claim to my attention; for an example, see K Dowding and M van Hees 'The Construction of Rights' (2003) 97 *American Political Science Review* 281, 286. However, even some of the extraordinary examples dreamt up to try to vindicate this claim can fit more readily than thought within the standard framework of a conflict of duties. If A and B have a right to the same scarce supply of medicine (one example along these lines), the duty typically associated with this will be a duty on all others not to interfere with the respective taking of the medicine by A or by B. Yet A and B will each interfere with each others' taking of the medicine if they exercise their right, so there may be said to be a conflict between the simultaneous realisation of the relevant duties. If C, stranded in a mountain storm, has a right to life that gives him a right to break into D's unoccupied cabin to get food and shelter (the widely-discussed example originates from J Feinberg, *Rights, Justice, and the Bounds of Liberty: Essays in Social Philosophy* (Princeton, Princeton University Press, 1980) 230), we can still analyse this in terms of duties. D's right to property creates a duty on others not to interfere with his property even when he is not there. C's right to life creates a duty on others not to interfere with (or even to help) his obtaining the basic necessities for emergency survival, including a duty to give an implied waiver of aspects of their right to property as necessary for C's emergency survival. That D is not present does not remove the conflict of duties, and thus of rights, implicitly existing in the example. So, on the concept of a right with which we have been working, a conflict of duties account does explain conflicts of rights, though we need not rule out the possibility someone working with a different conception of a right could have a different approach to conflicts.

[24] J Raz, *Practical Reasons and Norms* (Princeton, Princeton University Press, 1990) 39.

[25] Specification is sometimes described as a means of resolving conflicts between rights (eg in the claim that '[t]he general strategy would be to adjust the content and use of such rights to minimize conflict' (M McDonald 'Collective Rights and Tyranny' in G Lafrance (ed) *Pouvoir et tyrannie* (Ottawa, Éditions de l'Université d'Ottawa, 1986) 122). But it differs from modes I will discuss in section III, below, in being, given correct specification, a denial that any conflict exists.

Angelo Cortlett describes it, based on a logical principle of non-contradiction, 'where claims to a right are in conflict, at least one of the claims is invalid'.[26]

A Non-Specificationist will maintain that there is a conflict because a correct description of the rights can consistently permit conflicting duties. In the example, a Non-Specificationist will say that the duties to pay fully both creditors cannot simultaneously be fulfilled, so the associated rights conflict. In general, a Non-Specificationist will hold to a view that duties may conflict, perhaps drawing from other parts of Raz's writings, such as his claim that 'we are subject to duties we are unable to discharge'[27] and his description of rights as 'reasons in their own right, albeit not ultimate reasons'.[28] We might note, of course, that this position does not mean that rights have no internal limits – not every limit on vocalisation (or any other action, for that matter) is a limit on a right of free expression – but the position is rather that rights, even if internally limited, may nonetheless come into conflict.

Some Non-Specificationists argue that a Specificationist position renders the concept of rights useless. As Claire Finkelstein puts it

> such [Specificationist] strategies determine whether it would ultimately be permissible for the person to act as the right allows before making the assignment of right. . . . But then it is difficult to see what work the notion of a right is doing. So on this view, it will not be possible for us to explain why agents may do various things in terms of the fact that they have rights.[29]

She puts it abstractly, but the concern is that any claim that specification would solve every rights conflict would be tantamount to saying that all conflicts are resolved by reference to the underlying interests without any importance accruing to the existence of rights. This solution would allegedly denude rights of any use in decisions on controversial cases where the content of the rights themselves would be disputed.[30]

There is no doubting that the Specificationist position makes the content of rights more subject to dispute. This effect takes away from one function rights could have, that which Raz identifies in his discussion of how assertions of rights can serve as intermediate conclusions around which there can be agreement despite 'a great degree of haziness and disagreement concerning ultimate

[26] A Cortlett, 'The Problem of Collective Moral Rights' (1994) 7 *Canadian Journal of Law and Jurisprudence* 247, 248.

[27] J Raz, *Ethics in the Public Domain: Essays in the Morality of Law and Politics* (Oxford, Clarendon, 1995) 9.

[28] J Raz, *The Morality of Freedom* (Oxford, Clarendon, 1985) 181.

[29] C Finkelstein, 'Two Men on a Plank' (2001) 7 *Legal Theory* 279, 287–88.

[30] One commonly asserted secondary argument against the Specificationist view is that it cannot account for residual moral claims that give rise to compensation when rights are not fulfilled (eg ibid, 295). We can argue, though, that this criticism is not right. Aside from any claim that rights are generally disjunctive (of the form 'Do X or pay compensation'), which raises problems of regress if too general (see ibid, 296), there could be another mode of specification. For instance, why could not the correct specification of a particular right, as opposed to rights generally, be disjunctive and thus compelling compensation for the right not fulfilled in its primary form? This possibility negatives the claim that such a view *cannot* account for residual moral claims. If there is a serious problem with the Specificationist position, it is the concern about what meaning it gives to rights.

values'.[31] In the face of moral disagreements, Specificationists will fight matters out at the level of interests and ultimate values, rather than in trying to determine which rights claims prevail. Their complete account of any general right would occupy a multi-volume book. But there is nothing logically inconsistent about such a position; it is simply one in which the concept of a right has a place as more of an ultimate conclusion than an intermediate conclusion.

Accordingly, we need not decide definitively as between the Specificationist and the Non-Specificationist positions. These positions describe two concepts of a right. Specificationist rights are rights, all-things-considered, whereas Non-Specificationist rights are based on deep, but not complete, consideration of all relevant circumstances, interests and values. The present argument can rest on either of these concepts.

Taking up one branch of the Specification Pincer, if we are concerned with Specificationist rights, then we know by stipulation that there are no actual conflicts between individual and collective rights. We could rest there. However, the question that might remain would be whether any collective rights still exist, or whether correct specification of collective rights denudes them of all content. The answer to this question will be the same as the answer to the question of whether any Non-Specificationist collective rights avoid pervasive conflict with individual rights. So, I proceed to consider the Non-Specificationist branch, both to face up to the question under that branch and to resolve any lingering worries under the Specificationist concept.

The remainder of this chapter, then, will face up to the issue of rights conflict on the assumption that the Non-Specificationist position holds, showing the argument stands against this greater challenge. Alleged conflicts between individual and collective rights do not undermine the argument. This answer, I will argue, arises from the particular nature of collective rights and an ability to distinguish *simple conflicts of rights* from *pervasive conflict.* To make matters clearer before I sketch the argument, it will help to make these terms more precise.

On Waldron's conception of rights that may conflict, rights generate what he calls '*waves of duties*',[32] meaning that any given right typically grounds an array of duties of various sorts, including other duties grounded in circumstances where the initial duties are not fulfilled. In the Financial Predicament, the credit card company's right to be repaid grounds a duty to pay. If this is not fulfilled, there might be a duty (with corresponding derivative right) to submit to having some of one's assets seized to pay the debt. And so on. Many rights will have associated duties that in some way conflict with duties associated with other rights; conflicts of rights, at some level within the waves of duties, will not be uncommon.

This point incidentally might lead to a slight modification of the theory of rights with which the book started. Although Raz's minimalist definition remains true in that a right will exist when an interest is sufficient to ground a duty, with the right

[31] Raz, *The Morality of Freedom* (n 28) 181.
[32] Waldron (n 20) 212–13.

describing the moral protection applying to that interest, most rights will be more substantive than such a minimalist right and will ground waves or bundles of duties. An individual's interest in not being tortured will ground to some degree a bundle of duties on the state not to torture him, on particular officials not to torture him, on the state to punish any officials who do torture him, on the state to educate police officers about the importance of not torturing persons, and so on.[33] A failure to carry out certain duties will be less serious than a failure to carry out others, and there can thus be reconciliation of this right with other rights in circumstances where rights conflict. The interest, then, does ground 'a duty' and meets this minimal requirement for the existence of a right. But it is more interesting than that because it grounds many duties and even grounds reasons to create new duties. Many rights will be of this sort. Indeed, many interests will go beyond the minimalist definition. Rights typically enshrine bundles of (potentially overlapping, substituting, and otherwise interacting) duties.

With this preliminary, it is possible to distinguish simple conflicts from pervasive conflicts. Classes of rights *pervasively* conflict, one might say, when there is an array of conflicts between rights within these classes such that the duties in conflict are so quantitatively prevalent and/or qualitatively weighty that one would reasonably question whether the core interests protected by the rights can simultaneously be protected to any meaningful extent. Returning to the Financial Predicament, there might be a pervasive conflict between the class of rights held by Popper's creditors to be paid and the class of rights held by various persons to whom he has made binding promises to do things (for example, Tiny Tim, to whom he promised to give oboe lessons). Such pervasive conflicts might arise, for instance, if his time constraints are such that he cannot both earn the money he needs to pay his creditors and do the things he has promised. If the time constraints are serious enough, it might be that Popper cannot simultaneously meet even a fraction of these two classes of duties, so the protected interests cannot be protected to any meaningful extent.

The Financial Predicament, of course, might seem of limited relevance, dependent on particular circumstances. But the same kind of analysis can apply even to inherent conflicts between more fundamental rights. Members of racial minority groups will have equality rights, the waves of duties from which might include duties on other members of society not to promote hatred of the groups and duties on the state to act against those promoting hatred. At the same time, members of extremist political organisations have rights of free speech, which might imply (we will later see reasons why not) duties on other members of society and the state not to interfere even with their hate-filled speech. Here, we have the makings of an inherent conflict. The rights conceivably conflict because of the non-contingent content of the rights, though whether such conflict disturbs the societal fabric may depend on whether the rights-holders try to use them. We will return to this *Hate Speech Example* to ask if one or both of the rights is more limited than its asserted form. It is,

[33] *Cf* ibid.

however, conceivably a pervasive conflict – depending on the assumptions we will later examine that relate to what the core interests protected by rights are – as we might conclude that there is both a duty to suppress speech so as to protect fundamental aspects of the dignity interests of some and a duty *not* to interfere with speech so as not to interfere with the expression interests of others.

In the absence of pervasive conflict between particular classes of rights, there is no inherent difficulty reconciling conflicting rights. Moral life, on this view, is filled with potentially conflicting duties (which might or might not be grounded in rights), and this fact need not paralyse us. Waldron's waves of duties analysis makes clear, first, that some perceived conflicts will not in fact be conflicts at all, as there will be ways to find duties that do not conflict. Moreover, even where this is not the case, in the specific case of conflicting duties that are, for instance, elements of the outer waves of rights around certain interests, there is the possibility that the duties are not especially weighty, and there may be no great moral loss in one being unfulfilled. Matters become more difficult only with pervasive conflicts, which might reasonably call into question the meaningful existence of one or more class(es) of rights at stake. In the specific issue concerning classes of individual and collective rights, any pervasive conflict would lead to the kind of *reductio* problems raised earlier. Thus, for the argument to survive, it is necessary to establish that individual and collective rights do not pervasively conflict.

Although many theorists have begun to address issues concerned with conflicts of rights, almost none have examined these issues in the specific context of alleged conflicts between individual and collective rights. I will begin, in the second section, by examining the argument of one who has, Leighton McDonald.[34] He argues, in essence, that the possibility of internal relationships between rights means that there are no necessary conflicts between individual and collective rights. In this chapter, we will see that his argument has something right in spirit but that his claim is insufficient to address the problem at hand and is contradicted by the arguments of other theorists for the necessity of conflicts. However, I will argue that we can say more, and what we need to say, by capturing a key insight from his argument.

In the second section, I will set out his argument and show how it is insufficient to deal with the problem posed. Then, arguing against McDonald's claim that there are no necessary conflicts of individual and collective rights, I will turn in the third section to consider arguments that there are necessary conflicts of rights. I will actually begin by considering briefly a standard suggested by Hillel Steiner for a system of rights that demands compossibility of rights.[35] Steiner conceives of this requirement as avoiding a certain kind of logical vortex, which I will examine. I will argue that this argument cannot imply the non-existence of conflicts of rights. On the contrary, making use of social choice analysis can make clear that

[34] L McDonald, 'Can Collective and Individual Rights Coexist?' (1998) 22 *Melbourne University Law Review* 310.

[35] H Steiner, 'The Structure of a Set of Compossible Rights' (1977) 74 *Journal of Philosophy* 767. See also H Steiner, *An Essay on Rights* (Oxford, Blackwell, 1994).

there are powerful arguments against even the possibility of compossibility. I will examine briefly the relevant arguments of Amartya Sen[36] and several more recent commentators. The conclusion will follow that McDonald is mistaken if he is arguing that there are no necessary conflicts of rights.

However, in the fourth section, I will develop further what is right in McDonald's argument, and in Waldron's, that enables a rejection of any conclusion that there are pervasive conflicts between individual and collective rights. In particular, realising the internal relations between individual and collective rights makes clearer that the interests at stake will generally be compatible rather than conflicting, and that they are morally required to be. In other words, after having seen good reason to accept the claim that conflicts of rights almost inevitably exist, we will see that the relation between individual and collective rights has particular features that actually minimise conflicts in this context.

II. CLAIMS FOR THE NON-NECESSITY OF CONFLICTS

McDonald describes the purpose of his argument as to show that there is nothing peculiar about collective rights such that they will be generally irreconcilable with other rights.[37] His argument, however, does not refer to any particular feature of collective rights. It tries to offer reassurances that collective rights do not have anything special about them that results in their generally having negative consequences for individual rights. So, he begins by suggesting any process of choice between conflicting rights cannot be decided by simple aggregation, meaning that the value of any collective right to a large number of persons does not automatically trump individual rights.[38] He further argues that because both individual and collective rights protect important interests, no violation of the humanistic principle is involved in recognition of collective rights.[39]

McDonald raises two specific examples of collective legal rights to show that some concerns often raised are exaggerated. Thus, he suggests first that compromises between language groups in Quebec do not represent a clash of collective and individual rights, but a finding of middle ground between two linguistic communities, with collective rights on both sides.[40] And he suggests close attention to the reasons why any given collectivity is taking steps limiting individual rights, suggesting in this regard that if an aboriginal collectivity has membership rules discriminating against women, the reasons behind this may actually be a previous disregard for the collective interests, such as through the provision of an unjustly restricted resource base to be shared amongst community members.[41] McDonald

[36] AK Sen, 'The Impossibility of a Paretian Liberal' (1970) 72 *Journal of Political Economy* 152; AK Sen, 'Minimal Liberty' (1992) 59 *Economica* 139. See also AK Sen, 'Liberty and Social Choice' in *Rationality and Freedom* (London, Belknap, 2002).

[37] McDonald (n 34) 323.

[38] Ibid, 324.

[39] Ibid.

[40] Ibid, 326.

[41] Ibid, 325–26.

goes on at much greater length, but we can take it that some elements of his argument usefully correct certain exaggerations about the claims collectivities make.

What is perhaps more useful for present purposes is McDonald's suggestion that there are solutions to many cases of apparent conflicts of rights. He makes this point by way of an example similar to our *Hate Speech Example*. McDonald suggests that there can be internal relations between two rights that resolve many apparent conflicts. For example, he draws on Chief Justice Dickson's reasoning in the Canadian hate speech case of *R v Keegstra*: 'one may quite plausibly contend that it is through rejecting hate propaganda that the state can best encourage the protection of values central to freedom of expression, while simultaneously demonstrating dislike for the vision forwarded by hatemongers'.[42] Dickson CJC describes the right of free expression as resting on the fundamental values of promoting a helpful marketplace of ideas, promoting self-actualisation through expression, and furthering democratic discourse.[43] These values are not independent of the values that criminalisation of hate speech promotes, since hatemongers favour exclusion of some from democratic discourse, seek to undermine their self-actualisation, and undermine the marketplace of ideas.[44] Thus, if restrictions on hate speech favour equality rights over free expression, on this line of resolution, they do so because the rights are *internally related*. That is, the values and interests undergirding one right are not independent of those undergirding another. So, in a conflict arising between the duties implied by the two rights, one needs to look behind the rights to see how these interrelations can affect the appropriate solution.

The equality of groups targeted by hate speech impacts on their ability to engage in free expression, and the expression of groups seeking to engage in hate speech is limited by any such restrictions in ways not striking at the core interests giving rise to the right but in ways upholding others' core interests. The example, of course, is a more complex and contested one than can be discussed fully in the present context.[45] Anyone not liking the specific example can imagine one illustrating the same point. We can see the important possibility of internal relations between rights such that conflicts can be resolved through careful attention to these internal relations.

McDonald here makes a key point that he does not fully develop, which is that:

> Once it is accepted that collective rights and individual rights are both grounded by important human interests, there is no principled reason why the interests protected by particular collective rights might not be internally related to interests protected by particular individual rights.[46]

[42] *R v Keegstra* [1990] 3 SCR 697, 764; McDonald (n 34) 330. *Cf* also Waldron (n 20) 223 (suggesting protected free expression must relate to opponents' views in a manner making room for both sides).

[43] *Keegstra* (n 42) 762–64.

[44] Ibid, 764–66.

[45] See eg FM Kamm, 'Conflicts of Rights: Typology, Methodology, and Nonconsequentialism' (2001) 7 *Legal Theory* 239, 246 (arguing that the free-speech right is sufficiently extensive that it cannot be limited based on the speech rights of others).

[46] McDonald (n 34) 330.

But a further comment raises the important possibility to which I will return later in the chapter. McDonald also claims that such internal relations are inherent in Kymlicka's theory, in that it grounds the value of cultures in their promotion of individual autonomy.[47] Kymlicka's theory, then, could be taken to imply that there are inherent internal relations between individual and collective rights, though Kymlicka obviously could not maintain as much in a moral context since he argues against collective moral rights and for only group-differentiated rights based on individual moral rights. Nonetheless, the suggestion is rich with possibilities to which I will return.

For the moment, we can also take it that McDonald's argument contains an important suggestion as to why conflicts between individual and collective rights might be susceptible of resolution and not inherently irreconcilable. However, his internal relations approach is drawn by analogy from the legal sphere, and we can also draw from the legal sphere several other approaches that might point to reconciliations between conflicting rights. First, it may be possible to explain conflicting rights not as internally related within the rights themselves but as less directly geared to protecting the same background value. For instance, certain constitutional courts seek to deal with bills of rights in terms of a background value of dignity, thus finding that a right manifests no conflict with other rights if the background value of dignity weighs against the claimed extent of the right. In the South African constitutional discourse on hate speech, for instance, the Constitutional Court has explained such a rationale as applying to free expression and permissible limits.[48] This explanation in terms of a background value, of course, is but an extension from an internal relations discussion.[49]

We also have the old standby of 'balancing', seeking to reconcile conflicting rights by reference to the weight of their underlying interests, the effect on rights of particular policies, and so on. Balancing, of course, presumes that there cannot be reconciliation through some other means that avoids the conflict. We need not, of course, here develop a full theory of rights-balancing, but we might note that the understanding of a right as an interest-grounded bundle of duties can help us to understand how balancing might take place. There can be a close examination of the degree to which different, more peripheral elements of different bundles actually advance the interests in question, and a weighing off between these more peripheral elements according to the degree to which they contribute to the core interests at issue, their implications for the other rights at issue, and so on. Balancing need not surrender to some arbitrary process but can be based on a careful analysis which could be further developed in a project with that focus.[50]

[47] Ibid.

[48] *Islamic Unity Convention v Independent Broadcasting Authority* 2002 (4) SA 294 [32].

[49] In some legal contexts, these methods will support specifications of legal rights. I do not discuss those here because we are now concerned with Non-Specificationist approaches.

[50] For a discussion of legal rights balancing as between individual and collective rights, see Morse, Groves and Vermette (n 10). On similar lines, one might provide a further moral account of why Sen's famous goal-rights concept might make sense (A Sen, 'Rights and Agency' (1982) 11 *Philosophy and Public Affairs* 3, 15). However, such an account would need further elaboration and is not my concern here.

McDonald, of course, need not be taken as being committed to any view that analysis of the internal relations between rights is the only, or even the primary, means of reconciling conflicting rights. But his argument toward the assumption that there are no necessary conflicts takes for granted that such internal relation analyses are generally applicable. So we might think that he makes a mistake of taking one means of resolving rights conflicts as the whole of reconciliation theory. If rights cannot always be reconciled through their internal relations, then rights conflicts remain.

Moreover, McDonald's argument does not resolve the problem at issue. The claim we need to challenge is that there are pervasive conflicts between individual and collective rights. Even if it were established, a proposition that there are no necessary conflicts between individual and collective rights might shed some light on relevant issues, but it would not defeat the thesis we need to challenge. Logically, there could still be pervasive but non-necessary conflicts of individual and collective rights. So, though McDonald's argument may usefully correct certain misunderstandings concerning collective rights, his proposition does not engage sufficiently directly with the claim at issue. Moreover, as will be apparent in the next section, there are yet further problems even with his more minimal claim that there are no necessary conflicts of rights.

III. REJECTING COMPOSSIBILITY

In this argument, I have referred to 'pervasive conflict' as the potential concern. In so doing, I have implicitly rejected a particular requirement on a set of rights. Hillel Steiner has famously suggested the requirement that a just set of rights must be 'compossible'.[51] A set of rights, on Steiner's account, must not simultaneously describe a particular action as *permissible*, as falling within the rightful range of actions protected by X's right, and as *impermissible*, as falling with the rightful range of actions prohibited so as to protect Y's right. In this section, I will make use of this claim as a foil for discussion of possible necessary incompossibility of even Non-Specificationist rights, arguing toward a conclusion that, contrary to McDonald's attempt to resolve the problem, at least some rights necessarily conflict. I will begin by showing that drawing further distinctions actually undermines Steiner's demand for compossibility as a requirement of justice. I will then go on to draw on social choice theory and its recent arguments concerning compossibility, with these arguments suggesting that there is necessary incompossibility – that is, some rights necessarily conflict.

Conflicting rights, on the conception developed here, are not (at least typically) contradictory in a *logical* sense. We can draw here on Matthew Kramer's distinction between modal logic, concerned with possibility, impossibility and necessity, and what he calls 'jural logic', concerned with permissibility, impermissibility and

[51] Steiner, 'Structure of a Set of Compossible Rights' (n 35).

obligation.[52] On the latter, the existence of a duty that conflicts with another duty in the sense suggested need not preclude the existence of the other duty (as would be the case were we concerned with propositions of modal logic).

To make this clearer, there is nothing logically contradictory about the fulfillment of one duty making impossible the fulfillment of another duty. We saw this earlier in the quotidian context of the Financial Predicament. That example was just a special case of the creation of conflicting duties by two or more promises that cannot all be fulfilled. A teenager might promise his friend to go to a particular party and promise his mother not to go to the party, and (on a Non-Specificationist concept, which does not read the duty to the friend as implicitly limited by filial promises of which the friend is unaware) he now has conflicting duties. If a duty is simply a weighty moral reason arising out of a certain relation to circumstances or out of some inherent obligation, then it does not cease to exist simply because it cannot be fulfilled. In the sort of circumstances described, there may well be waves of duties if the primary duties cannot be fulfilled; the teenager who breaks the promise to his mother must make amends to her. In any event, though, there can be a conflict of duties without logical contradiction.

This argument could be developed in a different manner, making use of Bernard Williams's observation that duties do not agglomerate.[53] And one must indeed be cautious of certain mistakes one might make based on apparent grammatical parallels without equivalent conceptual parallels. If on Old McDonald's farm, we have the two true propositions that 'Old McDonald has a cow' and 'Old McDonald has a dog', we can of course correctly reason to the proposition that 'Old McDonald has a cow and a dog'. However, we cannot reason from 'Old McDonald has a duty to milk the cow' and 'Old McDonald has a duty to walk the dog' to 'Old McDonald has a duty to milk the cow and walk the dog'. That is, the duties cannot agglomerate. The single duty that requires both acts might or might not be an applicable duty, depending, say, on whether he has the time to do both while behaving consistently with other moral requirements. We more properly say that Old McDonald has two duties that might need to be reconciled through some means as discussed earlier, whether through analysis of internal relations or through a balancing between the duties.

This reasoning on the different mode of agglomeration of duties can reveal something about Steiner's requirement as well. Steiner refers to the logical contradiction of conflicting rights leading to some act being both permissible and impermissible. We can conceptualise this scenario, however, as simply an extreme case of the alleged agglomeration of duties. If someone has a 'duty to do X' and a 'duty to do not-X', we cannot infer that she has a 'duty to do X *and* not-X' so much as that she has non-agglomerated conflicting duties. Nothing about this

[52] M Kramer, 'Rights Without Trimmings' in M Kramer, N Simmonds and H Steiner (eds) *A Debate Over Rights* (Oxford, Oxford University Press, 1998) 19.

[53] B Williams, 'Ethical Consistency and Moral Dilemmas' in *Problems of the Self: Philosophical Papers 1956–1972* (Cambridge, Cambridge University Press, 1973) 170ff.

conflict need make the set of rights grounding these duties logically incompatible and thus inherently unjust. Steiner's requirement of compossibility need not be taken as a rigid requirement. It ought not to trouble us in any logical sense. An aspiration for compossibility might nonetheless weigh upon us, as we do not enjoy potentially tragic choices, whether between freedom of expression and equality rights, between the rights of different creditors in the financial predicament, or between particular rights in a whole host of scenarios.

Nonetheless, the present reasoning suggests that compossibility is not logically demanded. This is fortunate, for I will argue next that compossibility of rights (on the Non-Specificationist concept) is impossible. We will begin with Waldron's argument, which is merely probabilistic. We will then turn to the more necessity-based arguments of social choice theory and game theory.

Waldron, we may recall, suggests that conflicts of rights in the real world are nearly inevitable because interests conflict and because it is unlikely that the set of interests 'associated with the special level of concern that rights indicate . . . just happened to be coextensive with [the set perfectly compossible with one another]'.[54] Again, this argument is merely probabilistic and does not show that matters could not 'just happen' contrary to it. Indeed, Waldron's argument raises anew the distinction between interests and rights. The mere existence of conflicting interests tells us nothing about the existence of pervasive conflict, our broader concern. We must seek a firmer argument.

Amartya Sen has offered a classic argument, often termed the 'Liberal Paradox', which has some similarities to, and arguably inspirations in, the Arrow Theorem that would support the argument in chapter three.[55] Sen begins with a social decision function, this being a function that specifies a social preference from a set of individual preference orderings. As a necessary condition if rights are to exist, Sen suggests that a condition of minimal liberalism (ML) must hold. ML mandates that the society contains at least two individuals such that for each individual, there is at least one pair of alternative social states over which the individual is decisive (determines society's choice). That is, each of two or more individuals has at least one choice that is protected in that the preferences of others will not be able to override that choice in the determination of social preferences. Sen's Liberal Paradox is a proof that ML cannot be satisfied simultaneously with a Pareto condition (a condition that a strict preference of all individuals should also be a strict preference of society) and the condition of universal domain (that a social preference exists for any possible set of individual preferences). If the latter two conditions are reasonable, then the decisiveness of one individual over a pair of alternatives is actually incompatible with anyone else having any rights at all.

[54] Waldron (n 20) 205.

[55] See note 36, above, for the relevant references to Sen. For the Arrow Theorem and the argument of ch 3, see DG Newman, 'Collective Interests and Collective Rights' (2004) 49 *American Journal of Jurisprudence* 127.

Several theorists have recently offered arguments for the non-compossibility of rights in terms of game theory.[56] However, it is not clear that these arguments offer anything beyond what has already been put in the social choice arguments.[57] As a result, we need not consider these arguments separately and can contemplate the significance of Sen's result. To claim that rights cannot be described mathematically would be no answer, as the mathematical form of Sen's argument is but a compressed form of something that could be expressed through further-elaborated verbal discussion. Although Sen goes through a longer, more mathematically oriented proof, we can gain an intuitive sense of the workings of the Liberal Paradox with an example of its operation, helpfully and succinctly put by Robert Nozick:

> [S]uppose that person A has the right to decide among (X,Y) and person B has the right to decide among (Z,W); and suppose their individual preferences are as follows (and that there are no other individuals). Person A prefers W to X to Y to Z, and person B prefers Y to Z to W to X. By the unanimity [Pareto] condition, in the social ordering W is preferred to X (since each individual prefers it to X), and Y is preferred to Z (since each individual prefers it to Z). Also in the social ordering, X is preferred to Y, by person A's right of choice among these two alternatives. Combining these three binary rankings, we get W preferred to X preferred to Y preferred to Z, in the social ordering. However, by person B's right of choice, Z must be preferred to W in the social ordering. There is no transitive social ordering satisfying all these conditions.[58]

If we can express rights in terms of protected pairwise choices that influence a social decision function in this way, we reach a conclusion that there must be logical incompatibilities arising if rights cannot conflict and are absolute in the sense that they represent definitive individual or group control over certain pairwise choices. So, we seem to have a result that goes far in establishing necessary conflicts of rights, and perhaps even farther in its claim that the holding of a right by any one individual or group implies that nobody else can have a right over a pairwise choice, thus seemingly establishing a sort of pervasive conflict.

Nozick takes Sen's argument to imply that rights must be 'side-constraints' that cannot be part of a social decision function but must be constraints on it,[59] thereby incidentally making Sen's argument part of his famously distinct conception of rights. However, whatever the arguments for taking rights as side-constraints in some senses or contexts, employing that conception does not escape the clutches of the Liberal Paradox. Strip away the language of Sen's argument that seems to legitimate Nozick's escape, and set it out in the parallel terms relevant to our argument, and Nozick's argument ends up equally affected. If the 'social decision function' is, rather, taken to be a description of what is *morally best* for society, then

[56] See eg W Gaertner, PK Pattanaik and K Suzumura 'Individual Rights Revisited' (1992) 59 *Economica* 161; M van Hees, *Rights and Decisions: Formal Models of Law and Liberalism* (Dordrecht, Kluwer, 1995); KJ Arrow, A Sen and K Suzumura (eds) *Social Choice Re-Examined* (Basingstoke, Macmillan, 1996).

[57] Jonathan Riley has developed arguments that they are mathematically equivalent but has not, to the best of my knowledge, published these as yet.

[58] R Nozick, *Anarchy, State, and Utopia* (Oxford, Blackwell, 1974) 165.

[59] Ibid, 165–66.

rights must operate within this function and must demand the ML requirement, with Nozick having no basis to turn them into side constraints. Then, if this collective good must meet the requirements of having a universal domain and a requirement that something that is better for every individual member of society is automatically better for society, we arrive again at the Liberal Paradox. So, the solution seemingly must lie, rather, in there being something amiss in the conditions of universal domain or Pareto-optimality.

One might try to avoid the result by restricting interests (in the modified version of the Paradox) to those that do not conflict. But any real society does include conflicting interests. We rob rights of meaning if they cannot help adjudicate between conflicts of interests.[60] So, we might then conclude that the only way in which rights can exist with the ML condition is with a relaxation of Pareto-optimality; indeed, Sen himself suggested this approach.[61]

Such an approach actually flows logically from the earlier analysis. In chapter three, I argued that a collective interest, that which is better for a collectivity, is non-aggregative, which logically leads us to negative an attempt to describe what is best for society, essentially a collective interest, in terms of a function of individual interests. Any use of the Pareto condition to derive the collective interest from individual interests would be an attempt to use an aggregative function (since the Pareto condition in this context is itself an aggregative function), something which chapter three argued was a mistaken approach.

A collective interest is not defined by any aggregative function, including by a Pareto function. This realisation from chapter three liberates us, to a degree, from the Liberal Paradox. Were matters otherwise, we would be in a tough position indeed. One interpretation of the Pareto condition offered by some theorists is as a collective right, since it says that the group of individuals is together decisive over a pair of alternatives, with Sen's proof then establishing 'the noncompossibility of individual and certain *group rights*'.[62] But, given the non-aggregative nature of collective interests, we simply cannot accept that the Pareto condition describes any collective right. To whatever extent the general welfare of society itself gives rise to rights,[63] the interest protected by any such right is not to the fulfillment of the Pareto condition but to that which promotes the common good, the flourishing of reasonable and viable cooperation amongst the members, in accordance with the conclusions in chapter three. We might then claim to have escaped the Liberal Paradox by realising the non-applicability of the Pareto condition within the relevant parallel form of the Paradox, a simple corollary of the proper description of a collective interest being not a shared interest but based on a non-aggregative conception.

But this argument does not escape the possibility of seeming contradictions. As Alan Gibbard highlighted in an extension of Sen's argument, contradictions may

[60] *Cf* Dowding and van Hees (n 23).
[61] A Sen, 'Liberty, Unanimity and Rights' (1976) 43 *Economica* 217.
[62] Dowding and van Hees (n 23) 283 (emphasis in original).
[63] *Cf* ch 3, above; Newman 'Collective Interests and Collective Rights' (n 55), 163.

arise even without the Pareto condition, if individuals have certain kinds of preferences (which are implicitly permitted by the universal domain requirement).[64] Using Gibbard's example, let us suppose that each individual has a right to determine the colour of his or her own bedroom walls (each individual having control of one bedroom). There can be a Pareto-consistent inconsistency, however, if Denise wants her bedroom walls to match the colour of Leslie's walls but Leslie wants his bedroom walls to be a different colour from Denise's walls. Here, with each having pairwise control over the determination of his or her own wall colour, we can have no transitive social choice on the terms of Sen's original argument.[65] The real significance of Gibbard's argument for our purposes is the suggestion that even without the Pareto condition, certain individual preferences might lead to inconsistencies of the sort identified within Sen's Liberal Paradox. If rights are absolute pairwise determinations as between certain options, conflicts of rights necessarily arise that generate a sort of incompossibility. On a Non-Specificationist concept of rights, our conception of rights must be open to conflicts. Does this conclusion, however, imply pervasive conflicts between individual and collective rights?

IV. THE PERVASIVE COMPATIBILITY OF INDIVIDUAL AND COLLECTIVE RIGHTS

I have argued that McDonald is mistaken in his argument for the non-necessity of conflicts and that that argument, in any event, does not go far enough for the point needed. There is, however, something very much right in McDonald, from which the needed argument can be constructed. Recall McDonald's claim that:

> Once it is accepted that collective rights and individual rights are both grounded by important human interests, there is no principled reason why the interests protected by particular collective rights might not be internally related to interests protected by particular individual rights.[66]

There is actually a very important point here, though McDonald has made it more minimally than he should have.

We can go farther than saying that 'there is no principled reason why' the classes of rights in question 'might not be internally related' in such a way as to avoid conflicts. We can actually say that collective rights must be internally related to individual rights. This argument, notably, differs from Michel Seymour's argument that seeks alignment between individual and group rights on the basis that groups have developed in the course of human history in light of individual interests.[67] Rather, collective rights must be related to individual rights because of the

[64] A Gibbard, 'A Pareto-Consistent Libertarian Claim' (1974) 7 *Journal of Economic Theory* 388.
[65] Ibid, 397ff.
[66] McDonald (n 34) 330.
[67] M Seymour, *De la Tolérance à la Reconnaissance: Une théorie libérale des droits collectifs* (Montréal, Boréal, 2008) 602.

humanistic principle and the very bases for which collective rights exist, and the next three chapters will flesh out this internal relation at length. But to deal with the conflicts challenge, first, we need to sketch out, in a preliminary way, the principle that there must be such internal relations.

The humanistic principle implies that collective interests count only insofar as they serve individual interests; I will distinguish and develop this claim in chapter five. Already, however, the realisation in chapter three that a collective interest is inherently something meant to serve individual interests (in being an interest concerned with the reasonable and viable flourishing of a community that serves the individual members of the community) clarifies that collective and individual rights are necessarily interrelated. Internal relations are not mere possibilities, as in McDonald's discussion, but actually necessary requirements for any morally valuable collectivity. This means that arguments for the necessity of conflicts, and even Waldron's arguments for the likelihood of conflicts, do not apply, as they assume independently-defined interests, and the necessary presence of internal relations between individual and collective rights, then, undermines claims to pervasive conflict.

This point is clear at once when we consider the implications of the humanistic thesis for the moral value of individual and collective interests. Individual interests are inherently valuable, for they make better the lives of individuals, thus meeting by their nature the demands of the humanistic thesis. Collective interests meet the demands of the humanistic thesis only if other moral principles make the necessary link. A collective interest improves the life of a collectivity, something to which the humanistic thesis does not explicitly refer. There must be further moral principles ensuring that the flourishing life of a morally valuable collectivity improves the lives of individual members.

Part I already narrowed the range of collectivities permissibly holding rights, reasoning that only certain collectivities have the capacity to hold rights and identifying the sorts of interests that ground collective rights. The task of Part II will be, in a sense, to narrow further the range of collectivities holding rights and to specify moral conditions on the basis of which collectivities hold rights. Non-compliance with these conditions renders a collectivity's claims to right-holding morally illegitimate as no longer in accord with the humanistic principle. So, we appropriately develop additional principles, what I call the *Community Conditions*. Chapter five will develop the *Service Principle*, and chapter six will develop the *Mutuality Principle*. These principles will demand moral consistency between collective rights and the humanistic principle's ultimate concern with individual interests.

On such a theory, we necessarily have pervasive internal relations between individual and collective rights, thereby rendering conflict between individual and collective rights non-pervasive. We have not thus far said enough to make this so, but we have said enough to suggest how we avoid the challenges of conflicting rights. We cannot deny allegations of conflicting interests between individuals and collectivities, but we can maintain that, on either a Specificationist or a

Non-Specificationist concept of a right, there are grounds for maintaining that any conflict is non-pervasive and thus does not undermine our argument for collective rights.

Moreover, not denying the possibility of conflicting interests, there is a pervasive reality of collectivities making real contributions to the lives of their members.[68] As argued in chapter three, many individuals would lack full religious lives without the service provided by the religious collectivities of which they are members. This but manifests a broader reality in settings from the mundane to the profound. The ordinary book club, which meets the Community Conditions, enhances the educational and social lives of its members in real ways. Cultural-linguistic groups provide means of communication and modes of being. Indigenous nations, making members who they are, provide their members with cultural and spiritual connections in and through which they can work toward flourishing lives and better futures.

To all of these possibilities, we will return. But we distort our vision if we focus solely on the dangers of conflicts at the risk of ignoring all that is good about collectivities and their roles in individual lives. That said, we cannot ignore genuine conflicts of individual and collective rights. Such situations are important and interesting, however, because they are serious and exceptional. Part III will further develop from the principles in Part II certain additional norms concerning the reconciliation of such conflicts, particularly in situations of contested views on collective interests. We do well to note for now that these conflicts arise on only a limited basis, and also to suggest forthrightly that they are challenging to identify – more challenging than opponents of collective rights are apt to admit.

Consider the famed case of *Wisconsin v Yoder*,[69] one in which the Amish claimed that their community interests justified their removing their children from the public education system at an earlier age than previously permitted. I will return, particularly in chapter seven, to this case in more detail. For the moment, note that opponents of collective rights are likely to identify conflicts here and to claim that the Amish harm their children by limiting their opportunity to obtain an education about the outside world;[70] that they thereby harm their members by limiting their autonomy;[71] that they do so in a manner prejudicial against female members who receive training only in less marketable homemaking skills (thus preventing them from exiting as easily as male members);[72] that they threaten the education necessary for a liberal democracy;[73] and so on. The claim then becomes that *Yoder* is a paradigm case of conflicts between individual and collective rights. However, in themes to which the coming chapters will return, one properly com-

[68] *Cf* ibid, 602.

[69] *Wisconsin v Yoder*, 406 US 205 (1972).

[70] W Kymlicka, *Multicultural Citizenship* (Oxford, Oxford University Press, 1995) 162.

[71] L Green, 'Rights of Exit' (1998) 4 *Legal Theory* 165, 178–80.

[72] M Nussbaum, *Women and Human Development: The Capabilities Approach* (Cambridge, Cambridge University Press, 2000) 233.

[73] R Reich, *Bridging Multiculturalism and Liberalism in American Education* (Chicago, University of Chicago Press, 2002) 146ff.

plicates even this allegedly easy case. The claim that the policies of the Amish are against the interests of their members depends on a valorisation of autonomy interests over other interests. It depends, as well, on an assumption that the claimed religious interests of the Amish may be dismissed from the discussion, a claim not actually attentive to plausible claims as to individual interests. There is thus an inherent epistemic aspect to the question, and chapter seven will argue that certain requirements that have sometimes been advanced as necessary limits on collectivities are actually more in the nature of epistemically-helpful factors in determining degrees of deference to different collectivities. We can say for now, then, that we will develop a serious response to concerns arising in such cases, further undermining claims as to the pervasiveness of conflict.

Because there are necessarily internal relations between individual and collective interests, and thus between individual and collective rights, the conditions on which some would argue for necessary, or even probable, pervasive conflicts of rights do not hold as between these classes of rights. This conclusion protects the theory from being fundamentally undermined by this challenge. The task becomes simply to go on to develop the principles describing these necessary internal relations.

V. TOWARD A COMPATIBILITY APPROACH

Human rights lawyer Maxwell Yalden, without developing rigorous analysis on the relationship between collective and individual rights, offers this enticing image: 'The forest of collective rights . . . will be as sturdy as the trees within. That is why, in our immeasurably diverse societies, we must remain concerned with both [individual and collective rights].'[74] Of course, an awareness of the importance of collective rights must never make us doubt the continued importance of individual rights.

Yalden's image also implicitly contains other important truths. In particular, the relationship between a collectivity and its members does bear some resemblance to a forest and its trees. Just as the well-being of individual trees suffers if the forest suffers (through certain environmental interconnections), so too the well-being of individual members suffers if the collectivity suffers; at the same time, the forest flourishes only if its members flourish, and the collectivity flourishes only if its members flourish.

We have seen here that although conflicts between individual and collective rights are not pervasive but, rather, occasional occurrences in certain genuinely hard cases. In contemplating collective rights, we must flesh out the moral principles that assure this if we are to continue speaking of morally valuable collectivities, and it is to this task that we now turn. Potential challenges to collective rights have thus become important means of better defining which collectivities may

[74] M Yalden, 'Collective Claims on the Human Rights Landscape' (1993) 1 *International Journal on Minority and Group Rights* 17, 25.

hold which rights, and I turn to developing the Community Conditions in the next three chapters.[75] Although there is no need to return to the present chapter's argument in any explicit way, it sets both a groundwork and a standard for the subsequent chapters of this Part.

[75] *Cf* eg B Parekh *Rethinking Multiculturalism: Cultural Diversity and Political Theory* (Basingstoke, Macmillan, 2000) 217–18 (offering some principles for groups with parallels to those we will develop but without rationalising and justifying them at length).

5

The Service Principle

I. INTRODUCTION

IN THE LAST chapter, we saw that generalised allegations of conflicts between individual and collective rights do not interfere with the coherence of collective rights. This chapter endeavours to go beyond this conclusion to begin developing the compatibility model of rights that sustains and instantiates it. In particular, in this chapter, I will seek to develop the *Service Principle*, the fundamental principle concerning collectivities' internal relations with their members. In chapter six, I will seek to develop the *Mutuality Principle* that governs collectivities' external relations with non-members and with other collectivities. In chapter seven, I will show how these principles apply to the particularly important issues concerning individuals' rights to exit from collectitivities and membership control generally.

This chapter's principal claim is that the *Service Principle*, which is a normative requirement that collectivities serve their members' interests in a broad sense to be developed, both derives from the *humanistic principle* (the proposition that what ultimately matters is the well-being of individual persons) and is a fundamental normative requirement for a collectivity to make any legitimate claims. That is, I will claim that for a collectivity to legitimately mediate for its members, for the advancement of a collective interest to be consistent with the humanistic principle, it must provide goods morally worth preferring[1] over the goods that could be attained without it.

I describe the concern as one of *legitimacy* rather than simply *moral validity* because I am substantially concerned with why individual members should support the collectivity, particularly when some of its actions might seem opposed to some of their interests. Thus, the claim by Anna Moltchanova within her discussion about rights to national self-determination that '[i]ndividual members will have to bear with the results of collective decision making if it is based on legitimate collective deliberation in accordance with the constitution of the group as a collective agent'[2] is right, subject to some qualifications. But it requires

[1] My many intellectual debts to Timothy Endicott include these three words capturing a crux of the Service Principle.

[2] A Moltchanova, *National Self-Determination and Justice in Multinational States* (Dordrecht, Springer, 2009) 52.

justification beyond the recognition of group agents that she uses to attempt to support it. And I speak of what is *morally worth preferring* rather than what is simply *better* not out of some sudden reversion to subjective preferences, but considering the contingency of collectivities and the possible relevance of incommensurabilities. Collectivities are historical phenomena, and the fact individuals identify with particular collectivities will sometimes not be susceptible of moral judgment but simply reflect one morally permissible choice amongst several. Similarly, if incommensurabilities apply, some of the choices at hand may involve choices not fully determined by rational comparison. On these two counts, we cannot always speak of what is 'better' but only of that for which there are reasonable moral grounds, that which is *morally worth preferring*.

To be clear from the outset, to speak of what goods could be attained without the collectivity speaks of comparison not to a state of complete individualism but comparison to a state with other possible collectivities, which might include comparison with a state involving a reformed version of the same collectivity. Such comparisons, though, are subject to limits, which I will develop further in the later sections of the chapter.

The second section argues that the humanistic principle entails the Service Principle and argues against rival claims that the humanistic principle entails more substantial restraints on collectivities. The third section argues that the Service Principle is the principle required for the legitimacy of collectivities and that we do not have similar grounds for more demanding principles of equal regard for the interests of non-members. The fourth section reinforces the claims of the Service Principle as against arguments that collectivities must serve specifically the autonomy of members. The fifth section shows how the Service Principle can help to justify claims of cultural tradition in appropriate cases – making it capable of explaining elements in human experience that many competing principles do not – and reform of those traditions in others. The sixth section reiterates how demanding the Service Principle implicit in this latter point is, demonstrating the care it demands the collectivity take for every individual member's interests.[3]

[3] Individual interests, as discussed in ch 3, are normative relations that exist when certain objects make individuals' lives go better. On an extended conception of what makes an individual's life go better, or simply in the case of individuals who have adopted certain non-individual projects, it will be possible to speak of certain more distant projects being amongst individual interests. If Ursula the Norwegian has a profound concern for the environment and she joins a solidarity group promoting the preservation of bear habitats in Alaska, it is possible to speak of the collectivity serving her and other members' interests by acting for bear habitats, and thus still being subject to the Service Principle, even if this is not the typical sort of collectivity with which we are centrally concerned. Similarly, again on an extended conception of interests, it is possible for a collectivity to serve its members even by helping them to carry out their moral responsibilities, such as in certain community service organisations. Again, these are not the sort of collectivities with which we are centrally concerned, but it is significant that they too can face analysis under the Service Principle.

II. THE HUMANISTIC PRINCIPLE AND THE SERVICE PRINCIPLE

The *humanistic principle*, once again, is the proposition that the well-being of individual persons is what is of ultimate concern.[4] We must now confront a frequent myth about the implications of the humanistic principle, an alleged *priority* between individual and collective rights. For the purposes of this discussion, a particular interest or right will have *priority* if, by virtue of its nature as opposed simply to circumstances, it takes precedence in the sense of inherently having greater moral weight than the other interest or right in specified circumstances. Some noted theorists have taken the humanistic principle to entail an outright moral priority between collectivities and individuals, eventually coalescing into extravagant propositions along the lines that no collectivity can ever rightly act against the interests of one of its own members.

Their *inflexible individual priority claim* (*I2PC*), which effectively says that individual interests always have priority over collective interests, simply neglects the possibility that a collective interest could in an intermediate fashion take priority over individual interests for the sake of a greater purpose. This section will maintain that the humanistic principle actually entails only the more moderate *Service Principle*, a requirement that collectivities serve their members' interests in a general sense. This section will thus endeavour to develop a prima facie argument that the humanistic principle entails the Service Principle as the morally appropriate relation between a collectivity and its members.

Although I pursue this argument in a general manner, we need not think only abstractly. Chapter one put the initial case against Kymlicka's normative prohibition of internal restrictions (claims a group has against members) with reference to legislation by a cultural-linguistic community seeking to promote the ongoing flourishing of its language, including through means restrictive of individual members. The Québecois cultural-linguistic community claims that it legitimately imposes certain protections, such as regulations limiting francophones' access to English-language schooling within the Quebec territorial-political unit, so as to protect the survival of the French language in the face of English-dominated North America.[5] In this example, the humanistic principle mandates that it is the well-being of individual members of the francophone, anglophone, and allophone communities that is of ultimate concern. Any regard for the communities themselves that actually amounted to contempt for the individual members would be an immoral fetishisation. The theorists to whom I respond try to draw a conclusion that each individual's well-being must triumph over that of the communities in question.

These theorists would transform the humanistic principle's minimal claim that it is individual well-being that ultimately matters into a proposition that collective moral claims ought to yield to individual moral claims. Allen Buchanan (using the

[4] See ch 1.II, above; J Raz *The Morality of Freedom* (Oxford, Clarendon, 1985) 194.

[5] See ch 1.IV, above.

different term 'justificatory individualism' for what I have called the humanistic principle[6]) writes that:

> Justificatory individualism rightly rejects as implausible if not outright incoherent the notion that groups are possessors of moral rights and hence on a par, morally speaking, with individual human beings. When the justificatory individualist speaks of the interests of groups this is shorthand for the interests of the members of the group.[7]

Obviously, several different ideas percolate simultaneously through this passage. I dealt earlier with the associated ontological angst and with the existence of an irreducible collective interest. But a source of anxiety obviously remains in a concern over the idea that collectivities' claims might be 'on a par' with those of individuals.

This worry is clearer yet in a recent effort of Thomas Franck to develop theoretical perspectives to support his view of international law. Quoting Neil MacCormick's statement of a proposition equivalent to the humanistic thesis, Franck infers immediately that: 'Morally, individuals are entitled to priority.'[8] He goes on to state several times that individual claims ought morally to be preferred to collective claims,[9] including in his proposition that:

> [A] person's moral claim to rights derives from original, autonomous personage and not from the sorts of contingent external events that shape the rights claims of such entities as the state, society, or tribe. The rights of individuals, in this sense, may be said to have a natural or moral priority over the rights of a group or nation.[10]

Moral determinations, then, become subject to *I^2PC*.

Finally, we can turn to Kok-Chor Tan's development of an argument with certain strong resemblances to Will Kymlicka's.[11] Tan argues that the basis of ethical concern in individuals means that '[c]ollectivities are granted special rights because of their significance to their respective individual members and not because collectivities in themselves are the bearers of rights.'[12] Tan reasons that there cannot be legitimate collective restrictions on individual autonomy:

> [I]f this group wants also to restrict the rights of its members to reevaluate and revise its institutions and practices, we would say that these restrictions cannot be tolerated let alone be sanctioned as collective rights even if a majority in the group agrees to them.[13]

[6] A Buchanan, *Justice, Legitimacy, and Self-Determination: Moral Foundations for International Law* (Oxford, Oxford University Press, 2003) 255 (describing justificatory individualism as the position that 'all justifications for ascriptions of moral and legal rights (and duties) must be grounded *ultimately* on consideration of the well-being and freedom of individuals').

[7] Ibid, 256.

[8] TM Franck, *The Empowered Self* (Oxford, Oxford University Press, 1999) 252.

[9] Ibid, 252–54.

[10] Ibid, 253. *Cf* the more radical claim of Anthony Ellis: 'Because individual rights are ontologically prior to group-inherent rights, the moral significance of group-inherent rights is entirely a matter of the moral significance of the individual rights that compose them', 'Minority Rights and the Preservation of Languages' (2005) 80 *Philosophy* 199, 206.

[11] For example, K-C Tan, *Toleration, Diversity, and Global Justice* (Philadelphia, University of Pennsylvania Press, 2000) 125 (arguing explicitly against 'internal restrictions').

[12] Ibid, 106.

[13] Ibid, 126.

Again, based on something like the humanistic principle, a theorist claims that individual rights automatically have priority over collective rights.

Tan's argument is of course more subtle. It actually refers only to an allegation about priority concerning certain sorts of collective restrictions akin to Kymlicka's internal restrictions, which I discussed in chapter one. Tan derives this claim from the humanistic principle only with an implicit assumption about the normative significance of individual autonomy, so his claim falls to be considered in the same way as Kymlicka's. I will return to the autonomy aspect in the third section of this chapter.

Franck's assertions actually do seem to suggest a generalised priority of individual rights over collective rights, based on a reference back to certain ontological presuppositions. However, chapter two made clear the limited way in which we can speak about supervenience as between individuals and collectivities.[14] They each depend on one another in different contexts and different ways. In chapter three, we explored how although collective well-being supervenes on individual well-being,[15] this supervenience is non-aggregative; I also explored the point that individual well-being itself supervenes partly on collective well-being.[16] Now, the claim is that collective well-being must serve individual well-being. Franck's alleged priority can apply only in abstracted circumstances concerned with ultimate priority. Nothing about the nature of individual rights as opposed to collective rights dictates a priority as between them in contingent contextual circumstances. Note that this distinction of *ultimate moral priority* and *practical moral priority* is highly relevant. The two are not synonymous, or we could not imagine rights at all. Individuals have equal ultimate moral priority, but their practical moral priority will differ in particular circumstances based on their holding of moral rights. An assumption that individuals have ultimate moral priority over collectivities does not imply any general conclusion on practical moral priority. These two sorts of priority are distinguishable, and it is thus entirely conceivable that collective rights might take priority over individual rights in contingent circumstances, consistently with individual interests' ultimate importance.

Views of the *I2PC* sort, then, rest on a mistake. They neglect the possibility that a collective interest could in an intermediate fashion take priority over individual interests for the sake of a greater purpose. Though he goes on to criticise the morality of the legal position he identifies,[17] Franck acknowledges that posited law might involve collective legal rights taking precedence over individual legal rights in specific circumstances.[18] However, as soon as this acknowledgment is present, one should realise the analogous possibility of the intermediate collective moral right that serves individuals. If the flourishing of the Québecois community serves

[14] *Cf* ch 2.II, above.

[15] *Cf* J Finnis, *Natural Law and Natural Rights* (Oxford, Clarendon, 1980) 15.

[16] *Cf* ch 3, above; R Dworkin *Sovereign Virtue: The Theory and Practice of Equality* (Cambridge MA, Harvard University Press, 2000) 222–30.

[17] Franck (n 8) 253; *cf* also Buchanan, *Justice, Legitimacy, and Self-Determination* (n 6) 261.

[18] Franck (n 8) 253.

its individual members, it might rightly limit their educational choices to prevent a collective action problem that would undermine the achievement of a collective good.[19] The example, of course, has more complications, and I will return to it again, but it shows that the point here is not an abstract one.

A collective moral right, mediating ultimately for the interests of individuals, can reasonably take priority over an individual moral right in appropriate circumstances. Buchanan's shrinking back from the notion that collective moral claims could be 'on a par with' individual moral claims, in turn, has no definitive justification. The humanistic principle implies not an inflexible priority but a more general Service Principle. Here one can note that Joseph Raz explains as flowing from his account of the humanistic principle the conclusion that the ultimate value of fulfilling any group interest 'lies in the service to individual interests of advancing the interest of the group',[20] although he does not go on to develop that requirement further. Recognising the flaws in other theoretical approaches, I can now begin to argue for this Service Principle as the correctly derived entailment of the humanistic principle and develop it in the coming sections.

There is a prima facie argument for this Service Principle as the appropriate entailment. The humanistic principle says that our ultimate concern, putting it informally, is the advancement of individual interests. If we are concerned with the advancement of something, we ought logically to be concerned with advancing circumstances or conditions that facilitate its advancement. If collective legal rights advanced individual interests, then, we would logically advance collective legal rights. Analogously, if advancement of a collective interest would advance individual interests, then we ought to be concerned with advancement of the collective interest. We know from chapter three both that advancement of some collective interests does advance individual interests, and that collective interests are neither reducible to nor functional aggregates of individual interests. So, we have reason to call for the advancement of some collective interests independently as intermediaries for the advancement of individual interests.

On this reasoning, there is no automatic moral preference in particular circumstances for the moral claim of an individual over the moral claim of a collectivity. This proposition does not mean that there cannot be good reason to prefer the individual's moral claim. It says only that there cannot be an automatic priority. Even though individual interests are what ultimately matter, individual moral rights in particular circumstances do not automatically take priority over collective moral rights.

That being said, the very rationale for the present claims would be lost if we then inferred that we knew nothing about the interrelations of individual and collective rights. The collective moral right takes priority over individual moral rights only insofar as it serves as an intermediary for individual interests sufficient

[19] *Cf* ch 1.IV, above.

[20] J Raz, 'Rights and Politics' in J Tasioulas (ed) *Law, Values and Social Practice* (Aldershot, Dartmouth, 1997) 80.

to lead to that conclusion. In other words, its force is dependent on its service to these individual interests. In the process of arguing against stronger claims for the priority of individuals, I have developed a prima facie requirement that collectivities serve their members. Indeed, they have legitimate claims only insofar as they do so.

The humanistic principle does not imply an outright priority along the lines of *I2PC*. It instead implies a principle like that of the Service Principle. There is a prima facie argument that the collectivity has legitimacy insofar as it serves its members. But I need to develop this claim more fully.

III. THE SERVICE PRINCIPLE AND COMMUNITY LEGITIMACY

I have not yet fully explained how the humanistic principle, a general proposition about individual well-being, can yield a restricted relation between a collectivity and its members as opposed to all persons. This section will consider two arguments that the ambit of the Service Principle should, in fact, be larger. First, we can consider briefly arguments against *partiality*, those arguments in political theory claiming that an individual does not have special obligations based on particular relationships. Without needing to refute those arguments fully, we can, nonetheless, reject any alleged analogy between those arguments and the issue here by drawing a careful distinction between the obligations of an individual and the obligations of a collectivity. Secondly, we can consider the more directly analogical arguments of theorists like Allen Buchanan, who claims that a state ought not to act solely in its national interest but based on a broader concern for humanity. While accepting the attractiveness of the ideal of nations acting for all humanity, we can maintain that the first obligations of any collectivity are nonetheless to its own members, with further obligations falling to be resolved on other principles, for the collectivity's fundamental legitimacy depends on its service to its members. Collectivities' relations to non-members will be subject to further analysis in the next chapter, which will discuss the Mutuality Principle, but we need to make clear here that this distinction within the Community Conditions is morally right.

First, then, some political theorists have challenged the intuitive assumption that we have special obligations based on particular relationships, arguing that there can be no basis for circumscribing our moral concerns in such a manner.[21] Their arguments do not necessarily spell an end to justified partiality, however, for other theorists have persuasively responded that there are arguments giving force to obligations within particular relationships that have no force outside those relationships, so there can nonetheless be special obligations.[22] The earlier analysis of community clearly rested implicitly on the latter species of claim.

[21] For a range of views, see R McKim and J McMahan (eds) *The Morality of Nationalism* (Oxford, Oxford University Press, 1997).

[22] For example, J McMahan, 'The Limits of National Partiality' in McKim and McMahan (ibid) 107.

However, we need not revisit this larger debate. A collectivity's obligations are simply not directly analogous to an individual's obligations on this head. A collectivity's existence depends on individual members in the ways discussed in chapter two, and its moral responsibilities are particularly affected by the fact that it depends on individual members in this way. There is no automatic grounding for applying to it considerations that pertain to natural, non-contingent moral subjects.

We can turn, then, to an effort in international law theory to confront a seemingly more analogous question, this being Buchanan's argument that states should act based on considerations going beyond national interest. Buchanan argues from the assumption (which I will not challenge) that individual persons have a natural duty of justice toward other individual persons, which includes a 'limited moral obligation to contribute to ensuring that all persons have access to just institutions'.[23] On this ground, Buchanan argues that a state cannot be seen as a purely discretionary association for mutual benefit but must act in a manner consistent with the moral obligations of its members.[24] Accordingly, it cannot morally act simply on the basis of national interest without consideration of moral obligations to non-nationals. (Even an epistemic claim that a state knows its own interests falters, for its own interests will depend on moral determinations related to its own members, meaning obligations to non-members are not inherently less knowable.)[25]

An analogical application of this argument within the present, more general account of collective rights might then claim as follows: (1) A nation is a particular instance of a collectivity; (2) the preceding argument has claimed that a state must not act solely in its national interest but on a concern for the interests of all individual persons; (3) a nation would have similar responsibilities as a state; (4) we have no reason to distinguish between a nation and other collectivities on this point; (5) thus, we may conclude that other collectivities should act not on their collective interests, geared simply to serving members, but on a concern for the interests of all individual persons, whether members or not.

Leaving unexamined the disanalogy between a state and a nation – a state is a mere institution or instrumentality, whereas a nation may be a community – we can nonetheless question this application. Collectivities can and should maintain a concern for the interests of all individual persons, but that claim does not negative their special relation to their own individual members, one which has particular implications for the ongoing existence of any given collectivity. In particular, the argument in chapter three has shown that although we err if we try to identify particular collective interests by seeking shared interests amongst the members, if membership is to be secure and the collectivity's legitimacy stable, there must be a certain sharing of interest around a commonality of good that constitutes the collectivity.

[23] Buchanan, *Justice, Legitimacy, and Self-Determination* (n 6) 55.
[24] Ibid, 47–48.
[25] Ibid, 67–73.

We should distinguish this point from any empirical claim that members will protest or leave a collectivity when its flourishing is revealed as henceforth harmful to their interests or even when they have been perpetually systemically disadvantaged in their interests by their membership. Human beings are complex creatures and may remain in situations that the reasonable observer would urge them to abandon. Individuals' preferences might not correspond to their interests ('I want X even though I know X is bad for me'), so even if they act based on their preferences, they might not act consistently with their interests. And individuals' actions might not correspond even with their preferences ('I did Y even though I would rather have done Z'), so we have further possible disconnections on any such empirical regularities. So, these claims about security of membership and the collectivity's existence do not concern an empirical matter. They concern rather the collectivity's ongoing *legitimacy*, the moral validity of its claims and its morally valid pull on members' consciences.

A collectivity's legitimacy in this sense thrives insofar as it lives out the Service Principle and is threatened to whatever extent it fails to comply. As discussed in chapter three, there is no difficulty with the fact that various collective acts and even collective interests will be contrary to the interests of particular individual members. However, if the collectivity's flourishing ceases permanently to be in the interest of an individual member, we have a breakdown of the commonality of good that constitutes the collectivity. In such a situation, we need to say either that there is a schism such that the collectivity has lost some member(s), or that the collectivity itself has broken down and ceased to have the moral legitimacy to make claims.

A collectivity does not have a similar relation to non-members. I will analyse further in chapter six the ways in which a collectivity has obligations to non-members, but we must see at once that its first obligations are to its members. It is service to their interests that provides the essential basis for the morally legitimate existence of the collectivity.

Thus, the Service Principle is an ongoing moral requirement for collectivities. As stated, not every collective act or interest need conform to the interests of every individual member. But the collectivity must keep faith with their ongoing membership. Moreover, the Service Principle can offer epistemic guidance in the characterisation of particular collective interests and practical guidance in the assessment of particular collective acts, although the guidance to be gained is not as direct as one might first assume.

We might think that collective interests are legitimately identified as such only if they contribute to the ongoing reasonable and viable collaboration of members. A particular purported collective interest not itself complying with the Service Principle might seem not to contribute to the reasonable and viable collaboration of members. But to think in that way would be to turn collective interests into mere aggregates of individual interests, rendering each collective interest into a functional derivation from what would serve individual members, so any such position would be theoretically troubled. It would also be mistaken in a practical sense, for the present argument is that a collectivity may have an interest in and act in certain ways opposed to the interests of even all individual members, although not to all interests of all members.

In the Quebec example, the decision of the Québecois community to develop a language policy effectively limiting the opportunities of individual members to learn English may disadvantage each member in certain respects. It is against the interests individual members might have in the economic success they might attain with the English language. But it serves the interests of members in the continued cultural flourishing of the Québecois community, something that, depending on all the effects and circumstances, may well be morally worth preferring. Obviously, the guidance of the Service Principle is not simple to apply. The guidance, though, is that the Québecois community is valuable insofar as it is morally worth preferring to what could be achieved without the community's mediation and pursuit of collective interests.

Moreover, particular collective actions attain what legitimacy they have because of harmony with this Service Principle. An individuated collective action – one not affecting other policies not considered at the same time – may be evaluated by reference to the Service Principle, because a shrinking back in degree or kind from a collectivity's full potential on the Service Principle can always be grounds to call for different action, reform, or a reconstituted collectivity.

Violation of the Service Principle even in some widespread way does not mean that the collectivity in question could never again have a claim to rights; it would have claims insofar as it brought the actions and policies arising from its internal governance into line with the requirements of the Service Principle.[26] Cindy Holder thus widely cautions us against thinking of a 'vicious cultures' problem, the term other theorists use, when the real problem at issue in such contexts is more typically one of internal governance needing reform to bring a group into compliance with the moral principles that could make its claims legitimate.[27]

Any claims or actions of a group have legitimacy only insofar as they serve its members; we would otherwise be concerned with a fetishisation of collectivities rather than with the demands of the humanistic principle. However, as suggested already, matters may be more complicated. A collectivity can be compared against a reformed collectivity not advancing a particular claim or engaging in a particular action and seemingly morally worth preferring for that reason only if that reformed collectivity would be a genuine option. It is a genuine option only if the claims or actions at issue are severable from other claims or actions of the collectivity, and only if the reforms at stake are 'morally accessible'[28] in the sense that the reforms would not involve immoral disruptions of expectations based on

[26] *Cf* C Holder, *Rethinking Groups: Groups, Group Membership and Group Rights* (PhD thesis, University of Arizona Department of Philosophy, 2001) 180–81.

[27] C Holder 'Are Patriarchal Cultures Really a Problem? Rethinking Objections from Cultural Viciousness' (2002) 12 *Journal of Contemporary Legal Issues* 727, 756.

[28] The concept appears in another context in Buchanan, *Justice, Legitimacy, and Self-Determination* (n 6) 38.

the current form of the collectivity.[29] These requirements are not trivial. Reforms to gender-related elements of a collectivity's claims and actions, for instance, are more complicated than they might first appear. As Charles Taylor poignantly observes: 'The gender definitions of a culture are interwoven with, among other things, its love stories, both those people tell and those they live.'[30] This mere fact, of course, is no reason to resist reforms that do attain something genuinely morally worth preferring. But it does problematise simple claims about what is morally worth preferring, being one manifestation of the complex ways in which reforms may be less severable from other reforms and/or less morally accessible than they first appear. There needs to be careful analysis of the complex realities of collectivities before we can dismiss them as failing to comply with the Service Principle.

The Service Principle enables us to evaluate a collective action like the implementation of a language policy. If the policy in question serves the interests of the members, and does so in a manner morally worth preferring to other possible language policies, it is in harmony with the Service Principle. The Service Principle gives a basis for the collective action at issue. More complexities, of course, arise on how the language policy in our example affects other communities outside the Québecois cultural-linguistic unit but within the Quebec territorial-political unit, and we will return to some of those questions in our discussion of the Mutuality Principle in chapter six. Here, though, there are limits on the policy in that it would be illegitimate for the collectivity to develop a policy that could not be morally worth preferring to what could be attained without the collectivity's intervention.

If the leaders of the Québecois, counterfactually, developed a cultural policy whose sole content was to tax heavily all members of the collectivity so as simply to provide luxurious traditional Québecois foods (whether tourtière or poutine) to select minority groups of gourmands, there would be all kinds of things to say about such a 'cultural policy.' Amongst them would be serious questions under the Service Principle, demanding evidence that the policy promoted cultural flourishing in any meaningful way. If they had none, the policy might well be illegitimate under the terms of the Service Principle.

The fact the Service Principle gives indirect guidance does not mean it cannot give practical guidance. The requirement that a collectivity serve its members has one far-reaching consequence for practical collective action. Though it cannot indicate how to judge between complex bundles in some simple manner, it can generally offer guidance toward a collective policy that serves some members better without serving any members worse, so long as the alternatives are genuinely of that

[29] To acknowledge this element is not to reify existing collectivities, as some critics suggest theories of group rights risk doing (eg S Benhabib *The Claims of Culture: Equality and Diversity in the Global Era* (Princeton, Princeton University Press, 2002) viii, 4). The whole point of the analysis is to distinguish between collectivities worth protecting and promoting and those not having legitimate claims.

[30] C Taylor, 'Conditions of an Unforced Consensus on Human Rights' in J Bauer and D Bell, *The East Asian Challenge for Human Rights* (Cambridge, Cambridge University Press, 1999) 124, 139.

form and do not have further unanalysed consequences. On the stipulations here, there would seem no grounds on which the better situation is not morally worth preferring. Such a situation is a special and easy case.

Does this claim, which seems to import what some might see as a Pareto condition, contradict the conclusion in chapter three that a collective interest is non-aggregative? It might seem, after all, to be applying a functional condition to individual interests in developing principles concerning legitimate collective claims and collective actions. But it does not impose any aggregation to develop a collective interest. It says only that a collectivity's interests, claims and actions are subject to evaluation based on what they do for the individual members, something already inherent in our description of a collective interest as promoting viable and reasonable cooperation. So we can consistently recognise this important and far-reaching consequence of the Service Principle. A collectivity is subject to evaluation, amongst other things, on whether it could have provided better service. And easy cases on this criterion, while not quotidian matters, do arise.

To take one such instance, if at some stage the efforts needed to maintain a minority language become too burdensome for its members – when the policies that would be necessary to prevent the loss of their language and culture would impose on individual members economic or other costs that could not be justified based on the service to individual interests from the flourishing of the culture – then we would have reached a sad day. But it would nonetheless be one on which the cultural-linguistic community could not maintain its claims. Some sort of change process, whether ongoing cultural decay or major changes in economic factors, would have led to a stage of cultural loss. Continued linguistic and cultural preservation at that point would violate the Service Principle and itself spell a moral disintegration of the collectivity; if some within the cultural-linguistic community continued to use political instruments at that point to impose their policies coercively, they would do so tyrannically and wrongly. Augustus's descendants today have no moral basis to enact policies for the revival of the Latin language and Roman culture. More sadly yet, there are probably currently existing languages and cultures whose viability is beyond the point of no return, and there cannot be a moral argument for coercive policies to support those languages and cultures actually past the point of no return – although we do need to ensure that we do not abandon particular languages or cultures through inaccurate assessment of the point of no return. The assessment of that point of no return or 'tipping point', as one might think of it, is inherently challenging, interdisciplinary, and subject to various complex conflicts of interest on the part of those commenting on it, but it is also an unavoidable question if one is not to impose burdens inappropriately on individuals for the sake of lost hopes. These realisations do not deny that the loss of any such culture would be real, a genuine loss of a unique human creation, and one involving loss of the sort to be analysed further later in the chapter. They point rather to the appropriateness of earlier morally justifiable coordinative steps in other cases to avoid facing a similarly sad day in the future. The Service Principle can guide us throughout these various stages.

IV. THE SERVICE PRINCIPLE AND INDIVIDUAL AUTONOMY

The claim here has been that collectivities must serve members' interests generally. This claim seems to differ from a popular view that collectivities ought not to protect and promote interests generally but to advance *autonomy* (the ideal that each be '(part) author of his own life'[31]). On such a view, of course, there would be an independent justification for Kymlicka's pervasive emphasis on autonomy and readiness to dismiss the claims of any collectivity that limited autonomy.[32] The leading theoretical development of autonomy is, of course, that offered by Joseph Raz.[33] This framework, in turn, supports Raz's own arguments, four years before Kymlicka's first book, which discussed with which cultural groups ('inferior cultures',[34] as he terms them in a less conciliatory moment) it might be permissible for the political community to intervene. Raz, like Kymlicka, identifies those groups less supportive of autonomy as those facing further moral demands.[35] Some theorists have responded by asserting, although typically without developing the claim, that such a focus is too narrow and that groups can serve non-autonomy-related interests;[36] on these latter views, we need to develop richer ideas of the ways in which individual persons flourish.[37]

Without seeking to develop here a complete account of autonomy, it is worth making two points about this debate that reveal that we are right to maintain a focus on interests generally rather than simply on autonomy. First, I will argue that it is all too easy to make the mistake of thinking group members lose autonomy when they do not. Secondly, I will argue that other interests, that may or may not sit easily with autonomy, are valuable. Both points will go to show that groups may limit aspects of autonomy while meeting the moral demands of the Service Principle.

First, then, it is all too easy to think mistakenly that group members are losing autonomy when in fact they are not. So-called autonomy-limiting groups will typically implement what we can, following Jeff Spinner-Halev, call 'enabling

[31] Raz, *The Morality of Freedom* (n 4) 369. Raz fleshes this out further in terms of adequacy and awareness of morally accepting options: ibid, 370–89, although leaving aspects of his conception 'to be cashed' in a particular society (ibid, 375).

[32] See ch 1.III, above.

[33] Raz, *The Morality of Freedom* (n 4) chs 14–15.

[34] Ibid, 424.

[35] J Raz, *Ethics in the Public Domain: Essays in the Morality of Law and Politics*, rev edn (Oxford, Clarendon, 1994) 182–83.

[36] *Cf* D Weinstock, 'How Can Collective Rights and Liberalism Be Reconciled?' (1998) 23 *Public Policy and Social Welfare* 281, 294; D Weinstock, 'Beyond Exit Rights: Reframing the Debate' in A Eisenberg and J Spinner-Halev (eds) *Minorities Within Minorities: Equality, Rights and Diversity* (Cambridge, Cambridge University Press, 2005) 246; LW Sumner, *The Moral Foundation of Rights* (Oxford, Oxford University Press, 1987) 96; J Carens *Culture, Citizenship, and Community: A Contextual Exploration of Justice as Evenhandedness* (Oxford, Oxford University Press, 2000) 95 (each raising, but only minimally developing, the idea of important non-autonomy-related interests).

[37] *Cf* M Freeden, *Rights* (Milton Keynes, Open University Press, 1991) 76.

restraints'.[38] An enabling restraint is something that restrains autonomy in some ways but opens it in others. Of course, not every restraint is an enabling restraint, or at least not in any meaningful sense. Locking someone in a cell enables a mode of life that did not exist otherwise, but it does not enable a valuable life. So we need to consider an enabling restraint as one restraining autonomy in some ways but opening it in other valuable ways. In chapter one, I challenged Kymlicka's 'internal restrictions'/'external protections' distinction and his prohibition on internal restrictions.[39] However, I would agree with him that any policy having only an internally restrictive effect, with no offsetting advantage, would be illegitimate. This conclusion follows simply from the conclusion in the last Section that a Pareto-type failure of the Service Principle would be illegitimate.

However, the normal case, where a collectivity acts with reasons, will be one in which it pursues some interest at the cost of imposing some constraints on autonomy. The Québecois decision to restrict access of francophone individuals to English-language education is an example but merely typifies this pattern. Any such action will not be wholly against autonomy. Just as the rules of chess make it possible to play the game, what seem like limits on autonomy open other aspects of autonomy. [40] Notably, to put it in the very terms of the Service Principle, they open the opportunity to live a collective life morally worth preferring to the life without the collectivity. As Spinner-Halev puts it: 'All cultures and communities close off some options as they open up others.'[41]

Just as pursuit of a complete freedom from restraints would destroy the possibility of a game of chess, so too a rejection of all limits on autonomy, of all internal restrictions, undermines the possibility of particular relationships and forms of life. To have even the possibility of being a friend, a teacher, a neighbour, a lover, a spouse, or any of countless other life possibilities presupposes the taking on of certain constraints on one's actions in developed relations with others – and, in the process, the abandonment of some options.[42]

In the example, the Québecois community's use of constraints to promote a flourishing culture opens the mode of life in which individuals have the sense of purpose and meaning given by their culture. The reality that some constraints contribute to the fulfillment of a collective interest does not condemn it, for its fulfillment, aside from serving interests generally, opens new autonomy. The evaluation of which policy is morally worth preferring must consider complex bundles, but with neither having an outright advantage in terms of autonomy aspects of individual well-being.

This claim is generalisable to any collective action that is rooted in some reason, in the pursuit of something. The nature of legitimate collective actions under the

[38] J Spinner-Halev *Surviving Diversity: Religion and Democratic Citizenship* (Baltimore, Johns Hopkins University Press, 2000) 61.

[39] See ch 1.IV, above.

[40] Raz, *Ethics in the Public Domain* (n 35) 176.

[41] Spinner-Halev (n 38) 60.

[42] DA Bell, *Confucian Political Ethics* (Princeton, Princeton University Press, 2008) 51.

Service Principle is that they attain something not available without the mediation of the collectivity, so the fact that some aspects of autonomy are constrained, and others opened, is a complicating factor but not a condemning one.

When Kymlicka and Raz express concerns about the impacts of particular cultures on autonomy, they cannot mean that the actions of particular cultures are entirely against autonomy. All cultures open new options. Their concern must rather be a disagreement with the particular choices some cultures make insofar as they involve sacrifice of some interests for others, or a concern that these other cultures offer nothing of value. The evaluation of whether particular sacrifices are acceptable ones is an evaluation that can be guided by the Service Principle, and that can be open to the sort of contestation to be developed in chapter nine. But the prior point that some sacrifices may be acceptable is a point of moral theory, on which the analysis of public goods problems in chapter one has argued that some sacrifices may be acceptable.[43] Whether the particular sacrifices at issue attain something morally worth preferring, of course, can be a matter for serious analysis, but it must be a contextual analysis, not an a priori declamation about collectivities that supposedly limit autonomy.

But would we not make an a priori claim about collectivities that actually definitively restrict autonomy overall? This question raises the second point, that other interests are also valuable. It is not easy to identify non-autonomy-related interests. Interests we might give as examples of non-autonomy-related interests seem actually to contribute to autonomy. If we were to discuss, for instance, the idea of collectivities serving in some way members' economic interests,[44] we would realise immediately that even the economic well-being of individuals might contribute to their autonomy. Monique Deveaux's example of emotional security as an element of well-being actually in tension with autonomy[45] similarly could run up against the response that someone who is more emotionally secure will thereby be more autonomous.

That said, we might nonetheless distinguish between a motive of promoting autonomy and a motive of promoting interests more generally. To the extent that such a distinction can hold, there seems good reason to act for reasons other than the promotion of autonomy. If children in some underdeveloped state lack food, promotion of their future autonomy might be one good reason to seek to provide them with nourishment, but it will not be the only one. Indeed, it would be both possible and right (and maybe even more virtuous) to feed them simply because they are hungry. It would be not only possible but right to contribute to their having good lives even if doing so did not end up advancing their autonomy. Doing so will not guarantee them successful lives, but it has a value independent

[43] See ch 1.IV, above.

[44] Some have argued that socio-economic justice and the economic well-being of individuals might be an important reason for certain sorts of group-based claims: eg A Acharya 'Equality, Difference and Group Rights: The Case of India' PhD thesis, (University of Toronto Department of Political Science, 2001) 160.

[45] M Deveaux, *Cultural Pluralism and the Dilemmas of Justice* (Ithaca, Cornell University Press, 2000) 121–22.

of any autonomy-related value. Indeed, some of the very elements Raz includes in well-being are not necessarily autonomy-motivated, and there is no reason against them on this head. For instance, he later admits the 'pivotal importance of self-respect to the well-being of people',[46] which he notes gives powerful reasons to fight against such scourges as racism and sexism. It might of course be possible to give autonomy-based reasons for promoting individuals' self-respect. But the crucial point is that it might also be possible to promote self-respect for reasons of well-being not directly related to autonomy. If Ismael is a member of an ethnic group whose traditions limit autonomy to some degree, it will be right to discourage those who utter racist insults against him; the reasons for taking such action will be to help safeguard his self-respect, totally aside from autonomy-based reasons.

Bhikhu Parekh has criticised Kymlicka for settling on autonomy as the main value cultural groups can advance, with Parekh noting that Kymlicka himself had listed other contributions a culture can make in structuring the world for individuals, giving meaning to their lives, and building a valuable sense of community.[47] Again, not all of these contributions are separable from autonomy, but they might be to a degree. Indeed, insofar as Raz critiques some cultures for pursuing values other than autonomy,[48] he must presuppose that there are in fact choices on the matter. Insofar as he refers to duties to promote autonomy including duties to promote conditions that make successful activities possible,[49] he assumes that some things are good for persons that do not themselves consist in successful activities, suggesting a broader scope of interests, provision of some of which need not be motivated by autonomy. Although he says that it will be appropriate to provide individuals with material resources and a cultural environment and to promote generally conditions in which they have basic capacities and an adequate range of options,[50] with the purpose in doing so being to promote their 'chances of a good life' that they will live out autonomously,[51] he does not diminish the reasons for giving those resources and environment independently of autonomy.

Indeed, to deny the value of things other than autonomy would be paradoxical. Autonomy itself is an ideal that affirms the value of other interests in the very assertion of the value of autonomous choices – autonomy would be pointless and senseless if it were all that mattered. This conceptual point perhaps most tellingly undermines the notion that we can focus solely on autonomy. The Service Principle appropriately looks to interests more generally.

46 Raz, *Ethics in the Public Domain* (n 35) 26.
47 B Parekh, 'Dilemmas of a Multicultural Theory of Citizenship' (1997) 4 *Constellations* 54, 59.
48 Raz, *Ethics in the Public Domain* (n 35) 184–85.
49 Raz, *The Morality of Freedom* (n 4) 407.
50 Raz, *Ethics in the Public Domain* (n 35) 16–17, 23.
51 Ibid, 10.

V. THE SERVICE PRINCIPLE AND COMMUNITY SURVIVAL

This section will argue that a theory oriented around the Service Principle can support claims to community survival over time, claims of the sort Charles Taylor labelled *la survivance*.[52] Thus, unlike Kymlicka, whose failure to acknowledge moral reasons for preserving cultures over time was at issue in chapter three, we can maintain that there can be valid claims to *la survivance*. After first examining an argument that suggests the Service Principle is itself sufficient to rule out preservation of 'tradition for tradition's sake', I will argue that there are stronger arguments for the preservation of cultural traditions as living traditions.

A critic, whom I will call the Anti-Traditionalist (*A-T*), might challenge any claim that a cultural group has any right to maintain a cultural practice. *A-T* would say that a collectivity cannot make out any claim to carry out a traditional practice on the basis that it is traditional – whether this is observation of, say, cultural/religious prescription of certain modes of dress or certain aboriginal First Nations' performance of the annual Sun Dance. *A-T* says that such traditions serve no individual interest. Indeed, *A-T* might tell us that there can be no claim by an Israeli Ultra-Orthodox community to require its members to wear modest dress when this is uncomfortable on hot summer days, much less to require others passing through Ultra-Orthodox neighbourhoods to conform,[53] because there is no evidence that wearing modest dress rather than tanktops does individual members any good and such a requirement plainly limits autonomy. *A-T* might even tell us that the elements of self-inflicted pain in the Sun Dance mean that the First Nations who practise it can have no legitimate objection to legislation that prohibited it,[54] because they do not come with Western scientific evidence that their dancing does anyone any good. There can be, says *A-T*, no claim to tradition for tradition's sake.

To analyse matters carefully, we need to distinguish two interwoven elements from *A-T*'s position. First, *A-T* is purporting to describe the interests that individuals have, essentially saying that she understands better the interests of individual Ultra-Orthodox Jews or of individual Plains Cree than the groups themselves do. Such an assumption has, no doubt, been part of the historical reason behind legislative suppression of certain cultural traditions, as in the banning of the Sun Dance.[55]

It will sometimes be permissible to act based on such an assumption. Although I will return in chapter nine to principled grounds for deference and for interference,

[52] C Taylor, 'The Politics of Recognition' in A Gutmann (ed) *Multiculturalism: Examining the Politics of Recognition* (Princeton, Princeton University Press, 1994).

[53] For an argument for such a right, see A Margalit and M Halbertal 'The Right to Culture' (1994) 61 *Social Research* 491.

[54] Around the turn of the twentieth century, the US government prohibited a number of Native American spiritual ceremonies, including the Sun Dance: SS Harjo 'Native Peoples' Cultural and Human Rights: An Unfinished Agenda' (1992) 24 *Arizona State Law Journal* 321, 322.

[55] Ibid, 322–23 (with federal officials portraying themselves as 'civilizing' Native Americans).

some examples are clear at once. If someone were proposing policy steps to help prevent the followers of Jim Jones's cult from being brainwashed into committing mass suicide, there would be no question that the proposal was right. The cult's claims as to what is in its members' spiritual interests differs so substantially from what can be reasonably accepted, its consequences are so serious, and its brainwashing is so suspicion-raising that there are clear grounds for interference. But this is not the usual case, and we more often see the potential reasonableness of a group's claims.

I will return to deal with issues of deference more in chapters seven and nine, showing that we must defer even to some actions when we know how we could make things better. But a preliminary to that discussion is a recognition that *A-T*, speaking of traditions generally and with no specific understanding of the traditions of the Ultra-Orthodox or the Plains Cree, is no better placed than the groups to assess the values of their traditions. Traditions that have remained in place over the centuries begin with an initial presumption that they have served their members over time.[56]

Second, *A-T*'s position also deploys an assumption that there is nothing supporting maintenance of continuity in tradition absent clear service to individuals from a particular tradition. Here, too, we can challenge *A-T*'s assumptions. A culture presents itself to its present generation as a sort of web of traditions, neither precisely seamless nor a number of discrete traditions that can each be considered entirely separately. I will return in chapter nine to how members can argue within the present theory of collective rights for reforms of certain particular traditions. It is possible to note already, though, that members would be well-grounded in arguing for reforms that promote better compliance with the Service Principle, as discussed in the last section. The Service Principle can support calls for reform, but far from upholding *A-T*'s more abolitionist claims, it supports the general maintenance of traditions – not as traditions for tradition's sake but as traditions for the sake of living cultures.[57]

To see this point, we can usefully consider two particular individual interests. First, as Chaim Gans has highlighted, individuals have a weighty interest in the endurance of their projects and memory after their deaths, an interest in the meaningfulness of their endeavours. As Gans notes: 'A state of affairs that does not allow people to harbour this hope hampers their creative capacity. It leaves them with a narrow spectrum of alternatives, comprising hedonism on the one hand, and despair on the other.'[58] Much of the value of culture is precisely in its role as a vehicle through which one can transfer a mode of life to children and grandchildren.[59] Describing one collective tradition, Ronald Garet beautifully writes:

[56] Taylor, 'Unforced Consensus' (n 30) 124, 143–44.

[57] What is meaningless superstition to some is defining ritual to others: S Gilman, '"Barbaric" Rituals?' in J Cohen, M Howard and MC Nussbaum (eds) *Is Multiculturalism Bad for Women?* (Princeton, Princeton University Press, 1999) 57.

[58] C Gans, *The Limits of Nationalism* (Cambridge, Cambridge University Press, 2003) 53.

[59] J Nickel, 'The Value of Cultural Belonging: Expanding Kymlicka's Theory' (1995) 33 *Dialogue* 635, 639–40.

> This is the joy of those that share in the Seder meal, reenacting old histories so as to make them more than old histories, handing down both celebrations and commitments to children, who someday will preside at a different table in a different home, which yet will be the same home.[60]

Through traditions, we live out an intertemporal community with our forebears and our descendants, thereby fulfilling an important interest individuals have in the endurance of their efforts.

Second, individuals have an important present interest in the flourishing of the cultures of which they are members, as I have noted elsewhere, so a culture's flourishing serves their interest in identifying with it. The survival of a culture, and the maintenance of at least some of its traditions (to the extent necessary to preserve the cultural fabric, that precise extent being an empirical matter beyond the present discussion), serves these interests simultaneously, linking the members of a cultural collectivity from various points in time. Thus, in recognising the contribution of cultural traditions, and moral reasons for survival of cultures over time, the Service Principle renders traditions not into the 'dead faith of living people' or even the 'living faith of dead people'[61] but a living, intertemporal pattern of keeping faith, uniting the projects of our forefathers and foremothers and the present endeavours of each new generation. It can support tradition not for tradition's sake but for the sake of what tradition can provide for individual persons, identifying a place for tradition in compliance with the humanistic principle.

To say this much does not say that there ought not to be reinterpretations of traditions where moral reasons so demand. Failure to allow for the reinterpretation of traditions would amount to reification of cultures.[62] The interest individuals have in their efforts enduring is not an all-determinative command, so we of course strike paths between adherence to tradition and reforms to traditions to bring them into full compliance with the Service Principle, beginning with what Taylor beautifully describes as the 'possibilities of reinterpretation and reappropriation that the tradition itself contains'.[63] The Anti-Traditionalist has no valid general claim, but we need to turn to further analysis for when traditions can and cannot morally endure, evaluating traditions against the demands of the Service Principle.

[60] *Cf* RR Garet, 'Dancing to Music: An Interpretation of Mutuality' (1992) 80 *Kentucky Law Journal* 893, 909.

[61] *Cf* J Borrows '"Landed" Citizenship: Narratives of Aboriginal Political Participation' in W Kymlicka and Wayne Norman (eds) *Citizenship in Diverse Societies* (Oxford, Oxford University Press, 2000) 332–33.

[62] Benhabib (n 29) viii, 4.

[63] Taylor, 'Unforced Consensus' (n 30) 142.

VI. DEMANDS OF THE SERVICE PRINCIPLE: SUFFICIENT REGARD AND VULNERABLE INSIDERS

The Service Principle does not simply support an open-ended advocacy of tradition. It is a principle by which we can evaluate traditions, demanding that those traditions not genuinely serving the interests of members be subject to reform. The Service Principle is a demanding principle.

This aspect of the Service Principle also manifests itself in the implications of the nature of non-aggregative collective interests. As Robert George aptly writes:

> Under a non-aggregative conception of collective interests, [G1] no individual's interests may be left out of account by policymakers, [G2] nor may any individual's moral rights be trampled (by legislators, judges, or anyone else) without thereby damaging the collective welfare.[64]

Let us call the part of George's claim I have labelled G1 the Requirement of Sufficient Regard (RSR). We can note briefly why this principle is an aspect of the Service Principle and why, under further assumptions, it implies G2. By doing so, it is possible to both advance the claim that the Service Principle helps to meet chapter four's challenges concerning conflicting rights and to lay some groundwork for the analysis of later chapters.

We may restate the RSR as a requirement that no individual member's interests be ignored by the collectivity. For such a requirement to mean anything, we of course need to read in not only that said interests not be ignored but that they be given due weight. The rationale behind the Service Principle makes clear that this RSR is an aspect of the Service Principle. That rationale, the humanistic principle, specifies the well-being of individual persons as the ultimate moral concern. A collectivity has moral value because it serves individual interests, albeit in a mediated and irreducible form. But this moral value would not be secure were the collectivity to fail to give due weight to the interests of all individual members. So, the RSR is part of the Service Principle.

The formulation of this requirement necessarily remains abstract here. Just what 'due weight' is falls to be determined in the full context of a particular collectivity and its circumstances – and in accord with a complete moral theory. Without purporting to answer every question of moral theory, however, we can note several considerations on the weight due to particular interests. For the reasons developed in chapter two,[65] there will be particular weight due to members' individual interests that are associated with the structure and values of the collectivity. There is a particular weight to the interests of members as members; they may expect the collectivity to serve the interests it is meant to serve. However, other individual interests will also be of particular attention, namely those having the protection of

[64] R George 'Individual Rights, Collective Interests, Public Law, and American Politics' (1989) 8 *Law and Philosophy* 245, 252. *Cf* Finnis, *Natural Law and Natural Rights* (n 15) 218.

[65] See ch 2.IV, above.

rights, to which I will return in a moment. Individual interests neither expecting fulfillment on account of the structure and values of the collectivity nor demanding fulfillment on account of rights are not to be ignored either but do not attract the same levels of attention. A university, to draw on the example in chapter two,[66] has duties to its members, foremost to serve interests connected with its academic mission and to serve interests having the status of rights; this said, it cannot properly ignore other interests either, and its legitimacy might come into question if it wreaked financial devastation on its members. Again, however, the application of the RSR demands close contextual attention to many more factors and complete elaboration of the demands of moral theory.

Even with the remaining abstractness of the RSR, the very existence of the requirement is significant. It reinforces the point that the Service Principle is a demanding one, placing real requirements on collectivities. The requirement also helps make clearer the fact that the Community Conditions have meaningful implications for the harmony between individual and collective rights demanded by chapter four. George went on to make claim G2, suggesting that a collectivity could not 'trample' an individual's moral rights without 'damaging the collective welfare'. Depending on what George means by 'trampling', G2 might simply restate G1 in a different context. If 'trampling' involves disregarding or not giving due weight, a failure to give due weight to rights will be a failure to give due weight to the interests that underlie them, and trampling of rights will automatically be a violation of the RSR. But George seems not to have intended so limited a sense of 'trampling'.

Indeed, both in interpreting G2 and in showing how a more robust interpretation of it flows from the Service Principle under certain conditions, we can draw on a caveat George includes on the same page: 'I refer to fully specified moral rights in asserting that violations of rights damage the common good.'[67] Limiting his claims to the Specificationist concept of a right, George's caveat seems to imply a more robust interpretation of G2. If individual moral rights are fully specified, then they implicitly already take account of the common good and the feedbacks between rights and the common good, with the common good taking account of individual moral rights. The result is that any infringement of a fully specified individual right would automatically also damage the common good. On a Non-Specificationist concept of a right, the same result might not seem to follow. After all, we might infringe an individual right that has not fully taken account of the common good and the interactions between the common good and individual rights, without thereby damaging the common good. However, as chapter four explained concerning the Non-Specificationist concept, rights might be partly specified, with individual interests taking collective interests partly into account. If they are, infringements of individual rights may also damage the common good, although not every infringement will. So, G2 can represent a valid claim, even with a more robust sense of 'trampling' to include at

[66] Ibid.

[67] George (n 64) 252.

least some infringements. The Service Principle thereby also implicitly limits the degree to which a collectivity may infringe individual rights.

This statement, of course, remains abstract. We might wonder if we can say more about the limitations the Service Principle prohibits. In doing so – though admitting that we can say only a limited amount without a more complete elaboration of the values at stake in a particular case – we can draw on what was earlier unveiled. The Service Principle demands service to the interests of members in a broad sense (not without the possibility of some individuals benefitting more than others, or even at the expense of some interests of others), but it says more because it says that a collectivity's claims have legitimacy only because (and if) it can provide goods morally worth preferring over those that could be attained without its mediating presence. The RSR makes clear that any such evaluation must give due weight to the interests of all members, although this does not mean it is possible or right to seek never to act against any individual interest. As any infringements of individual interests or rights become more quantitatively or qualitatively significant, though, they can call into question compliance with the Service Principle's substantial demands.

Avigail Eisenberg has written on the related question of criteria for acceptable recognition of identity claims, albeit without the same overarching framework, and she has articulated three conditions for such claims. The first, a 'jeopardy condition', addresses whether failure to respect the identity claim puts the identity in serious jeopardy. The second, a 'validation condition', asks whether a particular identity claim has been supported by the relevant decision-making system within a community. The third, a 'safeguard condition', assesses whether the claim threatens to generate serious harm.[68] The second and third of these principles are generally consistent with the Service Principle, particularly as developed in the RSR. A community's rights claims can be assessed against standards of showing adequate regard for all members, of not causing disproportionate harm to some members relative to the overall advantage to the collective interest, and of not showing any generalised lack of respect for some members.

The Service Principle is one that both recognises possible value in the claimed values of collectivities and calls for their re-evaluation on appropriate facts. Its application will give rise to different views on particular cases. Susan Moller Okin asserts that the Catholic Church and Orthodox Judaism should face special taxation until they end internal discrimination against women.[69] If the claim allegedly justifying this treatment were that these religious traditions fail to serve women, there is reason to reject it. It is important not to exaggerate particular limitations on service; for instance, although the Catholic Church draws gender-based distinctions by denying women access to the priesthood, the obvious

[68] A Eisenberg, *Reasons of Identity: A Normative Guide to the Political and Legal Assessment of Identity Claims* (Oxford, Oxford University Press, 2009) 32–38, 79ff.

[69] SM Okin, '"Mistresses of Their Own Destiny": Group Rights, Gender, and Realistic Rights of Exit' (2002) 112 *Ethics* 205, 230n.

response from the Church is that women play important roles in the Church and it in fact does serve many women.[70] The presence of certain gender-based distinctions does not automatically spell a violation of the Service Principle, unless the distinctions in question are sufficient to spell a violation of the Requirement of Sufficient Regard we discussed earlier.

Some, perhaps Okin among them, might wish to challenge any such benign characterisation of these religious traditions. Indeed, some have prominently argued for prioritisation of gender equality over any group norm. On some accounts: 'Autonomy for religious groups in cultural matters almost always results in the subordination of women',[71] and there have been strong voices for the absolute prioritisation of gender equality.[72] However, there are profound reasons for caution in overgeneralising about religious or cultural groups. There have been long histories, for instance, of non-feminist authors using allegedly feminist arguments simply for the purpose of demonising particular minority cultures.[73] There are reasons to consider seriously the possible distinctions between practices that involve different roles but ultimately maintain equality, practices that may have symbolically problematic or at least complex effects but also ultimately maintain equality, and practices that create real inequality in a manner violating the Requirement of Sufficient Regard.

These judgments will be complex and fact-specific and will involve deep understandings of varying perspectives on different cultural and religious frameworks. Many factual situations will bring to the fore a complex mesh of interests and rights.[74] To cite just one example, the South African courts have struggled over recent years with a constitutional reaffirmation of African customary law – whose ongoing development had in many cases been partly frozen during the apartheid era – combined with the constitutional affirmation of sex equality. There would be much more complex claims to make about this area of legal development, but in essence the South African Constitutional Court has – rightly, on the account I offer – aspired to support communities' dynamic development of their internal law in ways that accord with constitutional values that protect members within

[70] *Cf* S Macedo, 'Liberalism and Group Identities' in W Feinberg and K McDonough (eds) *Citizenship and Education in Liberal-Democratic Societies* (Oxford, Oxford University Press, 2003) 423.

[71] G Mahajan, 'Indian Exceptionalism or Indian Model: Negotiating Cultural Diversity and Minority Rights in a Democratic Nation-State' in W Kymlicka and B He, *Multiculturalism in Asia* (Oxford, Oxford University Press, 2005) 288, 297. *Cf* S Song, *Justice, Gender, and the Politics of Multiculturalism* (Cambridge, Cambridge University Press, 2007) 3.

[72] G Bouchard and C Taylor, *Building the Future: A Time for Reconciliation: Report of the Commission de consultation sur les pratiques d'accomodement reliées aux différences culturelles* (Quebec, Gouvernement du Québec, 2008) 175ff. See also the related discussions in P Eid, P Bosset, M Milot and S Lebel-Grenier (eds) *Appartenances religieuses, appartenance citoyenne* (Quebec, Les presses de l'université de Laval, 2009).

[73] See A Phillips, *Multiculturalism without Culture* (Princeton, Princeton University Press, 2007) 2–3.

[74] For another particularly complex context not as closely connected to the main argument here, consider the recent decision of the Ontario Court of Appeal, albeit not explicitly addressing collective rights issues, in *R v NS*, 2010 ONCA 670, in which a challenge was put to a Muslim woman's right to wear a veil while testifying as a sexual assault complainant.

the community,[75] thereby facilitating a fulfillment of the Service Principle rather than ongoing clashes of rights.

Later chapters will thus return to other facets of the fate of what some would label 'vulnerable insiders' within collectivities.[76] Vulnerable insiders, for these purposes, are those members of a collectivity who are at risk of being systemically disadvantaged in the advancement of their individual interests by the collectivity. The role of the RSR in the Service Principle makes clear that the present account does not leave them to their fate but protects such individuals, while seeking to do so in a manner avoiding new injustices.

In this chapter, I have shown that the humanistic principle entails the Service Principle, a requirement that collectivities serve the interests of their members. Collectivities have legitimate claims because they enable the pursuit of goods morally worth preferring to the goods available without their mediation. This requirement mandates substantial demands on collectivities, requiring that they not abuse but unite their members.

This chapter has gone far already in removing risks of pervasive conflict between collective and individual rights. Once we see that collective interests must be aligned with the individual interests of members, that collectivities must serve their members, we see that we have intricate interrelationships between individual rights and collective rights that remove many of the dangers of conflict. In the course of elaborating the Service Principle, I have defined an important source of some such interrelationships, thus facing up to the prospect to which other theorists have merely alluded[77] of finding such a solution. That solution, as also noted, is not yet complete, as I need to develop the Mutuality Principle concerning the relation of the collectivity to outsiders. To that task, I now turn.

[75] See generally *Bhe v Magistrate, Khayelitsha*, [2004] ZACC 17, 2005 (1) SA 580 (CC); *Shilubana v Nwamitwa*, [2008] ZACC 9.

[76] See eg A Shachar, 'The Paradox of Multicultural Vulnerability' in C Joppke and S Lukes (eds) *Multicultural Questions* (Oxford, Oxford University Press, 1999).

[77] See eg L McDonald, 'Can Collective and Individual Rights Coexist?' (1998) 22 *Melbourne University Law Review* 310.

6

The Mutuality Principle

I. INTRODUCTION

THE SERVICE PRINCIPLE, a requirement that a collectivity serve its members in a broad sense, prescribes a necessary relation between a collectivity and its members based on the deeper humanistic principle (that the interests of individual persons are what ultimately matter). But does this principle speak to the relations of a collectivity with other collectivities and non-members generally? In this chapter, I will argue that, although the Service Principle itself does not directly address relations outside the collectivity, its rationale does indeed do so, implying that the Service Principle has the *Mutuality Principle* as a necessary partner.

The Mutuality Principle does not provide a justification of the collectivity's legitimacy in the same way that the Service Principle does. The Service Principle prescribes the morally required relationship between the collectivity and its members such that the collectivity does something for its members. The collectivity need not do anything for non-members, but it equally cannot wreak harm upon them, or there would again be a violation of the rationale inherent in the humanistic principle. Thus, the Mutuality Principle must restrict a collectivity's legitimate claims such that the collectivity does not inappropriately trench upon the interests of non-member individuals or other collectivities. What constitutes 'inappropriate trenching upon' is what we must here develop.

In this chapter, I will argue that the Mutuality Principle demands that collectivities respect something akin to the principle Joseph Carens has labelled 'evenhandedness'; I will argue that a collectivity's claims to rights must be respectful of equivalently weighty interests of non-members.[1] Because the equivalently weighty interests of non-members include those they have in the flourishing of collectivities that serve them, this Mutuality Principle also has within it a requirement of respect for other collectivities that serve other individuals. Or, as Thomas Pogge puts it, a group's demands for accommodation 'must be on principles by which they would be prepared to judge the demands of any other groups as well'.[2] By

[1] *Cf* J Carens, *Culture, Citizenship, and Community: A Contextual Exploration of Justice as Evenhandedness* (Oxford, Oxford University Press, 2000) 12–13.

[2] T Pogge, 'Accommodation Rights for Hispanics in the US' in W Kymlicka and A Patten (eds) *Language Rights and Political Theory* (Oxford, Oxford University Press, 2003) 122.

exploring why there are moral constraints on how a collectivity interacts with non-members, it will be apparent that this Mutuality Principle correctly describes these moral constraints.

Indeed, efforts to describe the morality of collectivities have often proceeded based on an assumption that collectivities must be constrained from harming others by rules imposed on collectivities, thus resulting in an account where the interests and rights of collectivities must simply be curtailed so that they do not enter into conflict with rights of those outside the collectivities. Such accounts feature particularly strongly in accounts of the rights of peoples to self-determination, one area of legal doctrine that has resulted in particularly vibrant discussion of collective rights,[3] and more generally in accounts of the rights of peoples. In particular, John Rawls's recent account draws on requirements of stability to develop moral constraints on peoples.

In this chapter, I will seek to show the inappropriateness of this approach, arguing that the principles constraining groups from harming others are actually endogenous to the principles that allow groups to hold rights. The second section elaborates the account offered by Rawls, develops possible similar accounts, and endeavours to show several specific problems with such accounts. The third section develops the Mutuality Principle from the same bases as the Service Principle, arguing that collective rights are internally premised on the sort of respect for other collectivities and individuals demanded by the Mutuality Principle. The fourth section uses the example of international legal doctrine on secession to illustrate some implications of this approach. The fifth section then illustrates the wider applications of the Mutuality Principle, illustrating how it engages with hard cases that raise the challenge of how to coordinate collectivities with competing demands.

II. IMPOSED CONSTRAINTS ON GROUPS

In *The Law of Peoples*, Rawls tries to establish principles for reasonable coexistence between peoples, a coexistence in which there is a fair law facilitating cooperation between peoples that have reasonable differences between them.[4] His account has met resistance largely from individualistically-minded theorists questioning his account's grounding in peoples having corporate moral agency.[5] In chapters two and three, we faced such challenges as related to this book's account of the moral agency of collectivities. So, we can, without hesitation, make use of Rawls's provocative structure in thinking about the moral constraints on collectivities. In this section, I will show how Rawls's account typifies a manner of thinking about

[3] See eg J Crawford (ed) *The Rights of Peoples* (Oxford, Clarendon, 1988). *Cf* A Xanthaki, 'Multiculturalism and International Law: Discussing Universal Standards' (2010) 32 *Human Rights Quarterly* 21.

[4] J Rawls, *The Law of Peoples* (Cambridge MA, Harvard University Press, 1999) 11–12.

[5] *Cf* generally M Nussbaum, *The Frontiers of Justice: Disability, Nationality, Species Membership* (Cambridge MA, Belknap Press, 2006) Part II:3.

constraints on collectivities, one that sees constraints concerning the interests of non-members as arising exogenously and as being moral constraints imposed on collectivities from the outside.

Rawls's account is both rich and subtle, and I can develop only one aspect of his account here, leaving aside many of the interesting questions with which he engages. Particularly interesting, for present purposes, is the fundamental requirement applying to a people that it participate in these principles of reasonable coexistence, and, more specifically, the rationale behind these fundamental requirements. Upon examination, it will be clear that Rawls roots these requirements in what is necessary for reasonable coexistence but that, in doing so, his account gives no answer to claims from peoples that reject reasonable coexistence; thus, his account ends in a sort of circularity. I will then seek to raise the same concern in some arguments analogous to that of Rawls in this respect, arguing that exogenous impositions struggle to satisfactorily explain how or why groups should be restrained from harming others.

Rawls's approach in *The Law of Peoples*, building on elements of his earlier works, envisions a sort of second original position in which the representatives of peoples develop principles for the relationship between peoples.[6] As with the familiar original position of *A Theory of Justice*,[7] this original position is a 'model of representation',[8] a device for elaborating principles that would be reasonable without assuming that there is any real contractual basis for these principles.

His initial account of this original position is one conducted between representatives of liberal democratic societies so as to model 'what we would accept as fair – you and I, here and now – in specifying the basic terms of cooperation among peoples who, as liberal peoples, see themselves as free and equal'.[9] He later extends this original position to include representatives of certain non-democratic peoples, those meeting requirements of what he calls 'decency'. To be part of this compact as a decent people, Rawls suggests, a people (1) must not have aggressive aims; (2) must secure basic human rights; (3) must have a system of law concerned with justice and imposing bona fide obligations; and (4) must be guided by an ideal of justice reasonably believed to be guided by the common good.[10]

We may interpret the three latter elements as concerned with the people's internal adherence to justice, especially as Rawls extends them into the requirement of a decent consultation hierarchy,[11] and thus as concerned fundamentally with ensuring that the people legitimately express the needs of its members, which my account has described more broadly in terms of the Service Principle. The requirement that a people not have aggressive aims adds something further, speaking to a requirement that applies to the relationship between peoples.

[6] Rawls, *The Law of Peoples* (n 4) 32–34.
[7] J Rawls, *A Theory of Justice* (Oxford, Clarendon, 1972).
[8] Rawls, *The Law of Peoples* (n 4) 30.
[9] Ibid, 33.
[10] Ibid, 64–67.
[11] Ibid, 71–72.

Although Rawls describes this element as flowing simply from the idea of decency as reasonable persons would understand it,[12] we can arguably better rationalise it within his theory as a requirement for the stability at which he aims.

Although Rawls does refer to the principles developed through this model embodying what is 'fair', his concern for fairness is at least partly instrumental to a further value of stability, which we may take to be his key aim. He seeks stability beyond a mere *modus vivendi*, preferring a stability resting on respect for the fairness of the principles motivating the stability.[13] Stability and avoidance of harm are paramount in Rawls's calls for respect between peoples: 'Lapsing into contempt on one side, and bitterness and resentment on the other, can only cause *damage*.'[14] The concern is with what generates stability rather than with injustice per se. In the end, the restrictions on which peoples may enter the original position are based on the aim of lasting peace:

> The interests which move peoples (and which distinguish them from states) are *reasonable interests* guided by and congruent with a fair equality and a due respect for all peoples. As I will note later, it is these reasonable interests that make democratic peace possible, and the lack thereof causes peace between states to be at best a *modus vivendi*, a stable balance of forces only for the time being.[15]

Thus, in Rawls's account, the requirement that peoples have non-aggressive aims is a requirement concerned with lasting peace, a stability not based on a temporary modus vivendi.

Rawls, of course, goes on to develop the implications that he says arise from such an original position, resulting in familiar international legal principles of sovereign equality of peoples, duties of non-intervention, non-use of force except in self-defence, respect for human rights, and respect for humanitarian principles governing war.[16] More controversially, he includes a duty to assist other peoples living under unfavourable conditions.[17] These implications, however, need not detain us, for the interesting element of the argument for present purposes is the prior constraint that excludes some peoples from the original position. 'Outlaw states' and other peoples not meeting the necessary requirements[18] are excluded essentially because they upset the possibility of lasting peace. This claim becomes apparent when Rawls explains why liberal and decent peoples within the original position have good reasons not to tolerate outlaw states: 'Outlaw states are aggressive and dangerous; all peoples are safer and more secure if such states change, or are forced to change, their ways. Otherwise, they deeply affect the international climate of power and violence.'[19]

[12] Ibid, 67.
[13] Ibid, 44–45.
[14] Ibid, 62 (emphasis added).
[15] Ibid, 44–45 (emphasis in original).
[16] *Cf* ibid, 37.
[17] Ibid.
[18] See ibid, 4, 63.
[19] Ibid, 81.

However, Rawls's foundations might here begin to appear problematic.[20] Assuming for the moment that we accept his general assumptions that there will be peace between liberal and decent peoples, his reasoning explains to liberal and decent peoples why they have good reasons not to tolerate outlaws. But it does not explain to outlaws what is wrong with their position. An outlaw state rejecting the aim of lasting peace in favour of some other principle of justice – not an obviously unreasonable position since we might reasonably pose questions of whether peace fully trumps justice – receives no answer within Rawls's account as to why it must not be aggressive.

This concern might seem odd when Rawls himself seeks to explain that the Law of Peoples is 'not ethnocentric' and 'asks of other societies only what they can reasonably endorse once they are prepared to stand in a relation of fair equality with all other societies'.[21] However, aside from a rhetorical question ('In what other relation can a people and its regime reasonably expect to stand?'[22]), Rawls does not explain to non-decent states why their position is unjustified. His aspiration is limited: 'in developing the Law of Peoples within a liberal conception of justice, we work out the ideals and principles of the *foreign policy* of a reasonably just *liberal* people'.[23] He goes on to discuss non-liberal but decent peoples 'not to prescribe principles of justice for *them*, but to assure ourselves that the ideals and principles of the foreign policy of a liberal people are also reasonable from a decent non-liberal point of view'.[24] In other words, the entire project is actually internal to liberal, non-aggressive principle, and it contains no explanation to a non-decent society (other than if we read in an implicit but undeveloped suggestion that it should be a decent one). The non-decent society is prohibited from participating in the hypothetical original position, rendering yet more uncertain any hold this original position could have over it. The requirement that a people be non-aggressive, then, does not receive a moral explanation within the theory but appears as an externally imposed limit on states that might reasonably ask why they must comply.

Analogous to Rawls's approach, in this one respect and admittedly not others, are certain accounts of limits a liberal state may place on rights. The 'harm principle' of JS Mill,[25] of course, could be considered a likely contender as a principle defining where rights end, or at least where they may be ended by the state. Under this principle, harm to others justifies limits on rights. What constitutes 'harm', of course, becomes a contested matter, and contestation on this matter does not end even when we accept Joel Feinberg's widely-used account of harm as a setback to interests.[26] But, leaving those battles aside, we might nonetheless seek to claim that Mill's principle could be applied by analogy to a collectivity claiming rights.

[20] *Cf* H Shue, 'Rawls and the Outlaws' (2002) 1 *Politics, Philosophy, and Economics* 307, 308.
[21] Rawls, *The Law of Peoples* (n 4) 121, 122.
[22] Ibid, 122.
[23] Ibid, 10.
[24] Ibid, 10.
[25] For discussion see R Crisp, *Mill on Utilitarianism* (London, Routledge, 1997) ch 8.
[26] See eg J Feinberg 'Harm and Self-Interest' in PMS Hacker and J Raz (eds) *Law, Morality, and Society: Essays in Honour of HLA Hart* (Oxford, Clarendon, 1977) 285.

I will return in the next section to a more direct comparison of the harm principle to the Mutuality Principle, but I can note for now simply that nothing in the harm principle as enunciated by Mill would directly clarify to a potentially harmful collectivity why its harmful aims are not morally permissible. Leave aside how we explain such a constraint to genuine outlaw collectivities, like certain vicious gangs. Some collectivities might make reasonable-sounding claims along the lines that we (either now or generally) are in the midst of a 'culture war' and that collectivities that are to be faithful to their beliefs and the rationale for their existence must continue to act on their beliefs even if their actions are incompatible with the ongoing flourishing of others to whose beliefs they are opposed.[27] Such a collectivity (let us call it the Cultural Warriors) might maintain that its actions retain the status of moral right even if they impose some sort of 'interest setback' on non-member individuals or other collectivities.

We might be tempted to respond, as presumably Mill might, by pointing to the consequences of such attitudes for life together generally, but any such response simply imposes further presuppositions of moral theory, meaning that we cannot presume the collectivity will accept these presuppositions, and we would need further argument for them. We need an explanation that actually shows the Cultural Warriors why it cannot have a claim to rights so long as it threatens to harm others.

We might take a different tack. Perhaps we have such an explanation in the concept of a right. Recall that a right is a normative relation existing when an interest is sufficient to ground a duty. The Cultural Warriors claims rights grounded in its collective interests. But can it rightly claim that anyone is under duties to it? If its collective actions, and very collective existence, causes harm to others, one might wonder whether these others could be under duties to it. Such an explanation might seem promising. However, appealing as it sounds, it would need much further elaboration. Clearly, the existence of many duties causes 'harm' in the sense of an interest setback to the duty-holder. The very nature of a duty is that it prescribes something to be done, whether or not doing so is in one's interest. If one has promised to sell one's car for 100 rupees in a manner giving rise to a duty to do so and now would be better off by doing otherwise, this fact, without more, does not undermine the duty. So, we would need an elaborate account of why the particular harms the Cultural Warriors would wreak are of a sort that would imply that nobody could be under duties to suffer or permit these interest setbacks. The contingency of these matters makes it difficult to see if some sort of analogy to the harm principle could give the required explanation.

These accounts have struggled in substantial part because they require something apart from what the collectivity itself claims. But so far as they stand as external impositions on collectivities, I have said enough to show that they struggle to explain how or why certain constraints apply to collectivities. In the next

[27] *Cf* B Peters 'Communal Groups and Cultural Conflict' in LH Meyer, SL Paulson and TW Pogge (eds) *Rights, Culture, and the Law: Themes from the Legal and Political Philosophy of Joseph Raz* (Oxford, Oxford University Press, 2003) 210–14.

section, I will seek to show how to root constraints in the claims that collectivities themselves make.

III. TOWARD A MUTUALITY PRINCIPLE

The Service Principle, a requirement that collectivities serve their members as a condition of their holding rights, depends of course on deeper propositions of value. It supposes that the value of collectivities resides in their contribution to the lives of individuals rather than in any entirely independent value of collectivities themselves without regard to their service to individuals. I developed the necessary ontological claims in chapter two. Although some have claimed that certain collectivities have priority over individuals, I distinguished in chapter five between different sorts of priority and showed that we should reject claims to the ultimate moral priority of collectivities. Although collective interests may serve individuals in an irreducibly collective manner, it is the interests of human individuals that matter ultimately, and groups matter only insofar as they serve individuals.

In this section, we can see how these deeper foundations undergirding the Service Principle imply the Mutuality Principle as a partner. In chapter five, I examined the primary requirements that a collectivity serve its members, with failure to comply with this principle threatening the very legitimacy of the collectivity and its actions. In developing that claim, however, I left a further point undeveloped. Because a collectivity's value depends on its effect on what is ultimately of value, the well-being of individual persons, its effects on non-members are also relevant to its moral standing.

We thus reject, first, the alternative proposition that no Mutuality Principle applies. The rationale undergirding the Service Principle is that individual interests matter ultimately, and collective interests matter for the contribution they can make to individuals. This rationale does not distinguish between different individuals, between members and non-members, but says simply that individuals' interests matter ultimately. How a collectivity affects non-members remains relevant. This claim does not mean that partiality to members is prohibited, for reasons developed in chapter five. But it does mean that a collectivity's effects on non-members are morally relevant and, indeed, that respect must be shown for the interests of non-members, including for their interests in other collectivities' flourishing. There must be some form of Mutuality Principle.

Could this Mutuality Principle demand that a collectivity have no negative effects on non-members? Such a strict thesis would demand a universe without conflicting interests, a vision rejected in chapter four, and surely lead to the rejection of all real collectivities. We must seek a description of the Mutuality Principle that yields an intermediate position.

The legitimacy of collective interests presupposes a way in which collective interests can be legitimate, since their legitimacy is not primary. Accordingly, the legitimacy of any particular group's collective claims presupposes that other groups' collective claims could be legitimate if they met the same, necessary basis of legitimacy. In the absence of any reason for such distinctions, this basis of legitimacy cannot distinguish between different individuals or groups. If it does, then the claims at hand are arbitrary, and the argument for them dissolves.[28] So, the legitimacy of any group's claims presupposes that other groups could also conceivably have legitimate claims.

Any group seeking respect for its interests, then, speaks arbitrarily if the claims it makes are not respectful of equally weighty claims that could be made by non-members or other groups. This arbitrariness would undermine any argument for its claims, rendering its seeking of respect for its interests into an ad hoc exercise of rhetoric or force, performatorily vitiating the claim. Thus, a collectivity's claims to rights must be respectful of equivalently weighty interests of non-members and other collectivities.

This point is clear in the abstract but might seem more complex in contextual circumstances. If the Taliban claimed that it was right to blow up Buddhist statues, it might try to claim that it still acted consistently with the demands developed here. After all, its defenders might argue, it acted consistently with a principle by which it would be content that all be judged, that true religions be protected and false ones attacked. How do we answer?

In developing the Service Principle, I identified a corollary Requirement of Sufficient Regard demanding that a collectivity consider and give sufficient weight to the interests of all members. This requirement is a procedural corollary demanded by the Service Principle. The Mutuality Principle similarly demands procedural steps to ensure compliance with the requirement that the collectivity respect the equivalently weighty interests of non-members. A collectivity cannot claim to be respecting the equivalently weighty interests of non-members or other collectivities if it does not attend to them and act in a manner respectful of their due weight. The sufficient regard at issue here, of course, cannot involve special considerations for interests relating to the structure and values of the collectivity, for we are concerned with non-members. But, even without elaborating a complete moral theory of the due weight of different interests, we would presume, of course, a special concern for interests of non-members that have the protection of rights, although there must be some concern for all interests of non-members, including their interests in the flourishing of valuable collectivities.

Applying this requirement to the Taliban question, it is apparent that the interest for which the Taliban demands respect is largely the value of religion generally and of persons' and groups' abilities to pursue religious enquiry and worship. This interest itself is valuable to individuals' lives,[29] independently of the truth of their beliefs. As I will discuss further elsewhere, we have grounds for respecting the religious beliefs of others not just out of uncertainty about their possible truth but also out of respect for their own religious enquiry, even if we think them wrong.[30]

[28] *Cf* J Finnis, *Natural Law and Natural Rights* (Oxford, Clarendon, 1980) 107–108.

[29] Ibid, 89–90.

[30] See ch 7.III, below; ch 9.II, below.

The Taliban cannot claim to be showing appropriate concern for the equivalently weighty interests of others when – without further facts other than an allegation of religious truth – they deliberately harm others' ability to pursue religious enquiry and worship, the very interest for which they claim respect. To the extent they will listen to reason, we can explain to them why there are limits on their actions that prohibit them from blowing up Buddha.

The application of the sufficient regard requirement in the context of the Mutuality Principle accepts the possible existence of genuine conflicts. Consider some issues that arise in the context of the Native American Graves Protection and Repatriation Act 1990, which mandates repatriation of Native American ancestral objects held by American museums and federal government agencies.[31] This legislation was intended to contribute to the renewed flourishing of Native American cultural and religious practices.[32] Native American groups have a stronger moral claim to ceremonial objects than do museums and government agencies. Museums might make a claim that these objects serve certain educational purposes and thus contribute to the flourishing of museums as sites of learning, but Native American groups have strong claims that possession of the objects is in the collective interests of the relevant Native American groups and that the interests at stake are of greater moral weight. The objects are specifically part of their cultural and religious traditions and can, in many cases, resume their full ceremonial role. So, there are strong moral rationales for this legislation, fully compatible with the Mutuality Principle.

More challenging moral issues arise, however, in the context of certain disputes, notably those involving ancestral objects now located on land controlled by different Native American groups than those claiming the objects. The legislation does not resolve matters when, for example, Hopi artefacts remain in unexcavated sites on Navajo lands, and the Hopi object to the resulting Navajo control of these objects.[33] If the Navajo claim a spiritual connection with their land, rejecting its excavation, and the Hopi claim a spiritual connection with the objects, demanding the excavation of the sites containing them, each group asserts a claim to defence of certain spiritual interests. In the result, they are in conflict with another group's claim. But, in the absence of evidence to the contrary, we have every reason to believe these groups would respect each other's claims were there a way to do so while still advancing their own. If we adhered to the stricter proposition considered earlier, we would say that the presence of conflicting interests between these groups undermines any claims they have to rights, a clearly implausible result. Instead, the Mutuality Principle illuminates that they can maintain their claims but that we have a challenging conflict to sort out.

A collectivity that will not abide by the Mutuality Principle gives up its claims to collective rights to the extent of the refusal. If the very being and existence of a collectivity is that it inherently acts contrary to the Mutuality Principle, as might

[31] Native American Graves Protection and Repatriation Act 25 USC 3001 et seq (1990).
[32] Ibid.
[33] MF Brown, *Who Owns Native Culture?* (Cambridge MA, Harvard University Press, 2003) 19–20.

be the case with an outfit like the Ku Klux Klan, then that organisation is eliminated from the realm of collectivities potentially claiming rights. In a different sort of case, where some interpretation of a collectivity's traditions or account of a collectivity's interests is opposed to the Mutuality Principle, there are moral reasons for the collectivity to reform itself, or it loses legitimacy in the pursuit of those claims infringing the Mutuality Principle. It does not, however, give up the possibility of claiming rights. Within the traditions of many groups, particularly the traditions of groups as internally rich with different possibilities as cultural groups, there is extensive scope for interpretation of traditions.[34] Such theorists as Bhikhu Parekh and Tariq Modood have challenged the common stereotypes of particular groups as homogenous and incapable of internal change,[35] and empirical scholars like Fred Kniss and Angela Campbell have demonstrated contestation even within communities sometimes stereotyped as relatively monolithic.[36] The scope for interpretation of traditions within any cultural group permitting gradual reinterpretations of its structure and values means that such a group can bring its claims and actions into accordance with the Mutuality Principle. We thus cannot generally condemn groups as 'vicious cultures', although in cases where issues arise we can reject their claims and actions as illegitimate insofar as they violate the Mutuality Principle.

We should note an important further element of this discussion, a sort of reciprocity between groups. Groups may legitimately oppose the existence of certain other groups, notably those that actually fail to comply with the Community Conditions. In doing so, they are opposed to other groups not meeting the conditions for the reciprocal claim. Activist churches that work against violent racist organisations do not sacrifice their claim as churches to hold rights but are shining examples of collectivities promoting interests of member and non-member interests. Any conclusion on a group's compliance with the Mutuality Principle depends, in turn, on the compliance of any groups against whom it acts with the Mutuality and Service Principles. Once again, this element follows because our ultimate concern is with the well-being of individuals; groups must respect other groups that promote the well-being of others but can rightly act against groups that disrespect the well-being of others.

[34] *Cf* eg B Parekh, 'A Varied Moral World' in J Cohen, M Howard and MC Nussbaum (eds) *Is Multiculturalism Bad for Women?* (Princeton, Princeton University Press, 1999) 69, 74.

[35] B Parekh, *A New Politics of Identity: Political Principles for an Interdependent World* (London, Palgrave Macmillan, 2008) 117. T Modood, *Multicultural Politics: Racism, Ethnicity and Muslims in Britain* (Minneapolis, University of Minnesota Press, 2005) 172. See also J Bowen, 'Normative Pluralism in Indonesia: Regions, Religions, and Ethnicities' in W Kymlicka and B He (eds) *Multiculturalism in Asia* (Oxford, Oxford University Press, 2005) 152 (warning of the dangers of misconceiving group claims through other lenses).

[36] See eg F Kniss *Disquiet in the Land: Cultural Conflict in American Mennonite Communities* (New Brunswick, Rutgers University Press, 1997); A Campbell, 'Bountiful Voices' (2009) 47 *Osgoode Hall Law Journal* 183. See also G Bouchard and C Taylor, *Building the Future: A Time for Reconciliation: Report of the Commission de consultation sur les pratiques d'accomodement reliées aux différences culturelles* (Quebec, Gouvernement du Québec, 2008) 69–73 (exposing the overwhelmingly stereotyped descriptions by media of minority group claims).

This point gives rise to a point explaining the name of the Mutuality Principle. The Community Conditions mark out a set of collectivities having mutually respectful legitimate collective interests. We seek a set of collectivities that can simultaneously exist in the manner required by Part I, can comply with the Service Principle, and can comply with the Mutuality Principle. Such a set might be difficult to find. It also might not be unique. To take an analogy from the economic realm, the conditions for what economists call a *general equilibrium*, which features simultaneous equilibrium in a number of markets that interact with each other, are strict indeed. We cannot automatically conclude that there is a single solution to the equilibrium problem here. There are very likely different sets of equilibria of mutually respectful legitimate collectivities. That said, even when communities are mutually respectful, there can still be tensions between them and conflicts in their interests, so long as these do not rise to a level actually calling into question their compliance with the Mutuality Principle. This problem would arise, for instance, if one community showed a generalised disrespect for another based on a refusal to understand it or created disproportionate risks of harm to another group or other individuals. This account provides no guarantee of stability and everlasting peace. There can be a 'culture war' between legitimate collectivities whose collective interests and visions differ.[37] But the war is at least a limited war, one in which the Mutuality Principle mandates some level of respect between the collectivities in conflict.

The question arises of what implications the Mutuality Principle might have for communities that have a measure of political power. The Bolivian Constitution of October 2008, which commits Bolivia to being a plurinational community, requiring the state to promote the ethical and moral principles of a plurinational society, and which entrenches specific guarantees of community rights and creates a plurinational legislative assembly, has provoked discussion in various contexts of the idea of a plurinational state.[38] Similarly, the Bouchard-Taylor Commission's consideration of policies of 'reasonable accommodation' of minorities within Quebec and its recommendation of extending policies of 'interculturalism' has also fostered discussion.[39] Does every community with political power need to develop policies of 'plurinationalism' and 'interculturalism'?

Because my account recognises rights held by majority communities as well as by minority communities, it is possible to answer that question with a 'not necessarily'. In some contexts, a nation-building scheme that draws in minority communities may be what is most consistent with the majority community's nature.[40] An American-style 'melting pot' option is not automatically off the table

[37] *Cf* Peters (n 27).

[38] See Bolivia, Nueva Constitución Política del Estado (October 2008) arts 1, 8:I, 30, 145ff. *Cf* Republic of Ecuador Constitution of 2008 (2008) (containing many analogous provisions).

[39] See discussions of 'interculturalism' at various points in G Bouchard and C Taylor, *Building the Future: A Time for Reconciliation: Report of the Commission de consultation sur les pratiques d'accomodement reliées aux différences culturelles* (Quebec, Gouvernement du Québec, 2008).

[40] *Cf* DA Bell, *Beyond Liberal Democracy: Political Thinking for an East Asian Context* (Princeton, Princeton University Press, 2007) 193–96.

and, in some circumstances, may actually respect the different interests and rights at stake.

However, such a set of relationships would be subject to the tests coming from the Mutuality Principle. Where they would not show respect to the different communities affected, the underlying policies would be subject to critique based on this principle. Although a community could have interests best fulfilled through a nation-building policy, the Mutuality Principle would recognise the same moral interests underlying the claims of other communities to a greater degree if the majority community had engaged in historic harms against these other communities, had taken on historic commitments to these other communities, or had taken in large groups of individuals from other communities without clarity as to the expectations on them. Thus, the United States might well justly pursue a set of policies based on a common American identity while nonetheless owing special regard to indigenous American communities that had faced historic harm, to certain religious pacifist communities who had been given assurances of freedom to pursue their traditions in freedom, and in more complex ways to the African American and Hispanic communities and perhaps some other immigrant groups. The Mutuality Principle, to some degree, can recognise the often-challenged distinction Kymlicka draws between national minority communities and immigrant ethnic groups[41] and give a morally principled basis for it. The analysis of particular relationships in terms of the Mutuality Principle will necessarily be highly contextual. However, there is nonetheless a general moral framework on the basis of which one can assess claims.

Although not every community need relate to other communities in an identical manner, the Mutuality Principle does enforce some fundamental moral requirements on communities. It will not be permissible to engage in national development that fails to give any regard to minority communities within the state where these minority communities have rights to participation and their own right to development. The African Commission on Human Rights powerfully enunciated limits on state action in the context of the right to development of specific communities in the recent *Enderois* case, in which the Commission affirmed the place of the right to development of minority and indigenous communities as against the development of the larger state.[42] The Mutuality Principle would be quite consistent with the sorts of concerns the Commission addressed.

Moreover, the conclusions here imply a general readiness by legitimate rights-holding groups to engage and participate in endeavours to attempt to reconcile rights. Other theorists have asserted as much,[43] but the Mutuality Principle offers

[41] See eg W Kymlicka, *Multicultural Citizenship* (Oxford, Oxford University Press, 1995) 10ff. *Cf* M Seymour, *De la Tolérance à la Reconnaissance: Une théorie libérale des droits collectifs* (Montréal, Boréal, 2008) 496–98.

[42] *Centre for Minority Rights Development (Kenya) and Minority Rights Group International on behalf of Endorois Welfare Council v Kenya* (decision of 4 February 2010) no 276/2003 (Afr Comm Hum Rts) [*Enderois* case].

[43] See NT Casals, *Group Rights as Human Rights: A Liberal Approach to Multiculturalism* (Dordrecht, Springer, 2006) 234; Carens (n 1) 12–14; B Parekh, *Rethinking Multiculturalism: Cultural Diversity and Political Theory* (London, Macmillan, 2000) 265–66.

a specific explanation as to why this is the case. Groups must show a respect for other groups that have underlying interests as worthy as their own.

This statement is not just a general principle but can have, in turn, specific implications. Consider, for instance, the context of rival claims over religious sites by multiple religious groups. It is not unreasonable to expect religious communities to recognise that other religious communities have parallel interests that may find fulfillment in the same site, where there is reasonable evidence of genuine commitments as such. The moral implication will be a preference for various kinds of site-sharing arrangements over those that preclude one group from being able to find fulfillment of its interests. Thus, a 30 September 2010 decision of the Allahabad High Court in India on title over the Ayodhya religious site awarding a sort of joint title to rival Hindu groups and Muslims all having religious interests in the site, marks a wise approach to such questions, preferable to one of making rigid determinations that would exclude some from use of such a site.[44]

On the same grounds, where a site is not divisible in an appropriate manner, the approach to some religious sites may require time-sharing arrangements. For example, there has been a long-standing campaign by some religious Jewish women to pray at the Western Wall in a manner consistent with egalitarian Jewish religious traditions but not accepted by some ultra-Orthodox Jewish practitioners who find the women's practices offensive and worthy even of violent response.[45] Judicial responses thus far have guaranteed the women's groups an opportunity to pray in their preferred manner only at a different site. However, in the context of the uniqueness of the Western Wall within Jewish religious tradition, and the Mutuality Principle's requirements to seek reconciliations of rights, there would be strong arguments for a morally preferable response being a granting of a specific regular time period during which the women could practice without interference their religion within their tradition at the Western Wall itself.

Some of the specific examples I have used will no doubt be contested, and I make no claim to have considered thoroughly all the factors in each of these cases. However, the Mutuality Principle's shaping of discussion in various contexts begins to become clearer. It provides a Principle originating from the very bases of collective rights themselves that speaks to inherent moral limits on the way in which communities interact with one another.

IV. INTERNALLY-LIMITED SELF-DETERMINATION

In the international law context, these issues play out practically on a larger stage in the context of international law doctrine on secession. This specific debate illustrates the disparity between moral arguments for self-determination and

[44] For a brief account of this and some similar disputes, see 'Unholy Rows', *The Economist* (9 October 2010) 85.

[45] See eg P Chesler and R Haut (eds) *Women of the Wall: Claiming Sacred Ground at Judaism's Holy Site* (Woodstock, Jewish Lights, 2003).

constraining principles of territorial integrity. If the constraints on self-determination resulting in secession were left as sheer implications of territorial integrity, theorists and peoples might claim that a moral right was being undermined by power politics, leaving matters in an undesirable position. By theorising more completely the limits necessarily internal to a people's self-determination, we may give a more satisfactory account of the limits on self-determination.

Legally grounded claims to secession, of course, originate in the international law right of self-determination. On a fulsome reading, this latter right would seem to ground a broad right of secession. As Judge Dillard memorably described the right of self-determination in the *Western Sahara Advisory Opinion*: 'It is for the people to determine the destiny of the territory and not the territory the destiny of the people.'[46] Such inspiring words incorporate no explicit limit. UN Declarations have similarly recognised self-determination in broad terms.[47] And the International Court of Justice has recently reaffirmed self-determination as 'one of the essential principles of contemporary international law'.[48] That said, the International Court of Justice has also shyed away from pronouncing on secession rights, with its recent *Advisory Opinion* on Kosovo's unilateral declaration of independence declining to answer many of the larger substantive questions naturally arising from questions that had been framed in terms of issues with an independence declaration, and leaving these larger questions to continue to be worked out in light of the more general statements on self-determination.[49]

At the same time, even these sources have typically included the right of self-determination alongside principles of territorial integrity, leading to claims that self-determination must be interpreted in a narrow manner, with a preference for internal self-determination practised without secession, so as not to interfere with territorial integrity. Three seminal judicial decisions on secession help to illustrate preferences for territorial integrity and rights of other individuals and collectivities.[50]

In two different cases in the mid-1990s, judicial bodies reached decisions limiting rights of secession. In *Katanga*,[51] the African Commission on Human and Peoples' Rights ruled that a people's right to self-determination generally had to be exercised in a form less disruptive to states' sovereignty and territorial integrity than secession. Thus, in the absence of grave human rights abuses, a people would be expected to exercise self-determination within an existing state rather than to secede. In *Bertrand v Quebec*,[52] the Quebec Superior Court contemporaneously

[46] *Western Sahara Opinion* [1975] ICJ Rep 12, 122.

[47] Declaration on the Granting of Independence to Colonial Territories and Peoples UNGA Res 1514 15th Session [1]–[4]; International Covenant on Economic, Social and Cultural Rights 1966, 993 UNTS 3 art 1(1); Declaration on Principles of International Law Concerning Friendly Relations and Cooperation UNGA Res 2625 25th Session.

[48] *Case Concerning East Timor (Portugal v Australia)* [1995] ICJ Rep 90 [29].

[49] *Advisory Opinion on the Accordance with International Law of the Unilateral Declaration of Independence in Respect of Kosovo*, ICJ Advisory Opinion of 22 July 2010.

[50] See also the International Court of Justice's application of the principle of *uti possidetis* in the *Frontier Dispute Case (Burkina Faso v Mali)* [1986] ICJ Rep 554 [25]–[26].

[51] *Katangese Peoples' Congress v Zaire* (1996) 3 IHRR 136.

[52] *Bertrand v Québec (Procureur général)* [1995] RJQ 2500, 127 DLR (4th) 408 (SC).

sided partly with a lawyer who brought a claim for injunctive relief against the province's plans to hold a referendum on secession. The lawyer argued inter alia that secession would take away his individual constitutional rights as a Canadian citizen. Although the Court refused to grant an injunction against holding a referendum, it did grant an unusual preemptive declaration: it declared that legislation providing for a secession referendum outside normal constitutional amendment procedures constituted a serious threat to citizens' constitutional rights, which would no longer be guaranteed after secession.[53]

Three years later, in attempts to clarify the law after a close referendum result, a national government reference to the Supreme Court of Canada sought to settle the issue of Quebec's legal right to secede. In the *Secession Reference*,[54] the Supreme Court of Canada, without referring to the *Bertrand* case, set out a broader legal framework for secession. The Court stated that international law recognised an international law right to secession only in cases of oppression (including colonial oppression) and that the international law right to self-determination was generally to be practised through internal self-determination.[55] However, the Court also stated that the structure of Canada's democratic constitution gave rise to an obligation to negotiate in good faith with a province seeking any major constitutional change, including secession.[56] The *Katanga* and *Bertrand* cases thus both limit secession rights so as to protect the interests and rights of other citizens and groups, and to protect state interests in territorial integrity. And, where the *Secession Reference* partly affirms a people's democratic right to self-determination, it does so only subject to its exercise in a manner respectful of other interests and rights at play.

State practice on recognition of seceding entities also reflects an effort to constrain secession with principles of territorial integrity. In particular, the European Community developed guidelines on the recognition of new states in Eastern Europe that required purported new states to respect human rights and not to be involved in any aggression or efforts to change frontiers other than by common agreement.[57] A separate declaration on Yugoslavia referred to requirements that any Yugoslav Republic to be recognised commit itself not to have territorial aims against neighbouring European Community states.[58]

Some have seen these sorts of restrictions generally as limitations on self-determination resulting from existing states preserving their power.[59] Indeed, this

[53] Ibid, [86].

[54] *Reference re Secession of Quebec* [1998] 2 SCR 217.

[55] Ibid, [126]–[135].

[56] Ibid, [88]–[91].

[57] 'EC Declaration on the Guidelines on Recognition of New States in Eastern Europe and the Soviet Union, December 1991' (1993) 4 *European Journal of International Law* 72; S Murphy, 'Democratic Legitimacy and the Recognition of States and Governments' (1999) 48 *International and Comparative Law Quarterly* 545.

[58] 'EC Declaration on Yugoslavia, 16 December 1991' (1993) 4 *European Journal of International Law* 72.

[59] See eg *Namibia Opinion* [1971] ICJ Rep 16 (sep op of Judge Ammoun); N Jayawickrama 'The Right of Self-Determination – A Time for Reinvention and Renewal' (1993) 57 *Saskatchewan Law Review* 1; R McCorquodale 'Self-Determination: A Human Rights Approach' (1994) 43 *International and Comparative Law Quarterly* 857, 884.

conclusion flows naturally from the apparent discrepancy between a legal principle going to the morality of freeing peoples from oppression, and a principle entrenching states' present territory. Need there be such a discrepancy, or can we improve the explanation of why self-determination must be limited in such a manner?

Rawls himself suggests that no people has a right to self-determination or secession at the expense of subjugating another.[60] He writes:

> A clear example regarding secession is whether the South had a right to secede in 1860–61. On my account it had no such right, since it seceded to perpetuate its domestic institution of slavery. This was as severe a violation of human rights as any, and it extended to nearly half the population.[61]

As we discussed earlier, Rawls's account in *The Law of Peoples* would presumably explain this further in terms of the need for stability, but we can explain it in a different way.

Secession can fulfill important interests of a people, but secession may also work contrary to the interests of other individuals and will certainly work contrary to the interests of other collectivities. As an example of the former, the secession of Ian Smith's Rhodesia had moral shortcomings because it was intended to help oppress individuals of non-European ancestry. As an example of the latter, the secession of the Katangese faced moral challenges because it would have trenched on the self-determination of the larger Zairean collectivity.

Allen Buchanan has recently reframed his writing on secession to emphasise a particular obstacle to any rights of self-determination giving rise to rights of secession:

> [A] moral theory of the right to secede must articulate the conditions under which a group is justified in asserting the right to try to set up a legitimate state of their own in a portion of the territory now claimed by an existing state.[62]

That is, any secessionist claim involves a territorial claim. Any secessionist claim inherently trenches on other collective interests in territory.

This reason for strong burdens on those advocating secession articulates a valuable insight, but it does not express fully the moral constraints on secession. Any secession of Quebec would be morally acceptable only if the Quebec government, in addition to other conditions, maintained appropriate protections for the collective interests of aboriginal First Nations within Quebec. And this moral constraint does not refer only to aboriginal First Nations' collective interests in certain territorial holdings. If, counterfactually, a Québecois sovereignty movement existed that intended to suppress aboriginal First Nations' cultural practices as part of a newly independent Quebec, any such movement would give up the legitimacy of

[60] Rawls, *The Law of Peoples* (n 4) 38.
[61] Ibid, 38n.
[62] A Buchanan, *Justice, Legitimacy, and Self-Determination: Moral Foundations for International Law* (Oxford, Oxford University Press, 2003) 16.

its claim insofar as its claim was inseparable from those plans. Were its secession akin to that of the American South or Rhodesia, it would give up its legitimacy at once. In reality, the Québecois community has sought to be respectful of indigenous claims and other minority rights. But other issues remain, insofar as any secession would affect the collective interests of Canadians.

We might try to describe these issues simply in terms of harm to other collective and individual interests, but we need not attempt to stretch the concept of harm in these challenging ways. The Mutuality Principle developed in the present chapter can provide a more powerful account. A people claims a right to self-determination based on its collective interests, but because the people itself has moral standing insofar as it serves the interests of individuals, the legitimacy of its claim to secession must rest on an internally-limited principle that yields to overriding interests of other individuals or groups that secession may harm. A people cannot claim a right that fails to respect the equivalently weighty interests of other peoples while remaining consistent with the bases for its holding rights.

Andrew Altman and Christopher Heath Wellman have recently proposed a vastly more permissive approach to secession, suggesting that the only restraint on secession is that the prospective state will adequately protect and respect individual human rights within the new state.[63] But this approach permits a claim to secession on a basis inconsistent with what justifies the claim. Altman and Wellman attempt to reverse the argument, saying a political community cannot claim rights over a separatist territory while simultaneously claiming self-determination against other states.[64] But that argument essentially ignores the reconciliation of interests mandated by requirements for internal self-determination.

Rights to self-determination often do not entail a right to secede. The account presented, however, does not constrain self-determination arbitrarily with limits imposed on potentially self-determining entities from power politics. Rather, it identifies internal limits on self-determination arising from the self-determining entity's own claim and demands that it respect these limits. Obviously, we could develop in further detail the precise implications for various situations of self-determination, but the point is made that such an account can resolve the moral discrepancy that otherwise undermines limits on self-determination. Ironically, this account, speaking to the self-determining group with a claim other than territorial integrity preserving existing power relations, offers hope of promoting negotiations better suited to the very stability at which external limitations accounts would aim. The internal limits on the right are simultaneously a protection for the self-determining group, whose interests must be reconciled in a general equilibrium of group claims, better promoting legitimate territorial entities. The account offered by the Mutuality Principle in the specific area of international legal doctrine on self-determination

[63] A Altman and CH Wellman, *A Liberal Theory of International Justice* (Oxford, Oxford University Press, 2009) 13.

[64] See ibid, 46–52 (trying various bits of prejudicial rhetoric by implying a claim against Quebec secession would deprive Canada of a right to independence from the United States and saying those opposing free secession must also logically have favoured Germany's annexation of Poland).

and secession is a particular instance of its generally more cogent structure, but a powerfully persuasive instance that offers greater hope on difficult legal and political challenges.

V. COORDINATING COLLECTIVITIES

Whatever hopes we might have that communities can live harmoniously together without difficulty, I would be presenting a mistakenly rosy view were I to make matters out to be replete with such harmony. Bernhard Peters, discussing cultural conflict, has drawn a useful distinction that can help to illuminate in what ways conflicts might remain for which there needs to be some coordination developed in line with further principles to be addressed in Part III. As Peters puts it, the need for a common normative framework (or what we can think of as a coordinative framework) arises when there is interdependence between groups – when they interact with one another, when they have harmful effects on one another, or when they compete for resources.[65] The latter two situations are those to which the Mutuality Principle applies and to which it can demand some sort of coordination to allow collectivities to continue acting in a manner that allows them to live out their purposes. Just to set out the challenge for Part III, let us see how each of these two kinds of scenarios can pose challenges under the Mutuality Principle. In the process, we will see how more complex conflicts exist than are often acknowledged.

First, groups can obviously have harmful effects on one another. We gain nothing with clear-cut examples here and turn at once to how these harmful effects can be complex and pose difficult challenges that theorists have been inclined to mask. Consider here the issue of religious proselytisation. One reaction, of course, might be to ask what the issue is. One might conceive of religious proselytisation as an obvious part of freedom of religion and something not raising any moral issues.[66] Natan Lerner helpfully problematises this view, noting that: 'What constitutes the sacred duty of evangelization for one group may be viewed by another group as improper proselytization.'[67] Saying that, of course, does not yet show how proselytisation could actually be not only disliked by other religious groups but actually harmful. But we can rapidly see more problematic features. Many of these have been powerfully highlighted by Makau wa Mutua, who describes eloquently how traditional religions can be woven into the life of communities (he writes specifically in the African context, though the argument could be broader).[68]

[65] Peters (n 27) 212.

[66] For such a view, see TM Franck *The Empowered Self* (Oxford, Oxford University Press, 1999) 102–103.

[67] N Lerner, 'Proselytism, Change of Religion, and International Human Rights' (1998) 12 *Emory International Law Review* 477, 488.

[68] M wa Mutua, 'Limitations on Religious Rights: Problematizing Religious Freedom in the African Context' (1999) 5 *Buffalo Human Rights Law Review* 75. The parallel amongst indigenous communities in the Americas is obvious. We might also note the parallel claims of some that Eastern Orthodoxy is inter-

When traditional religions have been delegitimised through missionary activities, this has historically led to the collapse of social norms and cultural identities.[69] Given the value we recognise cultural survival could have,[70] then there can be an argument that unrestrained proselytisation transgresses the bounds of the Mutuality Principle.

Fervent believers in a particular religious doctrine, of course, might not feel deterred by these concerns, arguing that the communication of their particular religious message is vital to the interests of those who have not yet had the opportunity to hear it. Notably, however, even were we to take the premises of the fervent believers as assumptions, there would still be grounds for some limits on unrestrained proselytisation. If proselytisation could take place in a manner less destructive to existing cultures and communities, there would be every reason to prefer a less destructive form of proselytisation, so as to avoid harm to human flourishing (indeed, many evangelical churches themselves do impose some restraints on their own proselytisation, communicating primarily with the 'unchurched' and exercising restraint in relation to those already part of another faith group). So, even on premises that would seem entirely supportive of proselytisation, we can find reason for limits. If, of course, the premises driving policy in the epistemic framework of a particular community did not include these religious premises, then it would conceivably be all the more ready to recognise the place of limits on proselytisation, seeking to reconcile the religious freedom to proselytise with the serious harms that may ensue from unrestrained proselytisation.

In saying this, I implicitly revisit Kymlicka's early attacks on '[t]heocracies on American reserves'[71] as insufficiently attentive (even if he does recognise possible contextual complexities to his dismissals[72]) to the complex coordination necessary between interests in religious freedom and interests in cultural survival in a context where missionary activity has undermined indigenous culture. It may well be vital to the cultural survival of certain indigenous communities that they have powers to promote the spiritual traditions of the community, even at the potential cost of some limits on the individual religious freedom of members who have converted to other faiths – something now recognised in some powers in the modern self-government agreements negotiated in Canada.[73] The coordination demanded by groups potentially harmfully affecting one another may be very complex and demand careful analysis.

woven into Russian culture. I will not here examine the complex features of late 1990s Russian legislation that had some limiting effects on individual religious freedom in order to help protect the Orthodox community (*On the Freedom of Conscience and Religious Associations* Federal Law No 125-FZ (26 September 1997) (Russia)), but we can note in advance the likely lack of full analysis in any view that would simply caricature it as tyrannical.

[69] wa Mutua (ibid) 75.

[70] See ch 5.V, above.

[71] W Kymlicka *Liberalism, Community, and Culture* (Oxford, Clarendon, 1989) 196.

[72] Ibid, 199.

[73] See ch 1.IV, above; Tlicho Agreement (4 September 2002) art 7.4.4.

Appropriate compromises will sometimes be easier to find. Returning to the example of Quebec's law on commercial signage,[74] an attempt to preserve a French-language *visage*, we can note additional considerations that arise in light of the Mutuality Principle. I defended the legislation earlier as one means of promoting cultural survival of the Québecois community.[75] However, the issues can now be rendered in a more complex form. Given that the initial legislation prohibited languages other than French on commercial signs, it went too far in restricting the ability of other cultural groups to maintain their cultural life.[76] Joseph Carens notes that there was usually non-aggressive enforcement of the legislation in immigrant neighbourhoods but points to the sheer insecurity of immigrant language communities on such an approach.[77] The problem is clear. There is a fine line between the Québecois protecting their language and culture against the English-language cultural threat posed by the rest of North America[78] and the Québecois themselves imposing their language on other communities seeking to survive within Quebec. The compromise later reached, one requiring only predominance of the French language on signage, lives out well the Mutuality Principle, letting the Québecois community flourish while respecting the flourishing of other communities. Similarly, the 1996 decision to prosecute Jewish shopkeepers for having kosher products sold for Pesach labelled in English or Hebrew rather than French failed to attend to their particular religious and cultural interests, and the subsequent development of an exemption lives out the Mutuality Principle.

A need for coordination can also arise from competition for resources between collectivities. There are almost inevitable conflicts in such viable claims as the claim that human societies drawing central elements of their life from particular territories have the relevant rights to those territories.[79] The cultural group claiming a cultural connection to a territory will rapidly find itself in conflict with the group that now draws economic sustenance from the territory. Competition for resources is thus evident in various contexts in which indigenous peoples and members of settler cultures would make use of the same natural resources. The resolution of some such conflicts will be easier under the Mutuality Principle than others. In *Sparrow*,[80] the Supreme Court of Canada adjudicated on Musqueam food fishing rights and recognised the priority of Musqueam food fishing over non-aboriginal use of the relevant fishery. The Court reached this conclusion based on the legal place of aboriginal rights under the relevant constitutional

[74] See ch 1.IV, above.
[75] Ibid.
[76] Carens (n 1) 126–27 describes the facts and issues well.
[77] Ibid, 127.
[78] See D Réaume, 'Justice Between Cultures: Autonomy and the Protection of Cultural Affiliation' (1995) 29 *University of British Columbia Law Review* 117, 136.
[79] B Slattery, 'Aboriginal Sovereignty and Imperial Claims' (1991) *Osgoode Hall Law Journal* 681 697; JM Valadez, *Deliberative Democracy, Political Legitimacy, and Self-Determination in Multicultural Societies* (Boulder, Westview, 2001) 286–88.
[80] *R v Sparrow*, [1990] 1 SCR 1075.

guarantees. But we can morally rationalise this priority in terms of the Mutuality Principle. The collective right of the Musqueam can prevail against the purely economic interests of other fishers consistently with the Mutuality Principle because, as James Tully usefully glosses the case, 'fishing a specific body of coastal water is constitutive of the cultural identity of the Aboriginal Musqueam nation' more deeply than for the non-aboriginal fisher community.[81] The Musqueam claim to priority in the fishery is consistent with the Mutuality Principle in that the Musqueam make out a claim to a more morally weighty interest.

The issue would become more problematic, however, if another collectivity had an equally weighty claim. This scenario might arise even in certain conflicts with a settler culture, such as where the interests of the settler group are sufficiently seriously affected in either cultural and/or economic terms so as to make these interests comparable with the indigenous group's interests at stake.[82] Such a scenario might also arise if more than one indigenous group made a claim to the same rights, as has arisen, for instance, where two aboriginal groups claimed the same fishery.[83] In such scenarios, there needs to be some sort of coordination. Appropriate coordination presumably must look first to the correctness of the claims – whether, in fact, both groups do have a claim to the fishery in question. In doing so, any coordinating body will wish to consider matters in a manner respectful of the nature of the claims and the circumstances; there may be reason to modify the rules of evidence, for instance, out of fairness to communities that have not made use of written documents but whose accurate oral histories can demonstrate traditional linkages with particular resources.[84] Any coordinating body will also wish to examine carefully the interests at stake and their moral weight. Some conflicting interests will be of clearly lesser weight, while others will be of at least potentially more equivalent weight. Compare, for instance, the conflicts arising over Native American spiritual sites between Native American communities and rock climbers as opposed to conflicts between Native American communities and sincere New Age spiritualists.[85] In the end, though, it may need simply to resolve the competition for resources in some manner as respectful of all as possible. But coordination will not be able to work miracles, and it will involve challenging choices that evoke contestation. To this contestation, we return in Part III.

The Mutuality Principle thus undermines the legitimacy of particular claims or actions that fail to accord with a collectivity's moral responsibilities to non-members. Only, however, where such claims or actions are inseparable from the meaning of a collectivity will the Mutuality Principle undermine a collectivity's claim to all rights; it eliminates altogether the claims of certain very pernicious

[81] J Tully, *Strange Multiplicity: Constitutionalism in an Age of Diversity* (Cambridge, Cambridge University Press, 1995) 172.

[82] Valadez (n 79) 288.

[83] *Hwilitsum First Nation v Canada (Minister of Fisheries and Oceans)*, 2001 FCT 936.

[84] See DG Newman, '*Tsilhqot'in Nation v British Columbia* and Civil Justice: Analysing the Procedural Interaction of Evidentiary Principles and Aboriginal Oral History' (2005) 43 *Alberta Law Review* 433.

[85] For references to these two types of conflicts, see Brown (n 33) 163, 168.

groups to any sort of collective rights. But it also allows us to call as illegitimate other claims or actions that violate the Mutuality Principle and, possibly, subject them to restraint – subject to the principles to be developed in Part III concerning when there can be principled interference with collectivities. These conclusions, together with the requirements of the Service Principle help to mark out sets of legitimate collectivities, those in compliance with these Community Conditions.

7

Rights to Exit and Membership Control

I. INTRODUCTION

SOME WILL ASK whether the Service Principle and Mutuality Principle include as further partners certain other principles they might like to see as necessary. In particular, claims have widely circulated that collectivities must allow members a realistic right of exit (*a right of exit*), that collectivities must allow their members to control collective acts in a more or less democratic manner (*a right of consultation*, or *consultativeness requirement*),[1] and that collectivities' degree of membership control must be limited. This chapter explores these issues, arguing that the Service Principle does not ground the sorts of claims alleged and that the Mutuality Principle permits substantial membership control by collectivities.

Unlike with some of the other analysis in this book, alleged rights of exit and consultation, as well as membership control, have been much discussed. Thus, this chapter can partly respond to theorists' analyses of these issues. That said, the relevant analysis of these rights for present purposes is oriented to whether they are partners of the Service Principle and Mutuality Principle, for this approach reveals whether the most immediate conclusions of the humanistic principle go on to entail these alleged rights. Thus, this discussion will not seek to engage with every argument on the right to exit, rights of consultation, or membership control.

I can thus set out the structure before further contextualising the argument with a brief account of that to which we respond. In the second section, I will analyse alleged rights to exit through recent theorists' efforts to develop arguments for realistic rights of exit, critiquing these arguments by making use of Albert Hirschman's analysis of what he calls 'exit' and 'voice' in the economic context. Drawing on Hirschman's analysis, we will argue that exit and voice (or provisions for consultation) can substitute for one another to a substantial degree. In the third section, I will extend this conclusion to examine some possible substitutions between exit and voice and argue that various bundles of exit and voice may be appropriate (depending very much on a contextual analysis of the circumstances of the collectivity and its members). We will then be able to recharacterise the

[1] This use of the term 'consultation' is distinct from consultation in the context of the duty to consult indigenous communities that is discussed at several other points in the book and in my other work eg DG Newman, *The Duty to Consult: New Relationships with Aboriginal Peoples* (Saskatoon: Purich Publishing, 2009). The consultation at issue in the present chapter is that with individual members within the community.

existence of rights of exit and consultation into non-mandatory derivative requirements of the Service Principle; the existence of exit or voice then becomes more of an epistemic indicator that may help to assess compliance with the Service Principle. In the fourth section, I will turn to parallel issues present in membership control generally and argue that a framework combining the Service Principle and the Mutuality Principle permits substantial collective powers of membership control. I will thus reach conclusions diverging from those often supposed, highlighting the power of the present account to cast new light.

A right of exit has been a central concern of a wide variety of political theorists writing on the relationship between individuals and groups,[2] although they have characterised it in different ways. Some have depicted rights of exit as being sufficient to excuse group conduct that would otherwise be considered unreasonably oppressive of individual members. As Chandran Kukathas puts it: 'If an individual continues to live in a community and according to ways that (in the judgment of the wider society) treat her unjustly, even though she is free to leave, then our concern about the injustice diminishes.'[3] Kukathas seems prepared even to excuse the potentially unjust treatment on the grounds that the right of exit is available. Others have depicted rights of exit as being in some way necessary to the protection of individuals. Joseph Raz, still arguing that groups should and may be encouraged to change repressive practices, nonetheless claims that 'the opportunity to exit from a group is a vital protection for those members of it who are repressed by its culture'.[4] Susan Moller Okin has gone so far as to say that: 'Any consistent defense of group rights or exemptions that is based on liberal premises has to ensure that at least one individual right – the right to exit one's group of origin – trumps any group right.'[5]

Exit rights, then, are thought to limit the repression of group members and to be either sufficient or necessary to comply with moral principles. I will argue, however, that rights of exit are neither necessary nor sufficient. To conclude that they were necessary would undermine the collective pursuits of groups and fail to realise the full value of groups. To conclude that they were sufficient would fail to live up to the full demands of the Service Principle.

That said, the demands of the Service Principle are also appropriately more complex than most simple positions on exit rights and membership control, many of which disintegrate quickly. The view expressed by some that membership

[2] See eg J Rawls, *Political Liberalism* (New York, Columbia University Press, 1996) 221; R Nozick, *Anarchy, State, and Utopia* (Oxford, Blackwell, 1974) 299, 312, 320, 330–31; S Benhabib, *The Claims of Culture: Equality and Diversity in the Global Era* (Princeton, Princeton University Press, 2002) 19–20; W Galston, *Liberal Pluralism: The Implications of Value Pluralism for Political Theory and Practice* (Cambridge, Cambridge University Press, 2002) 123.

[3] C Kukathas, 'Are There Any Cultural Rights?' (1992) 20 *Political Theory* 105, 133.

[4] J Raz, *Ethics in the Public Domain: Essays in the Morality of Law and Politics* (Oxford, Clarendon, 1995) 187 (though acknowledging that rights of exit are an 'imperfect' safeguard).

[5] SM Okin, '"Mistresses of Their Own Destiny": Group Rights, Gender, and Realistic Rights of Exit' (2002) 112 *Ethics* 205, 205.

should be as open as possible to enhance individual autonomy[6] unjustly ignores the impact on other members of individuals' movement in and out of a collectivity. At the same time, there is no simple allocation of membership control to a collectivity. An illustration makes this point clear. Within his rich and sophisticated discussion of membership control issues in Canadian law, Sébastien Grammond states at one stage that 'in order to justify the attribution to the minority of the power to enact membership criteria, its political institutions must allow for the participation of all members in the political debate'.[7] The point is punchy but of course circular insofar as the creation of membership criteria by members permitted into debate presumes a pre-defined membership. Turning to other approaches, views that demand support for every individual's opportunity to exit ignore the impact on the community and thus on the individuals whom it serves, but it would be similarly wrong to say that exit rights do not matter within a communitarian context,[8] or one would give up service to individuals. The demands of the Service Principle will be complex.

It is possible to approach the question by examining the recent arguments of several leading theorists, notably Green, Okin and Shachar, who have all offered important critiques of traditional understandings of rights of exit, claiming that arguments for a right to exit necessitate much greater interference with groups. In particular, they suggest imposing on groups requirements in some way parallel to (or mirroring)[9] those applying to political society, including requirements of respect for autonomy more extensive than background morality would demand of individuals in their private lives. The strain of argument present in Green, Okin and Shachar, I will argue, implies stricter demands on groups than on purely private actors, imposing further requirements on groups beyond the formal right of exit some theorists, notably Rawls, have urged.[10]

Green, beginning from the proposition that rights of exit are indeed necessary, argues that an effective right of exit in turn necessitates other rights, such as freedom of speech that will enable discussion of exit.[11] Okin highlights inattention to realistic rights of exit for oppressed subgroups, such as female members, and argues that formal rights of exit need to be supplemented by external defences of the individual rights of such members against the groups.[12] Shachar has questioned the logic of implied consent inherent in rights of exit arguments, repeatedly

[6] E Mitnick, *Rights, Groups and Self-Invention: Group-Differentiated Rights in Liberal Theory* (Aldershot, Ashgate, 2006) 150.

[7] S Grammond, *Identity Captured by Law: Membership in Canada's Indigenous Peoples and Linguistic Minorities* (Montreal, McGill-Queen's University Press, 2009) 44.

[8] A Chua in W Kymlicka and B He, *Multiculturalism in Asia* (Oxford, Oxford University Press, 2005).

[9] For prominent rejections of a mirroring requirement, see: Galston (n 2) 15–16; J Spinner-Halev, 'Autonomy, Association and Pluralism' in A Eisenberg and J Spinner-Halev (eds) *Minorities within Minorities: Equality, Rights and Diversity* (Cambridge, Cambridge University Press, 2005) 157, 166.

[10] See Rawls, *Political Liberalism* (n 2) 221.

[11] L Green, 'Rights of Exit' (1998) 4 *Legal Theory* 165. For a parallel but less developed argument, see A Mason, 'Imposing Liberal Principles' (1998) 1 *Critical Review of International Social and Political Philosophy* 98, 100–101.

[12] Okin (n 5) 206–207.

analogising it to old claims of alleged consent to domestic violence by women who did not leave their abusers,[13] and has argued for incentives promoting the dismantling of power hierarchies within groups.[14] I will, of course, explore these arguments in greater depth, but even a sketch makes apparent the question that arises. Does the prior assumption that there must be a right of exit from any group within political society imply yet further requirements on groups?

A closer analysis of these three recent critiques actually guides us to a better understanding of the moral principles governing collectivities. In this chapter, I will examine these critiques further to show that each of them has, in some way, incompletely analysed or failed to recognise the functions of exit. It will become apparent that exit actually does not play the precise role theorists have ascribed to it. We must seek a more complicated analysis of appropriate bundles of exit and voice that address the contingent circumstances of different collectivities. At the same time, I will show that these bundles are not sufficient for the legitimacy of a collectivity but are just further procedural mechanisms that may be helpful in promoting compliance with the Service Principle. This reasoning will also lay the groundwork for attention to important needs for collective powers to assert membership control, and I will show that the Community Conditions generally permit those powers.

II. FUNCTIONS OF EXIT

We can better conceptualise the recent arguments of Green, Okin and Shachar, and see where they have gone wrong, by drawing on a distinction from the economic writings of Albert Hirschman. Hirschman, describing consumer and member reaction to a decline in the quality of a firm's product, distinguishes between *exit*, the choice of consumers to cease buying the product or of members to leave the firm, and *voice*, the choice of consumers or members to express their dissatisfaction to management.[15] We can obviously generalise these concepts beyond the strict economic context of product quality to apply to alternative strategies that may be open to and pursued by members of a group. I will follow Green in taking exit to be an ability to withdraw voluntarily from the group's jurisdiction,[16] or, since we are not necessarily concerned with groups that have 'jurisdiction', from rights and obligations of membership or from identification with the group.

However, that traditional description of exit is overly general. Exit can come in a whole range of forms and powers. In the case of a group with jurisdiction in a

[13] A Shachar, 'The Paradox of Multicultural Vulnerability' in C Joppke and S Lukes (eds) *Multicultural Questions* (Oxford, Oxford University Press, 1999) 100; A Shachar, 'The Puzzle of Interlocking Power Hierarchies: Sharing the Pieces of Jurisdictional Authority' (2000) *Harvard Civil Rights–Civil Liberties Law Review* 387, 405.

[14] See generally ch 6 of A Shachar, *Multicultural Jurisdictions: Cultural Differences and Women's Rights* (Cambridge, Cambridge University Press, 2001).

[15] A Hirschman, *Exit, Voice, and Loyalty* (Cambridge MA, Harvard University Press, 1970) 4.

[16] *Cf* Green (n 11) 171.

certain territory, exit might mean mobility, an ability to depart physically from the territory. But there can be much more complex ways of exiting than a physical departure. A group member asking to have her name removed from a memorial acknowledging wrongs done to the group asserts a sort of exit. Exit can even be relatively passive, as in the instance of a homosexual who remains closeted by simply refraining from active steps to identify publicly with the relevant groups. So, 'exit' incorporates a broad range of ways of individuals distancing themselves from a group.

Voice is an ability to influence those determining the group's course of action by expressing one's preferences (which can amount to genuine participation and need not be confined by the analogy of 'complaining to the manager'). We of course presume that individuals can have preferences and can express them. Some would consider this point itself the beginning of an argument for greater protection for individual group members in instances where their preferences and expression are questionable, but any such contention would require a prior argument for voice.

The key point to observe is that exercises of both exit and voice can be reactions to what Hirschman calls a 'repairable lapse',[17] or in more general terms, responses to some policy of a group that fails to serve its members. Thus, exit and voice are not entirely independent concepts. Indeed, we might note at once the possibility that they could act as *substitutes*: voice might substitute for exit (or vice versa) insofar as it can be an alternative means of seeking a remedy – I will explore later in this chapter how substitutability might differ from interchangeability. However, they could also act as *complements*: they may be mutually supporting insofar as the availability or effectiveness of voice may improve the availability or effectiveness of exit (and vice versa). By gradually analysing these complex relationships between exit and voice, we can gain a better understanding of claims on rights to exit. I can begin by analysing the way in which these relationships are described in the recent arguments at question.

Green, rightly commencing his argument with some analysis of the functions of exit, has admitted a related distinction, noting that exit can have both a *protective* function and an *expressive* function.[18] The basic element of the protective function is that: 'If the group harms the member's interests as the member sees them, then leaving is a form of self-defence.'[19] However, within the protective function, Green includes another element: 'The possibility of exit may itself make the group responsive to the interests of its members.'[20] Although Green does not describe it as such, this latter element would actually seem to be an example of exit and voice interacting: the possibility exit might effectively *amplify* voice by providing an explicit or implicit threat of exit as backing.[21] Sufficient responsiveness to voice could render this element of exit unnecessary. Green describes the expressive function of exit in

[17] Hirschman (n 15) 4.
[18] Green (n 11) 171.
[19] Ibid.
[20] Ibid.
[21] *Cf* Hirschman (n 15) 82; Shachar, *Multicultural Jurisdictions* (n 14) 125, 143, 149n.

terms of an 'often exaggerated' claim that 'leaving is in a way to criticise the group, while remaining is to support it'.[22] Again, a collectivity's sufficient responsiveness to voice would obviously be a substitute for this expressive function of exit.

But let us turn to Green's argument, which actually seems to draw on a different potential function of exit from those he began by developing. That there is a further function latent in the analysis is unsurprising given that more recent commentary has arguably suggested a third function that could be masked in any analysis concerned solely with 'protective' and 'transformative' functions: a basic autonomy role of exit.[23] Indeed, Green adopts from Kukathas a freedom of association argument for rights of exit before going on to argue that rights of exit imply more freedoms than Kukathas was ready to admit.[24] Green states that exit is 'an insufficient safeguard for justice within groups'.[25] However, he presents exit as necessary when he offers his reintepretation of its function:

> Underneath the idea that no one can be required to accept a particular way of life lies, I think, the familiar notion of personal autonomy. The fundamental reason for thinking exit necessary is to fulfil the protective and expressive functions that enhance the capacity for a self-directed life, including the capacity to form, revise, and pursue our ends.[26]

Green then goes on to argue that conditions necessary for the right of exit are thus as necessary as the right to exit and that the value of autonomy independently grounds yet other rights. His argument, then, is based on autonomy, which both allegedly makes exit necessary, for both autonomy reasons and reasons grounded in autonomy, and allegedly grounds other rights (via exit and independently).

There are, however, good reasons to doubt Green's theses. First, as I have begun to do already, one can call into question the necessary link between the justifications for exit and a right to exit, instead seeing the link as contingent. To confront Green directly, even if we were to accept that a minimal concern for autonomy provides the key justification for rights to exit, a right of exit does not necessarily follow. As the foregoing analysis revealed, voice can act as a substitute for exit. Even if exit and voice function as complements in some circumstances, we do not know that they will do so in all circumstances, and it is thus contingent whether voice might not substitute completely for exit in some circumstance, potentially allowing individuals to lead the autonomous lives they would choose but without having to exit from the groups of which they are members. Recognising that there can be a substitution for exit immediately makes the requirement for exit contingent on the presence or absence of the possible substituting factor. Moreover, recognising a possible substitution itself reveals the contingency of exit; any right of exit is valuable not for its own sake so much as for the sake of something else. I will turn shortly to a further critique of Green's position concerning why we should understand that something else as not being restricted solely to autonomy interests.

[22] Green (n 11) 171.
[23] See eg O Reitman, 'On Exit' in Eisenberg and Spinner-Halev (n 9) 189–90.
[24] Green (n 11) 174–75.
[25] Ibid, 176–77.
[26] Ibid, 176–77.

First, though, I have claimed that depending on the way in which voice functions within some group, it might act as a complete substitute for exit. In saying this, I need make no general claim that substitutability always implies interchangeability. But we cannot exclude the possibility of a substitution between exit and voice that amounts in effect almost to interchangeability. Such a claim might seem difficult to maintain. After all, there is an inherent difference between exit and voice insofar as exit is an individual decision, and voice is a participation in a collective decision-making process.[27] It might seem natural to suppose that voice cannot provide protection in the same way as exit, particularly where the lives of some specific individuals are particularly adversely affected by their group membership. But whether voice provides protection equivalent to exit depends entirely on the nature of the decision-making mechanism. The resulting conclusions thus depend on contingent matters of particular circumstances and particular decision-making functions. So, the link between autonomy and rights of exit (and whatever other rights might be necessary to a realistic right of exit) is contingent rather than necessary. We can doubt Green's argument for the necessity of exit and rights flowing therefrom.

Someone might object that this challenge to Green's thesis proceeds too quickly. Could we not claim that autonomy demands an ability to exit no matter what effect a group has on its members, simply as a choice not to be identified with the group? Or could we not claim that having a choice over whether to exit a group is in an individual's interests, regardless of whatever other interests may be affected? However, the interest in not being a Z is unclear where being a Z has no effect on any other of an individual's interests. It amounts to a mere denial of an ascription but where the ascription is utterly without significance. We might also consider whether there are not cases where it is simply not meaningfully possible to cease being a Z, such as in instances of what we might call 'embedded individuals' who have grown up to identify wholly with the ethos of their group and will not leave it in any imaginable circumstance.[28] Any theory that depends on rights of exit as a protection for individuals may depend on the effectively impossible.

On the second limb of the argument, we can call into question Green's privileging of autonomy at the expense of other values – or even at the expense of autonomy itself.[29] Indeed, we might read Green as, without much explanation,

[27] *Cf* I Hunter, 'Individual and Collective Rights in Canadian Labour Law' (1993) 22 *Manitoba Law Journal* 145, 147.

[28] *Cf* Mason (n 11) 100.

[29] Although I will not develop this argument further, we might also see Green's focus on autonomy as leading him to privilege the importance of rights of exit unduly in some instances of moral reasoning. For example, when Green claims that rights of exit imply mobility rights, he concludes that 'groups cannot seek to restrict mobility in ways that would effectively hold people captive. The Taliban militia were therefore wrong to prevent women from driving cars' (Green (n 11) 177). We can agree with his conclusion while being tremendously concerned with his 'therefore'. The wrongness of the Taliban militia's preventing women from driving cars was not principally in the effect on the right of exit in the event that women would have used this right to drive out of the Taliban's jurisdiction. The Taliban simply went too far in their restrictions on members and offended the Service Principle more substantially than through the side effects on exit rights.

shifting from a concern with the interests of members in his initial account of the functions of exit to a concern with the autonomy of members.[30] Yet chapter five offered reasons why we ought to be concerned not simply with autonomy but with interests more generally.[31] Limitations on autonomy, as Green would surely admit, need not imply damage to individuals' overall interests.

Jeff Spinner-Halev, although arguing that the requirements of a right of exit are less than many theorists think, adheres to a proposition that we must 'insist that members of groups where autonomy is not prized have the right of exit, and that they can exit to a society that encourages autonomy'.[32] The restrictiveness of his proposition, however, reveals the possibility of autonomy within a group acting as a substitute for freedom to leave the collectivity. We might even develop other substitutions, between certain kinds of service to members' interests and what autonomy they might gain by leaving the collectivity. Members of a drug rehabilitation programme, for example, might well be better off in all ways without any right to leave the programme. An excessive concern with some aspects of individual autonomy (for drug addiction itself may limit autonomy) may not make individuals better off. Again, we can doubt Green's theses.

Someone could object, however, that a right of exit is either simply an instance of general freedom or else a particular counterbalance against groups having more than normal power over their members' lives and in either case a necessary implication of the freedom we hold dear. Again, however, the objection depends on a certain valuation of freedom for which more argument is needed. And, yet more devastatingly for the objection, it is not immediately clear how a lack of a substantive right of exit from a group automatically differs from something such as practical difficulties in changing career at some stage in life, something similarly closing off some options, but attracting no particular concern from liberal theorists. If the objector endeavours to argue that membership in a collectivity merits a different attention because it exerts a more pervasive influence on one's life or because it engages citizenship rights that are of particular concern, then the objection relies on contextually specific concerns. Again, there remain powerful reasons to doubt Green's theses.

Let us turn to Okin's argument, which makes a different criticism of theories on rights to exit. Taking realistic rights of exit as morally required, Okin's concern is the lack of realistic rights of exit for some group members, notably women.[33] As she puts the main point:

> For some individuals not to be able to choose an alternative mode of life, when others in the group are far more likely to be able to do so, is a serious violation of the equality of persons that is basic to liberalism.[34]

[30] *Cf* ibid, 171, 176.
[31] Ch 5.III, above.
[32] Spinner-Halev, 'Autonomy, Association, and Pluralism' (n 9) 57.
[33] Okin (n 5) 205, 206.
[34] Ibid, 206.

A large portion of her article is then concerned with demonstrating that gender inequality results in unequal opportunities to exit collectivities.[35] Okin considers, however, that some inequalities in rights of exit are intractable, or else that exit is sometimes an undesirable option ('What kind of a choice is one between total submission and total alienation from the person she understands herself to be?'[36]), and reasons that fair treatment within the collectivity is the key moral requirement.[37]

Okin's argument thus recognises the possibility of substitutions for rights of exit, fitting with the earlier analysis of possible substitutions between exit and voice or other substitutes. However, there is an unresolved tension in her argument insofar as this realisation actually complicates her otherwise more straightforward primary concern. If there are substitutes for exit, then a mere demonstration that some categories of members do not have equal access to rights of exit does not demonstrate 'a serious violation of the equality of persons that is basic to liberalism', and speaking of 'realistic' as opposed to 'formal' rights of exit does not change this conclusion. If there are substitutes for exit, they might be available in a way that offsets the alleged violation of the equality of persons. Of course, it may well be that the same groups that discriminate in allocating rights of exit also discriminate in allocating substitutes for exit. But that is no universal argument.

The possibility of substitutes for rights of exit reflects the derivative importance of exit. The concern with exit should not be some sort of fetishism that condemns any particular inequality in rights of exit but should look to the factors substantively affecting compliance with the Service Principle. We could imagine collectivities in which some members derive greater benefits from the collectivity than others without any automatic conclusion that such collectivities are wrongly constituted; no violation of the humanistic principle, or the Service Principle, would thereby follow. Indeed, the nature of collectivities would seem to be that they serve interests of individuals in ways that will plausibly vary from one individual to another. Those for whom a particular collectivity figures more prominently in an individual's life or identity will, *of course*, derive greater benefits from their membership in that particular group. And, just as variations in the service a collectivity provides to its different members do not condemn it, inequalities in realistic rights of exit are subject to no automatic condemnation; the wrongness of such inequalities actually requires further developed argumentation.

Shachar's reasoning on rights of exit develops themes similar to those of Okin, albeit with a different emphasis and orientation. Shachar, too, highlights the costs of exit, emphasising that:

> The 'right of exit' argument, however, obscures the very real hardships of leaving one's identity group (economic hardship, lack of education, skill deficiencies, or emotional distress, for example), and suggests that an injured insider, because she is

[35] Ibid, 216–22.
[36] Ibid, 229.
[37] Ibid, 207.

> maltreated in intragroup spheres, should abandon the very centres of her life, family, and community.[38]

Shachar is concerned that membership costs are not equally borne and that at-risk individuals may be least able to exit.[39] As with Okin, some of these concerns about the cost of exit may be very real concerns in the context of some actual groups, but they remain contingent.

We may read Shachar's argument, however, as going farther in some ways. First, Shachar highlights to a greater degree the notion that members *should not have to* exit in response to injustices. Secondly, Shachar provides further analysis on a problematic aspect of imposing this demand on members, arguing that such a demand refuses to solve systemic problems and instead insists on case-by-case decisions of individuals on whether to exit.[40] Thirdly, Shachar challenges the moral logic of those who suppose that a failure to exit implies consent to established collective practices, arguing that this logic is analogous to old reasoning that women consented to domestic abuse by not leaving their abusers.[41]

Let us begin with this last point. One might supplement Shachar's analysis by considering why the old reasoning was wrong, thus confronting why a notion of implied consent is morally dubious. The real problems in situations of domestic abuse have typically arisen because exit was too costly (either due to the nature of divorce legislation or due to the combination of such legislation with economic inequalities leaving an abused partner without means of living apart from the abuser) or because the pathology of abuse undermined an abused partner's ability to exercise the choice she might otherwise have made to leave.[42] Thus, old reasoning of implied consent to abuse was wrong not because a doctrine of implied consent never applies, but because no genuine consent obtained in the relevant contexts. Shachar's critique of the moral logic of implied consent thus applies only in a contextually specific way.

The contextual specificity of Shachar's critique is apparent also in her second point, in her claim that exit is an inappropriately individual remedy for systemic problems. This claim might be true in some situations; systemic solutions may sometimes be more effective. Noting that the discussion of Green and Okin questioned the necessity of exit rights, however, we must add that even if exit rights are not always necessary, they can still be important in some contexts. Where being a member of some collectivity has a seriously detrimental impact on some individual's interests, and where the individual has alternatives, exit may indeed serve its protective function. If individuals are better placed to know their interests than the collectivity (a matter to which I will return), a right of exit on a case-by-case basis may be an effective protection. And exit may be preferable to voice where those detrimentally affected are a smaller proportion of members,

[38] Shachar, 'Paradox of Multicultural Vulnerability' (n 13) 100.
[39] Shachar, *Multicultural Jurisdictions* (n 14) 69.
[40] Ibid, 41.
[41] Shachar 'Paradox of Multicultural Vulnerability' (n 13) 100.
[42] *Cf R v Lavallée* [1990] 1 SCR 852 (describing evidence on this point).

with interests not fitting with those of other members. We need not deny the attractiveness of Shachar's account in the specific contexts from which it has arisen, but we can say that its individual emphasis does not automatically make exit inappropriate.

This reasoning also challenges any universal claim that members should not have to exit in response to a lack of conformity between their individual interests and collective interests. Again, such a claim must be context-specific. In the right kind of case, an individual's interests may be so out of line with the individual and collective interests at stake that the individual should properly exit (if able to do so), for the individual's sake and the group's. A golfer who had somehow mistakenly ended up a member of a knitting group, who gains nothing from the group, and who is actually harmed by the group (losing golf time), should exit. I will return to these matters, however, in the last section of this chapter.

At the same time that she casts doubt on theories that exit rights can mitigate injustices within groups by questioning the genuine possibility of exit, Shachar also argues that members should be able to retain an exit option as a useful threat to enhance their influence within groups.[43] Indeed, as Oonagh Reitman's gentle, but potentially devastating critique has powerfully revealed, Shachar's attempts to offer solutions to the problems she has highlighted are themselves dependent on a jurisdictional division in turn reliant on the very sorts of exit whose usefulness she has questioned.[44] Although I will not here discuss this larger agenda at length, Shachar's project has been to develop a theory of 'transformative accommodation',[45] which makes use of a division of jurisdictional powers as between the state and groups to attempt to give patriarchal groups incentives to transform themselves so as to be more respectful of individuals' citizenship rights.[46]

For example, in the area of family law, Shachar would locate jurisdiction over demarcation (marriage and divorce) with a religious group and jurisdiction over distribution (property aspects) with the state,[47] with the possibility of opting out of the religious group's jurisdiction in a deadlock situation where an individual cannot obtain a divorce under religious law.[48] The aim is to create incentives for the collectivity to respond to the needs of individuals by giving more power to individuals to invoke the threat of exit.[49] Shachar suggests this policy can escape problems of traditional religious law giving a male partner power to refuse to consent to a divorce, which has traditionally undermined any fair distributive settlement, making the ex-wife 'pay emotionally and financially for the accommodation of her group's traditions'.[50] Reitman's reply, however, is that

[43] See eg Shachar, *Multicultural Jurisdictions* (n 14) 125, 143, 149n.

[44] Reitman (n 23). Okin attacked Shachar in a piece in the same volume for allegedly distorting Okin's position on the feminism/multiculturalism debate: SM Okin, 'Multiculturalism and Feminism: No Simple Question, No Simple Answers' in Eisenberg and Spinner-Halev (eds) (n 9) 67.

[45] See Shachar, *Multicultural Jurisdictions* (n 14) 117–45.

[46] Ibid, 140.

[47] Ibid, 132–34.

[48] Ibid, 134–35.

[49] Ibid, 137–38, 140.

[50] Ibid, 134.

Shachar's approach does not escape the fundamental problem: only women ready to exit from religious law gain the advantages of equal distribution of property, while others must potentially still negotiate sacrifices of the property to which they would be entitled in order to get a religious divorce.[51] In this sense, there are dangers that Shachar's very appealing argument simply relocates the problem.[52]

Shachar's theory is, more generally, in a tension-laden position on whether it demands abilities to threaten exit or abilities to actually exit. The former is, in some sense, dependent on the latter. Threats to exit cannot be meaningful when there is no actual ability to exit. A gunman's threat to shoot someone is effective only to the extent that he is believed capable of carrying out the threat (for instance, to have bullets and to be psychologically prepared to do so). Recognising this point does not deny that the threat of exit might actually be more effective in many instances. To take an economic analogy again, threats to exit from a particular economic relationship are often effective in getting another party to agree to some term. But their effectiveness in doing so is entirely dependent on the (at least perceived) ability of the party making the threat to carry it out.

We can problematise Shachar's argument in another way as well, noting that it does not confront all the complexities of how exit functions. I have noted that exit can act as both a complement to and a substitute for voice. The relationship between exit and voice reveals itself as yet more complicated, however, when we realise that the two remedies may also be in tension insofar as we can generalise Hirschman's observation that exit drives out voice.[53] Hirschman provides two reasons for this claim in market-type settings. First, he notes that:

> [T]hose customers who care *most* about the quality of the product and who, therefore, are those who would be the most active, reliable, and creative agents of voice are for that very reason also those who are apparently likely to exit first in case of deterioration.[54]

Secondly, he suggests that there can be a bias in favour of exit because individuals may base their choice to exit or not on past experience, when the effectiveness of voice may require future developments. That is to say, the effectiveness of voice in a consumer context may require the development of complaint mechanisms or even the stepping forward of an powerful advocate, but individuals might have already chosen exit. Thus, Hirschman concludes: 'The presence of the exit alternative can therefore tend to *atrophy the development of the art of voice*.'[55] Both reasons apply more generally. First, aside from strictly market-type

[51] Reitman (n 23) 201–204.
[52] Ibid.
[53] Hirschman (n 15) 76.
[54] Ibid, 46.
[55] Ibid, 43 (emphasis in original).

cases, those most at odds with a collectivity have the greatest incentives to leave, where they would have had the greatest incentives to advocate change within the collectivity. Indeed, as just noted, Shachar herself has suggested that at-risk individuals, those facing high costs to leave but great potential of facing abuse, are least able to exit, meaning that those most able to avoid the costs of the collectivity's decisions may be first to exit when they could have been the most effective advocates within the collectivity. Secondly, as follows straightforwardly from the fact that exit can be a substitute for voice, the availability of exit may undermine the reasons to develop voice where the development of voice is costly. It is thus unclear whether availability of threats of exit provides an amplifying force to voice in the kinds of situations where it would be most useful, for they mean that the availability of exit (necessary if the threats are to be meaningful) also undermines voice. Thus, we can question if Shachar's argument that threats of exit and voice must be available is consistent, first, with her critique of rights of exit and, second, with the nature of exit and voice.

Green, Okin and Shachar have all offered interesting recent analyses of rights to exit. However, the approaches of each of these theorists have failed to acknowledge dimensions of the ways in which exit functions. Green focuses rights of exit around individual autonomy claims, both mistakenly taking rights of exit as necessary to autonomy and unduly privileging autonomy at the expense of other values or even at the expense of other aspects of autonomy. Okin writes of inequalities in realistic rights of exit, underplaying the derivative function of rights of exit and neglecting potentially acceptable divergences in various collective contexts. Shachar develops concerns similar to those of Okin with additional dimensions, but again neglects the contextually-specific nature of exit and overlooks possible tensions between exit and voice, while also falling into difficult dual positions on the place of threats of exit. Through a gradual accretion of analysis, we have seen several ways in which exit can function and several, tension-laden ways in which exit can interact with voice. Through this analysis, we have seen that the frequent supposition that rights of exit are necessary is unjustified; that rights of exit need not necessarily even be equally allocated; and that much depends on a specific analysis of the way in which exit interacts with voice in the context at hand.

Matters are thus substantially more complicated than previous analyses admit, and rights to exit are less necessary than supposed, though they can be contextually important. This conclusion, in itself, poses major challenges to frequently presumed views and speaks of different possibilities for collective justice. In the next section, I will seek to make use of this critical groundwork toward a more constructive endeavour that will further develop the contextual nature of rights to exit. I will seek to consider, through a combination of theoretical reasoning and engagement with actual cases, what combinations of exit and voice can constitute morally acceptable bundles, or at least what we can say about such bundles. In the process, we will discover what was right in spirit in the recent analyses I have just critiqued.

III. ACCEPTABLE BUNDLES OF EXIT AND VOICE

1. Introduction

Writing of exit and voice in the economic context, Hirschman devoted an entire chapter to what he termed the 'elusive optimal mix of exit and voice', finding that each of these recovery mechanisms was subject to decay and that there was seldom any optimal, stable mix to be prescribed.[56] We cannot prescribe any precise, optimal mix of exit and voice that assures a collectivity's compliance with the Service Principle. Nonetheless, there can be principles on morally preferable bundles of exit and voice. We can begin from an insightful but otherwise undeveloped observation of Cindy Holder:

> [E]ntry into a community has consequences for not only the individual doing the joining but for the individuals already in the community as well. And insofar as an individual's decision to *leave* a community also changes the composition of the group, the relations between those who remain, and the options they have open, the same will also hold true for exit.[57]

Extrapolating from this observation, then, we need to contemplate the contingent effects of exit and voice in the actual circumstances of any given collectivity, recognising that the implementation of exit and/or voice has implications both for individuals directly and for the collectivity that ultimately serves their interests.

To bring the issues to life, consider the case of *Hofer v Hofer*,[58] in which the Supreme Court of Canada had to consider whether articles of association under which two individuals entered Hutterite religious colonies in Manitoba were unenforceable as against public policy. The articles provided for communal property ownership, in accordance with the religious beliefs of the Hutterites, and did not provide for exit payments – payments of some sum of money to enable individuals to exit – to those, like the plaintiffs, who chose to abandon the Hutterite faith.

Justice Pigeon, in a dissent that would have struck down the articles, expressed concern that members

> have no right at any time in their life to leave the Colony where they are living unless they abandon literally everything. Even the clothes they are wearing belong to the colony and . . . are to be returned to it as its property by anyone who ceases to be a member of the church.[59]

[56] Ibid, 124–25.

[57] C Holder, *Rethinking Groups: Groups, Group Membership and Group Rights* (PhD thesis, University of Arizona Department of Philosophy, 2001) 31–32.

[58] *Hofer v Hofer* (1970) 13 DLR (3d) 1 (SCC) [*Hofer SCC*].

[59] Ibid, 21.

He held that anyone subject to the articles would have effectively 'contract[ed] out of freedom of religion'[60] by having no realistic option to change his or her religion.

Jeff Spinner-Halev, generally a defender of group autonomy,[61] has nonetheless argued that the state should force groups like the Hutterites to establish exit funds that would exist so as to provide exiting members an amount of money not giving them an incentive to leave but helping them to enact the choice once made.[62] Those favouring realistic rights to exit as a mandatory requirement on groups would surely agree, and the spectre of religious dissenters condemned to wander the Manitoba prairie without even a scrap of clothing to their names surely elicits sympathy.

Yet the majority of the Supreme Court of Canada – and, I might add, the future Chief Justice Dickson sitting as the trial judge – disagreed.[63] In this section, although I am not undertaking a commentary specifically on the case, it will become implicitly apparent how the majority reasoning expresses the better moral position, upholding the opportunity of collectivities to pursue their collective interests. To analyse these matters, I will begin first with a general argument for the derivatively valuable role of exit and voice on the basis that they enable a collectivity to know better the interests of its members in the face of dispersion and asymmetries of information (clarifying in the process that there is not reason to call for an intrinsic role of voice in every collective context). Secondly, I will begin to complicate matters by considering some very real instances in which attainment of realistic exit rights and/or extensive voice will undermine collectivities' integrity and ability to pursue the non-individualisable interests they pursue, endeavouring to generalise toward a principle that exit and voice may be limited for reasons of group integrity. Thirdly, I will show the reasons why exit and/or voice might nonetheless be persisting moral requirements in the case of weighty individual interests, where exit and/or voice contingently best protect those interests. Fourthly, I will argue that there is nonetheless reason for substantial deference by the wider society to the decisions of collectivities in standard cases, with exit and voice essentially becoming a sort of epistemic tool for determining when there can be legitimate interference with collectivities.

2. General Argument for Exit and/or Voice

First, then, there is a general argument for exit and/or voice so far as their use leads to a better accord between what a collectivity pursues and what accords with interests of individual members. We can recall from above that exit has

[60] Ibid, 26

[61] See generally Spinner-Halev, 'Autonomy, Association, and Pluralism' (n 9).

[62] Spinner-Halev *Surviving Diversity: Religion and Democratic Citizenship* (Baltimore, Johns Hopkins University Press, 2000) 77–78. This seemingly builds upon the suggestion of Justice Hall that there should be legislation of that sort: *Hofer SCC* (n 58) 14.

[63] For Dickson J's opinion, see *Hofer v Hofer* (1967) 59 DLR (2d) 723 (Man QB) [*Hofer QB*].

fundamentally derivative functions and may help to ensure that collective and individual interests do not end up in such non-conformity that group actions violate the Service Principle. I have argued that voice can substitute for exit in such a function. We have not yet, however, further dissected voice to determine if its functions are solely derivative.

Recall that voice is an ability to influence those determining the collectivity's course of action by expressing one's preferences. Someone might claim that there is something intrinsically valuable about individuals having an opportunity to express their preferences. Whether or not this is so, however, individuals in any case do not have an intrinsic reason to express their preferences in every context, nor in every collectivity in which they are members. Voice is not automatically important to members in every collective context. So long as individuals have these opportunities in some other forum, non-expression of their preferences in the context of some collectivity is no intrinsic loss – and there may even be nothing wrong with a hierarchy that denies them the opportunity. If, say, some hockey team has a captain who can act with appropriate regard to the interests of individual members without running any particular consultation procedure, then this may be so much the better for their efficient decision-making.

Nonetheless, one can state as a political proposition that voice is generally highly desirable for reasons derivative from the Service Principle. If individuals' expressions of their preferences will enable the collectivity to better serve its individual members than if it did not receive such information, there are good derivative reasons for consultativeness. Dispersion and asymmetries of information – realities such that individuals know their own interests better than the collectivity knows their interests – thus establish derivative reasons for a consultativeness principle often being an effective contribution to fulfillment of the Service Principle.

In certain, extreme cases, individuals' preferences will not correspond to their interests; drug addicts' statements of at least some of their preferences may well reflect desires not actually in their interest, and it may be that the leaders of some collectivity can thus better fulfill the Service Principle without the pressures of voice. If analogous situations exist more widely, they undermine the derivative benefits to be attained from consultation and from voice. However, on the reasonable political proposition that individuals generally know best their own interests, consultation and voice are generally desirable because of informational dispersion and asymmetries. I will turn to exceptions later in the argument, but I can nonetheless state first the general case.

This general case does not demand a specific form of consultation procedure. Nothing in the argument says that the consultation procedure must be based on specific kinds of institutions, or, specifically, be democratic.[64] Rather, the derivative

[64] *Cf* J Rawls, *The Law of Peoples* (Cambridge MA, Harvard University Press, 1999) §9 (arguing that a people can be representative of the interests of its members so long as it provides for meaningful consultation and consideration of the 'important interests of all members of the people': ibid, 72.) Whatever is or is not demanded in the case of a people, the case is clearer that not all groups have a requirement of democratic consultation.

principle is that collectivities generally should consult with their members to elicit information as to their individual interests. Obviously, though, democratic consultation cannot be a requirement for all collectivities, since consultation itself is not even a requirement for all collectivities.

On the usual arguments in democratic theory, democratic consultation might be thought appropriate in the case of collectivities exercising coercive legal powers over their members.[65] This principle would explain such concerns as those found in recent Canadian case law on labour unions mandating specifically democratic organisation as a condition to unions having certain legally entrenched coercive powers.[66] Whether powers of legal coercion make out a case for democratic consultation will be crucial in certain collective contexts, but these claims raise complex questions which we need not develop further here. I can carry forward with the analysis, admitting that legal attribution of powers of coercion to certain collectivities would raise additional questions of democratic theory more generally, without losing the interesting questions that arise in cases where exit and/or voice are difficult simply for de facto reasons.

I have said that both exit and voice might be generally desirable as means of promoting compliance with the Service Principle. That being said, the earlier-established point that they might serve as substitutes for one another also makes clear that a bundle containing both may go beyond what is required. One or the other, even in some partly restrained form, may promote compliance with the Service Principle. That said, the analysis in chapter five has made clear that the Service Principle is a demanding one. Nothing about exit or voice guarantees full compliance with the Service Principle; they just promote such compliance.

3. Exit and/or Voice Not Appropriate to Some Groups

Secondly, one needs to add the reality that extensive exit and/or voice options may undermine in some respect the integrity of some collectivities in a manner destroying or negatively affecting valuable collective interests. It may be part of the very structure of certain collectivities (in that sense, integral to the collectivity)

[65] *Cf* Spinner-Halev, 'Autonomy, Association and Diversity' (n 9) 170.

[66] In the seminal case of *Lavigne v Ontario Public Service Employees Union* [1991] 2 SCR 211, the Supreme Court of Canada confronted the issue of whether there was a constitutional right not to be a union member. In the plurality opinion refusing to hold forced union membership unconstitutional, LaForest J stressed the importance of unions operating democratically if they were to be given rights to compel membership: ibid, 327. Similar indications appear in more recent Canadian cases, where requirements that unions be 'constituted democratically' have been taken as a condition of a union having well-functioning collective legal rights beyond the sum of the rights of individual members: eg *R v Advance Cutting and Coring Ltd* 2001 SCC 70 [27]. Note, though, that the democratic consultativeness required might need to be described along the lines of a constitutional democracy if protections are built in for minority groups within the union membership. Indeed, in some jurisdictions, it seems female members of a union will have the right to sue the union if it agrees to a collective bargaining agreement discriminating against women through wage rates not conforming to equal pay for work of equal value: eg *Canada Safeway Ltd v Saskatchewan Human Rights Commission* (1997) 150 DLR (4th) 207 (Sask CA).

that they tend to limit exit and voice options. And, in other instances, exit and voice options may give rise to free-rider problems that undermine the integral pursuit of collective interests.

We can recall now the *Hofer* case. Cartwright CJC starkly identified a further interest at stake in addition to the interests of the dissenting members:

> Unless the members are free to enter into contracts of the sort set out in the articles of association, it is difficult to see how the Hutterian Brethren could carry on the form of religious life which they believe to be the right one.[67]

Ritchie J and the trial judgment of Dickson J further flesh out this consideration. The Hutterian Brethren are a religious group that found sanctuary in North America after three centuries of transit from one European state to another to escape persecution for their communal form of life.[68] From the 1500s, a central tenet of the faith has been a belief that 'God from the beginning ordained naught private for man, but all things to be common',[69] with the baptismal vows taken by members including an acknowledgment 'that no one shall have any private possessions any more'.[70]

To impose on such a religious community a requirement that it provide for 'realistic rights to exit' would be tantamount to calling for the abandonment of an article of faith and would insist upon an end to the very purpose for which the collectivity exists. Even an apparently moderate solution like the required establishment of an 'exit fund' would enforce an ongoing requirement that this group violate its religious tenets and undermine its pursuit of religious community (in addition to being what amounts to an ongoing tax on the group). The majority reasoning upheld something very important that many theorists of exit rights simply do not discuss. Those demanding 'realistic rights of exit', and sometimes implying that they are an obvious, easy choice, must face up to the difficult choices that their position actually imposes on already long-oppressed groups.

This conclusion is not an isolated matter, arising uniquely from the particular nature of the Hutterites' religious faith. If the Amish seek to limit outside education in a manner that has effects on the realistic exit rights of members (and more so on the exit rights of female members due to their learning fewer skills offering outside employment options),[71] this is not for some malicious reason but because, as the United States Supreme Court recognised, the genuine faith of the Amish seeks a religious life uncorrupted by certain values of liberal securalist society.[72] If certain aboriginal groups limit voice by taking decisions that limit the internal opportunity of members to challenge the group's interpretation of culture and

[67] *Hofer SCC* (n 58) 4.
[68] Ibid, 6.
[69] *Hofer QB* (n 63) 729.
[70] Ibid, 730.
[71] *Cf* Okin, 'Mistresses of Their Own Destiny' (n 5) 217–18.
[72] *Cf* DG Newman, 'Liberal Multiculturalism and Will Kymlicka's Uneasy Relation with Religious Pluralism' (2003) 64 *Bijdragen* 265, 272–73.

spirituality (which may be intertwined with culture),[73] this may be because their cultures and religions are uniquely vulnerable given their long history of facing oppression. One could multiply the examples.

In some instances, establishment of rights of exit raises a different concern, not precisely related to direct effects on group integrity but related to a free-rider problem. In the union example, establishment of a right to exit would raise obvious free-rider problems,[74] so there is general acceptance of limitations on realistic rights of exit such that one's job will be lost if one attempts to leave certain unions.

We might similarly analyse other collectivities. For example, consider a threatened linguistic community with power over members' schooling, which can justify requiring children to have their primary schooling in the collectivity's threatened language on the basis that this choice best coordinates the interests of members in the flourishing of the collectivity as against the possible individual incentives to help children learn a more widespread language for individual economic gain.[75] Or consider a religious community that is granted a legal power to establish separate educational institutions; such a collectivity might be permitted to compel members of that religious community to direct their school taxes to the community's institutions, without an ability to exit to another school system, in order to ensure individuals cannot simultaneously derive the benefits of a flourishing religious-cultural community and those of choosing another school system.[76] In such circumstances, imposition of a realistic right of exit – depending what this means, given the possible range of ways in which individuals might exit – although not directly contradicting a fundamental value of the community at question, would impose serious costs on the community and threaten its ongoing pursuit of the collective interests that serve its members.

In at least some instances, exit may even actually be effectively impossible without rather drastic steps. As Jacob Levy has put a relevant point: 'Everything about a culture is an exit barrier . . . To have a culture where exit is entirely costless . . . is to have no culture at all.'[77] The cultural alterations necessary to establish the so-called realistic right of exit may well amount to cultural obliteration. The demand is doubly complex insofar as the communities to which an individual exits may still identify the individual as an ex-member of the prior identity group in the absence of particularly profound supports for the individual's transition.[78] The realistic exit rights arguments simply presume an acceptance

[73] Kymlicka has been in the forefront of the attack on the Pueblos on this ground (W Kymlicka *Liberalism, Community and Culture* (Oxford, Clarendon, 1989) 195–97).

[74] See eg S White, 'Trade Unionism in a Liberal State' in A Gutmann (ed) *Freedom of Association* (Princeton, Princeton University Press, 1998); M Olson, *The Logic of Collective Action: Public Goods and the Theory of Groups* (Cambridge MA, Harvard University Press, 1971).

[75] *Cf* ch 1.Iv, above.

[76] Ibid.

[77] J Levy, *The Multiculturalism of Fear* (Oxford, Oxford University Press, 2000) 112.

[78] KA Appiah, *The Ethics of Identity* (Princeton, Princeton University Press, 2005) 78 (discussing the identity status of ex-Mormons who continue to be treated as ex-Mormons by secular society).

into a broader society that may or may not be the case;[79] to impose the entire cost of such rights on minority communities would be harsh indeed. One could scarcely speak of a theory recognising rights of plural communities while demanding the elimination of every form of life not promoting entirely simple transitions to other communities.[80]

Accordingly, the appropriateness of exit and voice as derivative means of compliance with the Service Principle may depend on their respective effects on the community, either directly or indirectly. If either exit or voice, but not the other, would undermine the integrity of the collectivity's pursuit of its collective interests, that conclusion would offer an important moral reason to support the substitution that reality would imply. Similarly, if realistic rights of exit would create a free-rider problem, that conclusion might offer an important moral reason to prefer the thriving use of voice within the collectivity in question, in place of realistic rights of exit that would condemn its ongoing existence.

4. Exit and/or Voice as Persisting Moral Requirements and as Epistemic Indicators

Thirdly, however, we must limit this collectively-based approach with a further point that exit and/or voice might nonetheless be persisting moral requirements in the case of weighty individual interests, where exit and/or voice specifically contingently best protect those interests. We can note a basic autonomy function of formal rights of exit. We can note also the importance of exit and/or voice for individuals as potentially varying with: (i) the individual interests affected by a collectivity; (ii) the respective weights of the individual interests at stake and the individual value from the non-individualisable interests potentially attained by the collectivity; and (iii) the relative effectiveness of exit and voice given the homogeneity or heterogeneity of the collectivity.

Although the argument above refrained from the automatic privileging of autonomy interests, we also cannot deny the value of autonomy interests amongst the range of human interests. A 'merely' formal or legal right of exit may be important to the basic autonomy of individuals, and thus of far more significance than presumed by those who critique 'mere formalism'. We can have ongoing sympathy for those who leave the Hutterites without a penny to their names, but it is tremendously significant that they may leave. Even if at great cost, the individual members are free to change their lives. Taking a rare stance in defence of formalism, then, we can see the importance of formal exit rights to basic autonomy interests. It is in this narrow context that Anne Phillips's statement rings true that: 'Even the strongest advocate of cultural rights will not say that groups have the right to detain individuals against their will or force them to live

[79] *Cf* NT Casals, *Group Rights as Human Rights: A Liberal Approach to Multiculturalism* (Dordrecht, Springer, 2006) 123.

[80] *Cf* Appiah (n 78) 77.

according to prescriptions they no longer accept.'[81] There seems a radical failure of the Service Principle (conceivably dependent on the fairness of entry terms) if a group will not allow a member to walk out even when the individual is willing to walk out penniless.

We can also recognise a number of distinctions and accept that they may properly affect the analysis. First, there are obvious distinctions between collectivities that affect more or less central interests of individuals, which will correspond partly to those having broader or narrower effects on members' lives.[82] A collectivity that has little effect on a member's life will raise claims for less substantial exit and voice rights. A collectivity with more substantial effects on central individual interests will appropriately raise more substantial demands in terms of exit and/or voice possibilities. Secondly, what bundle of exit and voice these appropriately play out in will depend in part on the weightiness of the individual interests and the collective interests at play. Where the collective interests in question make a relatively more important difference to the lives of the individual members, this factor may provide a powerful argument for a bundle preferring voice to exit; here, a bundle emphasising exit would pose the terrible dilemmas Okin, Shachar and others have so rightly challenged. A bundle emphasising voice would offer individual members the opportunity to influence the pursuit of the collective interests so important to their lives. Thirdly, the bundle must also respond to the homogeneity or heterogeneity of the group in question. The relative effectiveness of voice and exit for individuals will depend on whether there is a reasonable prospect of the collectivity being able to respond to their individual interests. Where particular individuals' interests are dramatically different than those of other members, it may be most important that they have the opportunity to exit. All of these considerations, of course, are stated generally, but the thrust of the position should be clear: the appropriate bundle of exit and voice depends on a careful contextual analysis that takes account of the individual and collective interests at stake.

Nothing says, of course, that there is necessarily just one acceptable bundle of exit and voice in the context of a particular collectivity. Different collectivities in similar circumstances may develop morally appropriate bundles that are ultimately different bundles and should be permitted to do so, for their development of the bundle is central to the associative endeavours in which they engage and the pursuit of the collective interests at stake. But the presence of a reasonably defensible bundle is an important epistemic indicator (helping outsiders who cannot otherwise determine the matter directly[83]) that the collectivity is complying with the Service Principle; its absence will raise questions.

All of these considerations point to the rightness in spirit of aspects of the recent theorising of Green, Okin and Shachar. We may interpret these theorists partly as

[81] A Phillips, *Multiculturalism without Culture* (Princeton, Princeton University Press, 2007) 136–37.
[82] *Cf* DM Weinstock, 'Beyond Exit Rights: Reframing the Debate' in Eisenberg and Spinner-Halev (n 9) 235.
[83] *Cf* ibid, 232–33 (on exit's epistemic functions).

concerned with developing the conditions for effective exercise of voice. The development of effective voice as a derivative means of promoting fulfillment of the Service Principle may, in some circumstances, best strike a harmony between adequate respect for individual interests and adequate respect for collective interests that realistic exit rights would endanger. Green, Okin and Shachar also raise important issues by highlighting some of the additional policies that may have a substantial effect on the availability of realistic rights of exit – the education offered to members, for instance, may actually affect not only their effective use of voice but their access to rights of exit as well. However, as we saw earlier, Green, Okin and Shachar have still gone astray in neglecting some of the interactions of exit and voice and, more generally, that the importance of exit and voice is ultimately their contribution to the collectivity's service to its members. The acceptable bundles of exit and voice can encompass various combinations in various circumstances, the acceptable bundles in particular circumstances being circumscribed by the relation of the collectivity's integrity to exit and voice and by the individual interests at stake, and the presence or absence of an explicable bundle can be an important epistemic indicator on whether a particular collectivity complies with the Service Principle.

5. Exceptional Cases with Neither Exit nor Voice

Anyone evaluating a collectivity's compliance with the Service Principle receives some assurance of the collectivity's compliance if there is a bundle of exit and voice, the acceptability of which can be articulately justified as appropriate to the particular context of the collectivity and its individual members. They serve, then, an epistemic function for outsiders in determining their proper responses to certain collectivities. What, however, of contexts in which both voice and exit are restricted? Matters might seem easier, since we might express scepticism that a collectivity in any such context will comply with the Service Principle, but the issues are actually often more difficult, given that we have recognised both exit and voice as having derivative value only, and we are thus ultimately concerned only with the Service Principle itself. Recall that we earlier described the desirability of voice as not universal, but general. Claims that voice does not have its usual desirability are particularly likely to arise in contexts where there are claims that voice does not apply in the same way, such as in religious contexts where leaders may make a claim to supernatural truths affecting the interests of individual members but on which the leaders claim to have greater knowledge than the members. Such collectivities may also seek to act in ways that affect the realistic availability of exit options, and it is in these contexts that the most difficult moral dilemmas arise.

The Amish in the United States, while restricting internal exercises of voice, refuse to submit their children to the full course of public education, with the effect, some claim, of limiting their children's choices about exit (although they do offer an explicit, formal choice about exit at a certain age). The Amish claim to act in the defence of vital spiritual and religious interests, and the United States Supreme Court has effectively upheld the claims of the Amish group.[84] Examples of this sort need not come solely from religious contexts, though I will use the religious examples further.

Certain groups then claim that there should be deference to aspects of their collective life that result in limits on both effective exit and voice. One possible response is to conclude simply that these collectivities' limits on exit and voice render it unlikely that they comply with the Service Principle. But to do so is to ignore, without argument, the distinctive claims that these collectivities make as to the nature of the interests they protect. The claim on behalf of these groups is that they can comply with the Service Principle without depending on exit and voice.

There is, of course, a truth of the matter about whether or not such collectivities fulfill the Service Principle. It depends upon whether, for example, they genuinely serve spiritual and religious interests of their members. The members typically accept the claims concerning these interests, though there may be dissenters. How should outsiders respond? Absent definitive proof on the truth or falsity of such collectivities' religious claims (not easily obtained!), we nonetheless need to make choices as to interference or non-interference.

I will turn in chapter nine to reasons for deference and interference more generally, but on this issue specifically, there are powerful grounds for outsiders to defer to collectivities repressing exit and voice where these collectivities can articulate a reasonable account of the interests they serve and compelling reasons for repressing exit and voice. These grounds have epistemic force in the sense that a collectivity might have a reasonable explanation against the normal presumption that its members know their individual interests better than the collectivity does. These grounds can have pragmatic force in the sense that outsiders might be well-advised to defer to a collectivity in the absence of a genuine case that their interference would make matters any better. Outsiders thus owe and should show some deference to collectivities that have compelling justifications for their non-compliance with the general epistemic indicators of exit and voice. To refuse such deference is to risk undermining the non-individualisable interests of collectivities in an unjust fashion contrary to the interests of the individuals we otherwise purport to protect. At the same time, this deference may and must be limited where individuals are at risk of serious harm as understood by outsiders; in such instances, the collectivity's explanation for its non-compliance with exit and voice faces an additional hurdle insofar as the prima facie evidence outsiders might examine on the effect of the collectivity on its members runs contrary to a conclusion that it complies with the Service Principle.

Two examples may help illustrate how such deference might work in practice without involving deference to every cult that endangers life and limb in a manner and for reasons wholly inscrutable and inexplicable to all outsiders. There must

[84] *Wisconsin v Yoder* 406 US 205 (1972).

be a careful judgment on reasonableness, with an examination of evidence of interests of members adversely affected alongside the reasonableness of the claims of the collectivity. Let us consider first the case of an authoritarian religious-cultural community mandating education in the threatened language of the community, in whose flourishing members have an interest. Even if this education restricts their ability to exit and even if voice within the community is restricted, it is possible that, all things considered, the community's edict best serves the members overall. Members' interests in the survival of their language and culture might be reasonably served by such a policy, and the group might explain its authoritativeness in terms of claims to better knowledge of what will serve the members. We might judge this collectivity's claims as not unreasonable, as plausible, or even as reasonable, and we thus might defer to its refusal to provide the bundle of exit and voice we would usually expect. This case incidentally reminds us that such claims need not arise in religious contexts, for we might be able to imagine such claims succeeding simply in a culture with traditions of authoritativeness, though the religious claim obviously has more prospect of attaining the reasonableness threshold.

Let us consider, second, the case of *Thomas v Norris*.[85] In this case, Thomas was awarded damages for battery and false imprisonment after the defendants forcibly initiated him into Coast Salish spirit dancing, even though he claimed a right to exit from the aboriginal community and claimed not to be a member of the community. The evidence in the case showed that Thomas had been 'grabbed' (in a technical sense within the tradition) and kept in a longhouse against his will, hit with sticks, bitten on his sides, and so on, all in a manner corresponding to traditional initiation into Coast Salish spirit dancing. The judgment refers only briefly to testimony on the practice's traditional role and does not explore the justification further. In this case, there are obvious harms to the interests of non-consenting persons alongside a lack of an articulated justification for service to members' interests despite denial of a right to exit. On the evidence as presented, then, it would seem that the group's claims had not met a reasonableness standard. This being said, however, there are arguably lingering reasons for discomfort with a conclusion reached without any complete examination of Coast Salish spirit dancing. We must be cautious of presuming, say, that non-Western traditions do not have deeper meanings analogous to religious rites within Western cultures; a rite performed within a non-Western tradition might actually have some purpose, such as to ward off harm, analogous to the purposes of certain religious ceremonies within Western cultures, so there must be careful examination of relevant facts. In saying this, we need not think that further examination of the circumstances

[85] *Thomas v Norris* [1992] 2 CNLR 139 (BCSC). This case is not typical of the claims of aboriginal peoples in, for instance, their claims for exemption from the *Charter* under self-government agreements. For more typical claims, see eg D Russell, *A People's Dream: Aboriginal Self-Government in Canada* (Vancouver, University of British Columbia Press, 2000). The discussion of examples, as I have argued elsewhere (Newman, 'Liberal Multiculturalism and Will Kymlicka's Uneasy Relation with Religious Pluralism' (n 72) 268–69) can prejudice our discussions, but there is justification for discussing this particular case because it is already widely discussed.

would alter our conclusion in the case, but it might give us greater pause for thought and reveal better how there could be an articulate argument on the other side of the issue.[86]

An acceptable bundle of voice and exit serves as some procedural assurance of compliance with the Service Principle. Groups exhibiting an acceptable bundle of exit and voice should thus generally be accepted as in compliance with the Service Principle. Nonetheless, collectivities may be able to comply with the Service Principle even without a bundle of exit and voice. Collectivities with particular reasons for repressing exit and voice may well nevertheless serve their members, and it is the Service Principle that is primary. The judgment of outsiders about such collectivities should be constrained by deference to reasonable articulations of the interests such collectivities serve and their possibly compelling reasons for repressing exit and voice. Outsiders cannot demand that every collectivity provide a bundle of exit and voice, nor need every collectivity do so.

IV. THE MUTUALITY PRINCIPLE AND MEMBERSHIP CONTROL

Madhavi Sunder, arguing for support for dissenters within cultural groups, has objected fiercely to the 'legally authorized exile' that results when 'the leaders of a normative association have exclusive rights to define an association's meaning and to exclude those who would disagree'.[87] Exit theorists have generally shown minimal attention to this issue, either not mentioning it or doing so only briefly in an undeveloped form,[88] although ejection or exclusion of members represents the actual means by which many individual/group differences are actually resolved.[89] Hirschman showed the foresight, however, to note that for many organisations in which exit is 'either impossible or unthinkable, provision is generally made in these organisations for expelling or excommunicating the individual member in certain circumstances'.[90] In this final section, I will argue see that the issues on rights to exit are actually part of a larger set of normative issues concerned with membership control, on which we can comment but briefly here. Making use of Stuart White's initial foray into the issue of group rights to eject members, however, we will see the parallels between the issues of exit and exclusion, which will

[86] Some theorists have turned *Thomas v Norris* into a case challenging any contemplation of more group powers: eg W Kymlicka, *Multicultural Citizenship: A Liberal Theory of Minority Rights* (Oxford, Oxford University Press, 1995) 44.

[87] M Sunder, 'Cultural Dissent' (2001) 54 *Stanford Law Review* 495, 542.

[88] See eg D Réaume, 'Justice Between Cultures: Autonomy and the Protection of Cultural Affiliation' (1995) 29 *University of British Columbia Law Review* 117, 138 (asserting that prohibiting exclusion of a member refusing to accept a group practice 'comes perilously close to requiring the group to accept the dissident's interpretation'.)

[89] The *Hofer* case actually involved excommunication of the individuals who now dissented, though there is every reason to think they would have been content to leave on terms of exit offering them some resources for exit. Dickson J found the expulsion to be necessary, however, to preserve the 'full unanimity of faith, life and work essential to communal living': *Hofer QB* (n 63) 732.

[90] Hirschman (n 15) 76.

make the point that White's framework needs to be elaborated into a more complex form. I will seek to show how the Community Conditions allow collectivities fairly substantial membership control powers.

We can note at the outset the potential relevance of both the Service Principle and the Mutuality Principle. By the very nature of membership control issues, we are discussing those where a dispute exists on whether a particular individual is or should be a member of a collectivity. So whether an individual is a member or a non-member, whether the Service Principle or the Mutuality Principle applies, is precisely at issue. However, absent evidence of an exclusion manifesting bad faith, there will typically be reason to apply either the Service Principle or the Mutuality Principle based on whether the collectivity itself has previously considered the individual in question a member. Thus, if the issue is a collectivity's decision to expel a particular member about whose membership there has been no previous question, the decision must comply with the Service Principle. If the issue is whether to admit someone who has had no previous claim to membership, the decision must comply with the Mutuality Principle. Both of these guidelines embrace the primary claim of members who are already recognised as being members of the collectivity to control its ongoing shape. Their claim is primary because they have a sort of 'ownership' of the collectivity. They have been members and have built up expectations around the fact of their membership and the nature of the collectivity. So, even if one could imagine interesting reforms to a collectivity were it to take on new members, the existing members have a primary say, through their existing rules, over such a decision.

That said, some have challenged this argument, at least implicitly. Anne Phillips, for instance, argues that cultural outsiders have as much claim to an identity as cultural elites.[91] Reformulating that argument from its initially punchy form, it could be cast as an argument that those clearly recognised as members within a collectivity do not automatically have a stronger claim to membership in that collectivity than those who would like to be members of the collectivity. But that more attenuated form, moving away from a power differential issue within the group itself, that should of course not dictate membership, now moves to something not sufficiently sensitive to the importance of collective interests pursued by collectivities. If collectivities are to be free to pursue specific interests, they cannot simply be open to all comers but only those properly fitting with the nature of the collectivity and its specific realisation of its collective interests.

In seeking a broader analysis, it is possible to begin with one well-developed theoretical framework for questions of membership control. Stuart White has offered a seminal analysis of these issues.[92] He proposes a framework that strikes a balance between integrity interests and opportunity interests.[93] This framework has powerful potential from the outset, allowing White to go beyond earlier

[91] Phillips (n 81) 156.

[92] S White, 'Freedom of Association and the Right to Exclude' (1997) 5 *Journal of Political Philosophy* 373.

[93] Ibid, 374.

theories that denied any group right to exclude based on grounds individuals were not free to alter (a counter-intuitive approach in the context of a women's gym or in the context of veiled racial exclusion on religious grounds).[94] White thus reasons that the moral principles governing exclusion first defer to a purpose-protecting exclusion rule but that this can be overruled by opportunity interests of individuals negatively affected by exclusion from a group (whether economic opportunities of women excluded from a business club or community participation interests or suchlike), which can in turn be overruled (except in extreme cases) by individuals' integrity interests (as in their expression of a message through a group or in their intimate association).[95]

White's framework, though more specific to particular concerns, parallels the earlier recognition of the broad balance at stake between individual and non-individualisable interests, realised more or less appropriately through different bundles of exit and voice. At the same time, it must awaken us to a broader array of membership control issues. White's concern for the economic opportunities of those excluded, for example, seems to presume the appropriateness of all sharing in particular economic opportunities, when groups may exist for the very reason of defining who is entitled to share in certain opportunities. For example, in contexts like those of aboriginal rights, membership control may be important precisely because it affects the allocation of rights limited to members of aboriginal groups. Membership control policies are important, for instance, in the allocation of certain scarce resources.[96] Saying that much, of course, does not make clear the collectivity's concern for defining its own membership rules (allocation of scarce resources could also be in accord with government-defined membership). However, taking groups as concerned more broadly with realising weighty non-individualisable interests, we see that the process of self-definition may itself be crucial to the pursuit of these interests; if, for instance, one of the interests advanced by an aboriginal group is a cultural identity, it may well be essential to the success of this identity in promoting self-respect in members that it be an autonomously shaped identity rather than something imposed on the group through, for instance, colonial institutions. The array of issues at stake in the context of membership control is thus wide-ranging.

In serving its members generally, it might be better that a group eject or exclude particular individuals whose interests are not in conformity with those of the group. To take a less serious example where the point is clear, if Oxford's Jurisprudence Discussion Group exists for the sake of group discussion of jurisprudence (as the name implies), and the expectation on members is that they be ready to participate in, or at least listen to, the discussion of jurisprudence, those ceasing to find the non-individualisable interests the group promotes to be

[94] Ibid, 375–77 (arguing against the views of P Hirst, *Associative Democracy: New Forms of Economic and Social Governance* (Oxford, Polity Press, 1994)).

[95] White (n 92) 374, 382–86.

[96] For a discussion of such purposes of membership control and detailed discussion of some specific membership rules, see generally S Grammond, *Identity Captured by Law: Membership in Canada's Indigenous Peoples and Linguistic Minorities* (Montreal, McGill-Queen's University Press, 2009).

in accord with their individual interests would be well-advised to leave.[97] The group would do nothing wrong, and could comply with the Service Principle, in ejecting the marauding musician who desired to practise the tuba, or even merely to talk about the tuba, during the group's meetings. To conclude otherwise would be to prioritise arbitrarily the interests of some particular individual over the good of all. Everyone might be better off with such dissidents absent from the group, the remaining members through being able to carry on their life projects, and the dissidents themselves being able to carry on theirs.

This example reiterates the possible historical dimension to the rights of membership control, a further element not coming out in White's analysis. Although this dimension cannot overcome all other considerations – because legitimate expectations based on the past cannot trump all present justice concerns – the ownership claim of existing members is a factor to be considered along with the claims concerning what interests might be advanced through reform that would fit with new membership rules. In the example, the members of the collectivity who joined on the basis of its being a collectivity for discussion of jurisprudence have a claim to its remaining such that can morally overcome the interests of the dissidents in remaining part of a collectivity to whose principles they do not subscribe. Nothing, of course, says that a group may not evolve, but a dissenter may have no right to demand that it evolve in some particular direction. Ejection may disrupt certain settled expectations members had concerning their identities or lives more generally. So ejection is a serious step. But so is a decision not to eject those who threaten the expectations of others.

A refusal to recognise the possibility of rights to eject would be tantamount to refusing to take seriously the collective interests groups embody. It would deny appropriate recognition to the Boy Scouts' interest in expression of a moral message,[98] deny organisers of a parade the right to express the message they want and/or force them to express a message they do not want,[99] deny churches the pursuit of the spiritual interests they claim to pursue, and so forth. Even if we find unappealing the purposes some groups pursue, if they act in accordance with the Community Conditions, we cannot reject the membership control conditions they may need to facilitate their ongoing flourishing.

That said, some steps that collectivities might seek to take will violate the Community Conditions. If the elites within some collectivity corruptly sought to expel some member whom they disliked for personal reasons, they would act in violation of the Service Principle by blocking further service to someone who has a persisting claim to membership. If certain rules arbitrarily discriminated such that (certain classes of) members who married outside the group were immediately expelled, in the absence of a compelling case that these rules were vital to group purposes and fully justifiable, there would be grounds for challenging their

[97] *Cf* Holder (n 57) 32.

[98] *Boy Scouts of America v Dale* 530 US 640 (2000). *Cf* SV Shiffrin 'What is Really Wrong with Compelled Association?' (2005) 99 *Northwestern University Law Review* 841.

[99] *Hurley v Irish-American Gay, Lesbian and Bisexual Group of Boston* 515 US 557 (1995).

legitimacy under the Service Principle. If a particular collectivity had membership rules damaging the economic opportunities of non-members, in the absence of an identifiable necessity to the integrity of the group, these rules would violate the Mutuality Principle.

Partly by reminding ourselves of some of White's concerns, we can see that the Mutuality Principle may have different effects for groups in different contexts. For instance, where there are fewer other opportunities for non-members, the Mutuality Principle's requirement of respect for the equivalently weighty interests of non-members has a different force than where they have many alternative opportunities. Let us make this abstract claim more tangible. Consider again White's example of the exclusion of women from a business club, an issue that has arisen in case law as well.[100] The present approach allows us to recognise the claims of current members (that the club allows them a particular sort of social environment as a purpose of the collectivity and/or that they have persisting expectations as to the nature of the collectivity) and the claims of prospective women members (that they have economic interests at stake more weighty than the claims of some old men to smoke cigars without women around). Notably, what we conclude as to the demands of the Mutuality Principle will depend partly on the existence of alternative opportunities.[101] If, counterfactually, women in some community had not faced a legacy of discrimination, or, more simply, if there were a viable and equally beneficial women's business organisation (that would open equivalent economic opportunities) in the community, then there would be a stronger argument against the opening of the club to women. That point is perhaps clearer if we think of the inverse example; men generally have no claim to membership of a women's entrepreneurial network because men have many other economic opportunities (although we can also see why we have more sympathy on this issue for particular men for some reason excluded from those more general opportunities). The implications of the Mutuality Principle, then, may differ from one community to another.

This conclusion will apply outside the context of this example in a variety of interesting ways. In remote communities without the same alternative opportunities as in larger centres, non-members of a specific religious denomination who are members of related faiths might have a stronger claim not to be excluded from elements of its services.[102] Whether particular religious groups who not only expel certain dissidents but then go on to shun them do so legitimately will depend partly on context.[103] do so legitimately will depend partly on context. The analysis

[100] *Roberts v United States Jaycees* 468 US 609 (1984); *Board of Directors v Rotary Club* 481 US 537 (1987).

[101] Matters could be more complicated, for instance, if business networking in a particular community took place in a religious organisation that excluded women from membership based on established religious doctrine. The interests at stake would then no longer be simply social but would involve yet more weighty interests as well.

[102] A Gooley, 'The Eucharist and Ecclesial Communion' (2004) 2 *Australian EJournal of Theology* (arguing for relaxed rules on interecclesial communion in remote communities).

[103] For a fascinating discussion of lower-court decisions on such issues, see C Weisbrod, *Emblems of Pluralism: Cultural Differences and the State* (Princeton, Princeton University Press, 2002) 69ff.

will differ based on whether the effect of the shunning is simply to cut the individual off from participation in the religious community while preventing him from continuing to seek to influence its members, or whether it is to cut the individual off from contact with other members of his own family and all ongoing economic opportunities in the region. The Mutuality Principle mandates a general respect for the equivalently weighty interests of non-members, so it will call for constraints on shunning where it has substantial harmful effects on the ongoing lives of those who are no longer members of a community.

The implications of this analysis of membership control will seem potentially perplexing in some situations, particularly those in which outsiders do not understand well the rationales for a particular rule as to membership. But the tests applied to the justness of membership control policies must be based on the factors within the Community Conditions and not just some preconceived notion of what certain communities should be like based on what other communities are like. This latter concern applies to some of the reasoning in the recent United Kingdom Supreme Court decision in *R v Governing Body of JFS*,[104] which concerned a challenge against membership policies of an Orthodox Jewish school that were based on traditional Jewish law principles reaching back thousands of years and that involve matriarchal descent as part of Jewish identity. Some of the reasoning for a finding of discrimination on grounds of ethnicity read as follows:

> As far as we know, no other faith schools in this country adopt descent-based criteria for admission. Other religions allow infants to be admitted as a result of their parents' decision. But they do not apply an ethnic criterion to these parents. The Christian Church will admit children regardless of who their parents are.[105]

To suggest implicitly, verging on explicitly, that the membership criteria of Jewish *halakhic* law were to be judged by whether they matched well with Christian standards surely marked a low point in judicial consideration of membership control. So long as non-Jewish people (or, at least, those not recognised as Jewish by the Orthodox) continue to have reasonable opportunities for quality education in the locale at issue – something nobody questioned – the integrity interests of a community expressed in genuine and internally non-controversial principles about who is an Orthodox Jew must win out in decisions about membership criteria of the Orthodox Jewish community. Some cultural communities will be partly defined by descent within a particular background. An Irishman in London has no particular claim to be part of the London Ghanaian society.

The Community Conditions both allow a collectivity substantial membership control and require it to comply with moral conditions in its membership control practices. Before concluding this section, though, we need to consider two final objections that might confront this analysis. First, Sunder might seek to problematise the analysis, claiming that it inappropriately privileges cultural survival over cultural dissent. As Sunder puts it: 'Lacking a theory of cultural dissent, current

[104] *R v Governing Body of JFS* [2009] UKSC 15.
[105] Ibid, para 88.

law ends up authorising the exclusion of cultural dissenters because their speech conflicts with the speech of a cultural association's leaders.'[106] Does my approach reify collectivities in a form denying claims of dissent? The full striking down of such a claim will be apparent in Part III, where I discuss contestation within communities. But we can note for now that the present approach has not been insensitive to the claims of members who are in dissent; it has sought rather to acknowledge all the interests at stake. Secondly, Réaume would call on us to revisit the right to exit issue in light of a conclusion that there must be a right to eject. As she puts it, 'denying the right to exit would embroil the group's defenders in a mistake that is the mirror image of that made by the internal dissident claiming the power to determine the meaning of the group's practice'.[107] But I have explored in this chapter important differences between exit and expulsion, shown how there may be substitutes for exit, and how exit has only a derivative rationale. Membership control by the group may well be part of what it needs to flourish, or even exist, as a group, so it may have a strong grounding even in some circumstances where individuals do not have rights to exit but there are other ways in which compliance with the Service Principle is achieved. We can conclude, then, by reiterating the powerful account of membership control that the Community Conditions give us and by foreshadowing the further discussion in which I will engage concerning contestation within groups in Part III.

Difficult questions obviously remain. However, it is possible to develop more sophisticated analyses of rights to exit and rights to eject than have henceforth been offered. Many of the principles apply in a context-specific manner, undermining neat generalisations. But we can say that exit is not always necessary, that exit and voice both generally serve functions derivative from the intrinsically important attainment of the Service Principle, that different bundles of exit and voice may be appropriate in different contextual situations, and that there may be situations where outsiders should defer to groups that exhibit neither exit nor voice. Exit and voice can be derivative means of promoting fulfillment with the Service Principle, but they are not mandatory for all groups.

[106] Sunder (n 87) 508.
[107] Réaume (n 88) 139.

III

Realising Collective Rights

8

Imperfect Collectivities

I. INTRODUCTION

PART I DEVELOPED the claim that collectivities can hold moral rights. Part II analysed the series of moral conditions that collectivities must meet to hold rights legitimately. These Community Conditions consist of the Service Principle, explaining that collectivities hold rights only because they serve their members in a broad sense, and the Mutuality Principle, recognising the internal limitation on any collectivity's rights-holding requiring it to act with respect for the equivalently weighty interests of non-members and other collectivities.

Yet Part II may seem to leave us in a quandary. Perfect compliance with the Community Conditions is a rarity, and collectivities in the real world will, in various ways, diverge from those conditions. Part III seeks to face this challenge in the hope of establishing that the present account can have practical applications. In particular, chapter eight considers the implications of the reasonable assumption that many actual collectivities will fail to live up perfectly to the Community Conditions. And the concluding chapter nine considers some principles for when it is and is not permissible to interfere with collectivities to render them into communities fulfilling the Community Conditions.

To make these issues tangible, let us hone in on a particular example of how a collectivity might fail to live up perfectly to the Community Conditions. Recall from the earlier discussions that from the standpoint of the collectivity's claims, a violation of the Service Principle is, in one sense, potentially more serious.[1] As discussed in chapter five, even partial failures in service undermine a collectivity's claims. This is because the service provided by a collectivity can always be evaluated for whether it is morally worth preferring as against the service provided by other possible collectivities, including, where morally accessible, a reformed version of the same collectivity.[2] The Mutuality Principle already has some limits built into it, since a deviation from it marks only particular collective claims or actions as illegitimate, not undermining the very reason by which collectivities hold rights. Taking the harder case, then, we will consider the moral implications of a possible imperfection in a collectivity's compliance with the Service Principle.

[1] Chapter 5.III, above.
[2] Ibid.

A common concern expressed about collective rights is that 'those who control the group's rights may use this special power [granted by collective rights] for ends quite unrelated to the considerations that make the rights valuable.'[3] Kok-Chor Tan suggests that claims made for measures to support cultural survival are frequently inauthentic; he writes that they amount more often to 'measures to protect corrupt regimes or community elites rather than a culture's survival'.[4]

All of these claims concern suggestions that the leaders of a particular collectivity might, on some occasion, act corruptly rather than in service to the interests of members. Such a possibility of course exists, though we might emphasise at the outset that nothing about the possibility is inherent to any particular collectivities; Western political communities have also shown themselves very capable of corruption.

The Service Principle, of course, is a requirement precisely against deviations like those of corrupt regimes. If the leadership of a particular collectivity guide it wisely, they will maintain an ongoing site of flourishing that contributes to the lives of all. If they are corrupt and are stealing its resources for their personal benefit, the collectivity's actions will not be in accord with the Service Principle.[5] So the theory lends no support to corruption. But does it imply that no collectivity with even slight imperfections can continue to hold rights?

We will here see how two conclusions follow in the context of imperfect collectivities. First, I will show that mere imperfections in compliance with the Community Conditions do not undermine a collectivity's claim to hold rights. In this regard, the next section turns to what is sometimes called *partial compliance theory* and argues for what we can call the *approximation principle.* This principle states that collectivities *approximately* meeting the Community Conditions legitimately hold the collective moral rights they would hold if they met the Community Conditions. Some might not think this principle needs much argument but seems intuitive. Indeed, we will see an early statement of a similar principle by John Rawls citing intuition. However, we will also see how an area of economic theory known as the theory of second-best calls Rawls's suggestion into question. On further analysis of this economic theory, however, we will find that, contrary to first appearances, it actually sustains the approximation principle.

Secondly, we will see that there can be important duties in political morality for a *political community* (a collectivity holding certain kinds of power we will specify) to encourage compliance with the Community Conditions. The third section develops this claim generally as an implication of the Service Principle as applied to a community containing subcommunities within. The fourth section develops the implications for one specific kind of failure to meet the Community Conditions,

[3] A Buchanan, 'Assessing the Communitarian Critique of Liberalism' (1989) 99 *Ethics* 852, 863.

[4] K-C Tan *Toleration, Diversity, and Global Justice* (Philadelphia, Pennsylvania State University Press, 2000) 127.

[5] I am assuming here that the particular circumstances make the actions of the leaders attributable to the collectivity: that they are in fact collective actions, and not just individual actions wronging the collectivity.

that which arises when collectivities do not have appropriate institutional or organisational forms, and argues that a political community has duties to foster subcommunities that will contribute to individuals' lives. These conclusions, however, will be subject to reasons to defer to collectivities, to which I will turn in chapter nine.

II. PARTIAL COMPLIANCE AND THE APPROXIMATION PRINCIPLE

In this section, I will show why we should adopt the *approximation principle*. This principle states for present purposes (although the argument for it defends a more general principle applicable to other questions as well) that collectivities *approximately* meeting the Community Conditions legitimately hold the collective moral rights they would hold if they met the Community Conditions. This principle might initially seem intuitive. Aristotle wisely counsels that the same degree of precision cannot be demanded in all contexts.[6] Here, we are doing moral and political philosophy, not computer science, and to suppose that a simple, binary test applies to determine the legitimacy of a collectivity's claims has a science fiction character to it. The approximation principle makes room for epistemological uncertainties and moral greyness of the sort bound to exist in real life. However, the matters at stake are more complex than one might think. I will turn first to the nature of the principles we may use, then to Rawls's suggestion along the lines of the approximation principle, then to how the economic theory of second-best might seem to reveal gaps in that suggestion, and finally to how a careful consideration of this theory actually lends further support to the approximation principle.

Having begun in earlier chapters with what we might call *ideal theory*, that assuming the possibility of perfect compliance, we must now turn to what has sometimes been called *partial compliance theory*. As Rawls first describes it while writing about such topics as obligations to obey unjust laws, partial compliance theory 'studies the principles that govern how we are to deal with injustice.'[7] Or, as Murphy fleshes out this concept, the essential problem is 'a question, that is, of what a given person is required to do in circumstances where at least some others are not doing what they are required to do'.[8] Although particular questions within partial compliance theory, including the obligation to obey unjust laws question, have been addressed at length in existing literature, more general questions of partial compliance have often been underexamined.[9]

Such underexamination might be partly explained by suggestions that questions of ideal theory and of partial compliance are fully separable. For instance, in

6 Aristotle, *Nicomachean Ethics* I:3 1094b.

7 J Rawls, *A Theory of Justice*, rev edn (Oxford, Oxford University Press, 1999) 8. *Cf* ibid, 215.

8 L Murphy, *Moral Demands in Nonideal Theory* (Oxford, Oxford University Press, 2000) 5.

9 Murphy's work (ibid) now constitutes a leading study of the issues, though within a specifically utilitarian framework and thus not easily applicable here. See also G Sher, *Approximate Justice: Studies in Non-Ideal Theory* (Oxford, Rowman Littlefield, 1997).

A Theory of Justice, John Rawls raised briefly the subject of partial compliance theory, but he implied that it had no implications for ideal theory. Indeed, he drew a sharp distinction between ideal theory and non-ideal theory and argued that it was preferable to argue first in terms of ideal theory, suggesting that an ideal theory of justice can reveal 'a conception of a just society that we are to achieve if we can'.[10] Such an approach now faces challenges. In particular, Allen Buchanan's recent moral theory of international law disparages work on theory topics without attention to institutional issues, calling this effort 'Leaf-Blower Theorizing' that 'simply displaces problems to some location conveniently out of sight, without solving them'.[11] Buchanan thus maintains, for example, that any theory of secession must be an institutional theory, one specifying the institutional form to be given to any rights.[12]

There is a danger, of course, in the latter view that it might demand the practically impossible – a theory that simultaneously resolves all theoretical and institutional issues, presumably demanding the solution of a number of important empirical matters about human behaviour as well – and thus end in an argument against the possibility of theory generally rather than in an argument for a new form. Moreover, it might be that our controversies in institutional design arise from deeper moral problems, so we can make genuine contributions by addressing them.

Nonetheless, there are limitations in the former view also. Notably, if theoretical conclusions are of no use in real situations of imperfect compliance, theory's applications are undermined. We can already see the potential value in a middle road identifying principles under which we can guide the application of our ideal theory principle to imperfect collectivities. One may further justify such an approach by analysing Rawls's intuitive suggestions concerning the implications of partial compliance theory.

In suggesting that an ideal theory of justice can reveal 'a conception of a just society that we are to achieve if we can',[13] Rawls goes on to argue that we should judge existing institutions against this standard and act so as to bring them closer to conformity with it. Rawls asserts that this duty arises because: 'The lexical priority of the principles specifies which elements of the ideal are relatively more urgent, and the priority rules this ordering suggests are to be applied to nonideal cases as well.'[14] Rawls himself removes the jargon: 'Thus as far as circumstances permit, we have a natural duty to remove any injustices, beginning with the most grievous as identified by the extent of the deviation from perfect justice.'[15]

[10] Rawls, *A Theory of Justice* (n 7) 216.

[11] A Buchanan, *Justice, Legitimacy, and Self-Determination: A Moral Theory of International Law* (Oxford, Oxford University Press, 2003) 18.

[12] Ibid, 17, 205; see also: A Buchanan, 'Self-Determination, Secession, and the Rule of Law' in R McKim and J McMahan (eds) *The Morality of Nationalism* (Oxford, Oxford University Press, 1997) 301; A Buchanan *Secession: The Morality of Political Divorce from Fort Sumter to Lithuania and Quebec* (Boulder, Westview, 1991).

[13] Rawls, *A Theory of Justice* (n 7) 216.

[14] Ibid, 216.

[15] Ibid.

This attitude of course sounds intuitive, but it is potentially terribly mistaken – we will see in a moment that Rawls himself implicitly recognises this reality. What, though, is wrong with it? If one could attain a fully ideal result, there would be every reason to seek it. Rawls realistically accepts that circumstances might not permit attainment of a fully ideal result. We might even accentuate that point, which elicits widespread challenges. Allen Buchanan has rightly raised the particular challenge of 'moral accessibility'[16] of the recommendations of any theory meant to apply to practice – the steps required by the transition to any ideal must themselves meet moral standards. Here, Rawls's argument falters. Although it sounds appealing to choose one of a set of injustices with which to begin based on the grievousness of each injustice, such a strategy actually has no inherent logic to it and may have detrimental implications. I will offer more rigorous proof of this point with the economic theory of second-best, but we can see immediately the possible problem of unintended effects. We might refer, for instance, to Shachar's identification of widespread processes of 'reactive culturalism', under which many cultural groups become more conservative in response to efforts to impose reforms on them.[17] For Rawls to speak of turning simply to the 'most grievous' injustices does not take account of potential unintended effects of correcting injustices according to a supposed 'lexical priority'.

Indeed, Rawls himself implicitly realises the need for a different analysis. His brief references to partial compliance issues in *A Theory of Justice* grow in his later works, with the *Law of Peoples* most recently evidencing a serious encounter with partial compliance issues. First referring to ideal theory, Rawls envisions 'true peace among [liberal democratic peoples] because all societies are satisfied with the status quo for the right reasons'.[18] The Rawlsian project in *The Law of Peoples*, however, is one going beyond ideal analysis. Rawls's analysis centrally addresses how a democratic people should relate to other sorts of peoples, including *decent peoples* and *outlaws*. In dealing with decent peoples, those which might contain hierarchies but which still meet minimal requirements of consultativeness with individual members, Rawls argues that there should be toleration and development of mutual relations; in dealing with outlaws, those peoples that both fail to meet the conditions of democracy and are outwardly aggressive, Rawls holds that a democratic people may resort to war for reasons of self-defence or, sometimes, intervention to protect human rights.[19] A different political principle emerges because of constraints on the achievement of an ideal outcome resulting from implicit consideration of partial compliance issues.

Partial compliance analyses open different sorts of arguments. Consider the recent critiques of Rawls's *The Law of Peoples* published simultaneously by Martha

[16] Buchanan, *Secession* (n 12) 38, 215–17.

[17] A Shachar, *Multicultural Jurisdictions: Cultural Differences and Women's Rights* (Cambridge, Cambridge University Press, 2001) 35–37.

[18] J Rawls, *The Law of Peoples* (Cambridge MA, Harvard University Press, 1999) 47. The claim is empirically doubtful, but I will not pursue that objection here.

[19] Ibid, 91–94.

Nussbaum and Henry Shue.[20] Nussbaum attacks Rawls's argument that non-interference with decent peoples could be grounded in toleration, urging rather that any failure to change the hierarchies present within decent peoples has to be based on difficulties of intervention. Shue attacks what he perceives as Rawls's call for war with outlaws, arguing that we need rather to develop 'principles to structure non-belligerent relations between members [of the Society of Peoples] and non-members, at least sometimes'.[21]

Nussbaum is right that the difficulties of intervention may present a compelling moral reason not to interfere with the hierarchical structure of a decent people. Even before we get to the consequences of an attempt at intervention into Kazanistan (Rawls's imagined decent people), it might be near-impossible to design a way of intervening that would actually encourage the Kazani powers to alter their policies. Such difficulties of intervention are an important moral argument in the context of partial compliance – and even theorists who do not specifically put their argument in terms of partial compliance accept the relevance of such arguments, such as when both Kymlicka and Raz advance prudential reasons not to interfere with illiberal cultures.[22]

Though we need not address it at length, Nussbaum is arguably mistaken on her other point. In questioning whether toleration could extend to a decent people, she implicitly suggests that an ideal conception of toleration must not extend beyond peoples ready to 'respect certain stringent norms of political justice and graft them onto their comprehensive doctrine'.[23] It is unclear whether such a doctrine remains a conception of toleration at all. Moreover, Rawls's conception of toleration is open to decent peoples not because of any partial compliance analysis therein, but because decent peoples meet conditions that make them 'genuine corporate moral persons' that can respect and make claims of justice.[24] Rawls's conception, of course, is consistent with the Community Conditions, so we need not address this point further here.

Shue's argument seeks a different partial compliance approach in the relation with outlaws, in one sense going yet farther than Rawls in engaging constraints on ideal outcomes. As Shue puts it, 'what we need most are principles to structure non-belligerent relations' between liberal or decent peoples and other peoples.[25] Shue thus delves deeper into partial compliance (or even non-compliance), in this respect expressing concerns about the stability implications of retaining an ideal focus to the theory. Opening to partial compliance analysis thus substantially complicates analysis.

[20] M Nussbaum, 'Women and the Law of Peoples' (2002) 1 *Politics, Philosophy, and Economics* 283; H Shue, 'Rawls and the Outlaws' (2002) 1 *Politics, Philosophy, and Economics* 307.

[21] Shue (ibid) 308.

[22] W Kymlicka, *Multicultural Citizenship* (Oxford, Oxford University Press, 1995) 164–70; J Raz, *Ethics in the Public Domain: Essays in the Morality of Law and Politics* (Oxford, Clarendon, 1994) 185.

[23] Nussbaum (n 20) 293.

[24] *Cf* DA Reidy, 'Rawls on International Justice: A Defense' (2004) 32 *Political Theory* 291, 298.

[25] Shue (n 20) 308

We might try to defend the *approximation principle* in the present context through a further-elaborated analogy to *The Law of Peoples*, for chapter six explored important parallels between the present theory, particularly on the Mutuality Principle, and Rawls's work in this context. But there is actually a more general defence of the approximation principle available by pushing further into partial compliance theory. Specifically, I will show how the approximation principle emerges in the stated form from the challenge second-best theory poses to Rawls's earlier suggestion.

We turn outside political theory to a realm of discourse that has long considered the implications of partial compliance, the economic theory of second-best. The general theory of second-best received both its name and its classic statement in a famed article of Lipsey and Lancaster.[26] Lipsey and Lancaster analyse the achievement of Pareto optimality, a situation where no reallocation of resources offers a gain by one agent without a loss by another. A Pareto optimum may be achieved by the fulfilment of a number of Paretian conditions. Lipsey and Lancaster's contribution is a general proof within the context of a general equilibrium model (one incorporating multiple markets at once) that if a constraint blocks the fulfilment of one Paretian condition, then there is no longer a general argument for the desirability of the fulfilment of the other Paretian conditions. This differs from a possible layperson's guess that we should simply seek the fulfilment of as many Paretian conditions as possible, the intuition Rawls seemingly expressed.

Put less technically, Lipsey and Lancaster show that there can be no 'piecemeal welfare economics'.[27] Because one market potentially affects other markets, correcting inefficiencies in one market is certain to improve overall Pareto welfare only if there is simultaneous correction of all inefficiencies in all other markets. In the absence of this condition, assuring compliance with a 'first-best equilibrium', we must develop 'second-best policies' which, though not necessarily desirable in a first-best world, are the best that can be done, and these policies may not correspond to those of the first-best world.

On a strict reading of the economic theory of second-best, it poses questions to the approximation principle. As soon as one departs from the complete set of Paretian conditions, all bets are off on whether increased compliance with one condition will improve Pareto optimality. By analogy, an objector might argue, as soon as collectivities depart from the delicate balance of the Service and Mutuality principles, we cannot assume that getting closer to fulfilment of those conditions marks any improvement.

The economic theory of second-best has drawn attention in recent years for its potential claims against the approach of law-and-economics scholars. Some have claimed law-and-economics scholars ignore the fundamental insights of Lipsey and Lancaster by often identifying departures from Paretian conditions and then

[26] RG Lipsey and K Lancaster, 'The General Theory of Second Best' (1956) 24 *Review of Economic Studies* 11.

[27] Ibid, 17.

arguing immediately for reforms to particular policies giving rise to those departures without analysing other departures.[28] We have no direct concern here with the fate of law-and-economics analysis, but I might note in passing that such claims are surely exaggerated. Prominent law-and-economics scholars have shown themselves at least implicitly aware of the second-best issue when discussing certain proposed piecemeal reforms.[29]

In any event, the economic theory of second-best's implications also has an important limitation. Second-best theory can demand that we examine carefully any broader effects, but it cannot say that broader effects always exist. The conclusions of economic theory without second-best theory will continue to hold in markets that are isolated from others.[30] Similarly, if certain principles of political morality apply without side effects calling for changes in other principles, then they hold against objections of those deploying theories analogous to second-best theory.

Here, we can develop a more positive, general argument for the approximation principle. If a genuinely marginal change in compliance with a principle does not in itself call for adjustments to other principles, it can be considered an isolated change for purposes of the theory of second-best or partial compliance theory more generally. Marginal deviations are approximately independent from other principles and do not call for more complex applications of partial compliance theory.

Obviously, one might go through more definition of genuinely marginal deviations, analysing how substantial a deviation can be before it ceases to be marginal. We need not carry that through fully but can rely on the rough sense already offered. We can note, however, an important point that even mild, somewhat-more-than-marginal departures from the service principle are likely still to fit within the approximation principle. The real concern in accepting departures without evoking the whole array of potentially complex and complicating implications of second-best theory or partial compliance theory is that any departures from the principle not have substantial side effects that call other principles into play.

Small departures from the Service Principle affect the relation between individual members and a collectivity. Thus, they do not obviously, immediately imply problems for other relations. Even if the analysis in chapter five would have held departures from the Service Principle to searching scrutiny against other

[28] See especially RS Markovits 'Second-Best Theory and Law & Economics: An Introduction' (1998) 73 *Chicago-Kent Law Review* 3.

[29] See eg RA Posner *Law and Legal Theory in England and America* (Oxford, Oxford University Press, 1996) 72 (noting that 'you should not change a functioning part before examining the effect of the change on the operation of the system'); EA Posner and A Vermeule, 'Reparations for Slavery and Other Injustices' (2003) 103 *Columbia Law Review* 689 (using second-best theory as a principal element in assessing theories of reparations for historic injustice).

[30] *Cf* TS Ulen, 'Courts, Legislatures, and the General Theory of Second Best in Law and Economics' (1998) 73 *Chicago-Kent Law Review* 189, 216–17.

possible forms of action the collectivity might have taken, we see now reasons to be wary of assuming that every departure undermines rights-holding.

In the case of a collectivity with leaders engaging in corruption, whether the resulting violations of the Service Principle amount to pilfering or to larcenous fraud might matter greatly: it might determine whether this corruption undermines the legitimacy of the collectivity's actions. Corruption that does not detract from the approximation principle is morally wrong, but it does not undermine the collectivity's legitimate claims. Corruption that means the collectivity has ceased to act for its members, by contrast, fundamentally undermines the collectivity's present claims due to the failure of even approximate compliance with the Service Principle.

One could imagine appropriate uses of outside-imposed regulation promoting compliance with the Service Principle as against risks of actual corruption. However, any such measures must obviously be subject to a test, first, that they will achieve the aim of promoting compliance with the Service Principle and not counterproductively waste resources or in other ways take away from compliance with the Community Conditions. And they must be subject to a test concerning whether they will otherwise damage collective (or individual) interests when they purport to promote them.

These conclusions, I might reiterate, are no defence of corruption by anyone. But they are an indication of the importance of collectivities themselves developing the mechanisms to combat corruption or other analogous failures of the Service Principle. Collectivities working on challenges and through problems, notably, may retain the same rights they would otherwise have, so long as they fall within the parameters of the approximation principle.

Mild departures from the full spirit of the Service Principle affect the relation between individual members and a collectivity and do not immediately imply problems for other relations; departures from the Mutuality Principle, by contrast, immediately cause problems for other collectivities. So, although I described the Service Principle as having a sort of moral primacy in being the first concern of any collectivity, it is also one subject to greater degrees of approximation. Pilfering of a collectivity's own accounts might not undermine its collective claims; even mild pilfering from other collectivities just might do so.

A collectivity approximately meeting the Community Conditions thus remains legitimate as a rights-holder, although more significant departures from the Service Principle and even less serious departures from the Mutuality Principle do undermine the legitimacy of its claims. We have taken the intuitive claim of the approximation principle through important tests, and it emerges as a valid principle. That realisation is significant. The approximation principle renders realistic the holding of collective moral rights in real life where real collectivities will have their failings from time to time, making it all the more necessary to flesh out the implications of the existence of collective rights; these implications obviously include duties to refrain from violating rights, but the coming sections will make the point that these duties go farther as well.

III. POLITICAL DUTIES TO ENCOURAGE COMPLIANCE WITH THE COMMUNITY CONDITIONS

A political community is a collectivity holding a de facto institutional power to coordinate substantially the actions of its members and of subcommunities within (other collectivities within the sphere of the political community). Obviously, one individual might simultaneously be a member of more than one political community, for a member of a people that has coordinative power in a particular region might simultaneously be a member of a nation-state community that has coordinative power over a multi-region state and of an international political community. Nonetheless, we speak of the moral duties of a political community; where there are overlapping layers of political communities, each will be subject to duties concerning what is within its powers.

I thus respond to Will Kymlicka's important challenge to Ayelet Shachar, which questions her presumption that the state is the political community to intervene when individuals actually belong to many political communities.[31] Determining which political community should respond to a particular matter might involve separate reasons that one could develop in a theory with that focus. We can remain content with the general claim here by conceiving of our arguments as addressed to a particular political community, with the actions of other political communities taken as given for our purposes. Obviously, an extension of the present account could further examine the implications of a more dynamic account of multiple, simultaneous political actors. Leaving those complexities aside, this section develops further the duties of a political community arising from collective interests and collective rights.

One obvious implication of collective rights is the existence of duties correlative to these rights. We might call compliance with these duties *respecting* the rights. However, the existence of collective interests that have the particular moral force of rights actually has further implications. This section argues that a political community also has duties to *protect* and *promote* members' or subcommunities' interests, the first of these requiring it to take steps in accord with relevant moral reasons to discourage or prevent others from interfering with particular interests, and the second requiring it to take steps in accord with relevant moral reasons to fulfil or facilitate the fulfilment of, particular interests.

This view might seem intuitive in light of the rich concept of a right developed in Part II, in which an interest grounds not just a single duty but a bundle of duties, as well as moral reasons not necessarily having the stringency of duties, that may both complement and substitute for one another, depending on the particular interest at stake and the existing context and circumstances. This concept of a right makes intelligible the contingent possibility of the simultaneous truth of

[31] W Kymlicka, 'Comments on Shachar and Spinner-Halev: An Update from the Multiculturalism Wars' in C Joppke and S Lukes (eds) *Multicultural Questions* (Oxford, Oxford University Press, 1999) 117–18.

several appealing claims about rights. They can simultaneously be some sort of constraint on action, in that they give rise to certain duties and the duty-bearer respects rights, and be an impulse to action, in that there are duties to protect and promote the underlying interests.

A political community's duties to protect and promote members' and subcommunities' interests are a simple application of the Service Principle. The Canadian political community has, according to the Service Principle, a duty to serve the interests of its members. Some of its members have profound interests in the flourishing of subcommunities within – for example members of the Nisga'a First Nation will have interests in the flourishing of that community. The Canadian political community, then, has a duty to serve the interests of the Nisga'a First Nation insofar as it contributes, in turn, to the lives of its members.

If the ultimate measure of the morality of actions is their effect on the well-being of individuals, then the coordination carried out by any political community may be judged by that standard. Its protection and promotion of the interests of individual members and of subcommunities, insofar as they serve the interests of members, will be central to the application of this standard. The qualification on the latter point, however, is key. The primary duty is to the members of the collectivity. If they are, in turn, members of subcommunities that fail to serve them, the larger collectivity has some reason to interfere so as to protect and promote its members' interests. However, the range of factors that will affect whether or not interference is the moral course of action in response is complex. In chapter nine, I will turn at further length to a variety of competing reasons for interference and reasons for deference.

For the moment, we can note that the moral reasons for interference can sometimes ground regulation of fairly interventionist sorts, though we need to recognise simultaneously the risk to other collective interests. For example, the political community's use of legal authority may actually best promote certain forms of compliance with the Service and Mutuality principles. Although the example is complex, depending on the circumstances, legal prohibitions on and legal sanctions for corrupt use of a collectivity's funds might actually be an important way to promote use of funds in conformity with the Service Principle rather than for elites' own ends.

We might here draw a distinction between *supplantive regulation*, regulation replacing the regulation that the (well-ordered) collectivity's own decision-making processes would yield, and *supportive regulation*, regulation reinforcing the regulation that the (well-ordered) collectivity's own decision-making processes would yield. Supportive regulation may seem generally preferable from the standpoint of the rationales at stake, insofar as the collectivity itself will have informational advantages as to what promotes its collective interests. These informational advantages may be attenuated in an imperfect collectivity. However, the point remains that regulation reinforcing the regulation the collectivity would develop were it well-ordered has particular moral backing. This conclusion may then support a broader conclusion as to the desirability of consultation with collectivities regarding regulation that will support their collective interests. That said, when what is at stake is whether a collectivity complies with the Service and Mutuality Principles so as to have legitimacy in the first place, supplantive regulation may sometimes be appropriate. As noted, I will examine at greater length the reasons for deference and reasons for interference in the next chapter, which is obviously essential analysis for such choices.

For the moment, however, we can note one further qualification on any claims about a general preference for supportive regulation over supplantive regulation. The rationales against supplantive regulation lose some of their force in the context of the Mutuality Principle. In cases of conflicts with other collectivities, we have no reason to presume one collectivity knows another collectivity's interests better than the political community does. Accordingly, for purposes of the Mutuality Principle, not only are lesser degrees of departure permissible, but the political community has a stronger basis to coordinate rival claims. That said, given that each (ideal) collectivity knows its own interests best, there may be reason to contemplate sorts of 'consociation' in which inter-group fora, rather than the political community itself, develop coordination best respecting their interests. Complex policy choices remain.

Duties to encourage compliance with the Community Conditions, of course, must coexist with limits on appropriate state interference with collectivities. There obviously may be a number of reasons for such limits, whether based on the collective interests of collectivities themselves in certain degrees of noninterference, on necessary limits on the powers of political communities as against risks of abuses of power, or on the ability of the political community's interference to make any actual, positive difference to collectivities' behaviour. I will return to these matters in chapter nine, but we must first turn to a particular variation on the duty to promote compliance with the Community Conditions.

IV. POLITICAL DUTIES TO FOSTER CIVIL SOCIETY

In *The Law of Peoples*, John Rawls identified what he called 'burdened societies', those lacking the traditions or resources to be well-ordered, as raising particular moral challenges.[32] Here, we confront a matter with some parallels, those sub-communities that lack viability under their current institutional and organisational conditions.

This matter presents one particular policy challenge among many in institutionalising collective rights. Other less central policy challenges might include the possibility that the availability of collective rights encourages a proliferation of groups and escalation of claims beyond the genuinely justifiable[33] – Brian Barry

[32] Rawls, *The Law of Peoples* (n 18) 106. *Cf* also A Xanthaki, *Indigenous Peoples and United Nations Standards: Self-determination, Culture and Land* (Cambridge, Cambridge University Press, 2007) 38 (discussing the position of highly disadvantaged indigenous communities not able to meet all requirements on them).

[33] C Offe, 'Political Liberalism, Group Rights, and the Politics of Fear and Trust' (2001) 53 *Studies in East European Thought* 167, 181–82. DM Weinstock, 'Beyond Exit Rights: Reframing the Debate' in A Eisenberg and J Spinner-Halev (eds) *Minorities Within Minorities: Equality, Rights and Diversity* (Cambridge, Cambridge University Press, 2005) 241.

puts it more crudely as a problem of 'ethnocultural political entrepreneurs'.[34] But such a challenge is a familiar one where the political community must sort genuine rights claims from false ones to act justly.

The possibility that some subcommunities lack viability raises a more pressing concern in light of a reality that many real-world collectivities are not organised and institutionalised in ways easily permitting them to claim respect by political or legal institutions for their collective moral rights or even to seek their collective interests. James Nickel has powerfully analysed two specific sources of groups' lack of ability to 'play an active role in exercising, interpreting, and defending their rights'[35] – 'effective agency' and 'clear identity'.[36] We can read the same sources as more broadly interfering with their pursuit of collective interests and thus of objects that would contribute importantly to the lives of members through the flourishing of the collectivity and the service it could then offer to members. Nickel initially suggests that he will conclude that the lack of these features will ground an argument against giving groups legal rights in many instances, but he later modulates his claim by recognising that it is often possible to develop more effective agency and clearer identity.[37] Indeed, this latter approach may well be the more appropriate course.

Issues related to groups' effective agency, clear identity, and well-developed representative mechanisms have arisen, for instance, in contexts related to requirements of consultation with indigenous communities.[38] It would be an unreasonable approach for states and mining companies to simply rule out the possibility of consultation with particular indigenous communities on the basis that the communities were not sufficiently organised. There can be, rather, even an obligation to help foster the requisite capacity to engage in consultation.

Nickel suggests that sometimes, 'part of the work that group [legal] rights would have done can be accomplished by giving individual [legal] rights to members of the group', which he suggests we can call 'the "privatization" of group rights'.[39] However, the earlier arguments have made clear that the very nature of the collective interests with which we are most concerned is that they cannot be 'privatized' in this sense, so the challenge becomes one of fostering effective agency and clear identity, of encouraging collective organisation that allows pursuit of and claims for collective interests, or what we will call *civil society*. Civil society, for present purposes, is the organisation and institutionalisation enabling a collectivity to meet the Service Principle.

[34] B Barry, *Culture and Equality: An Egalitarian Critique of Multiculturalism* (Cambridge MA, Harvard University Press, 2001) 21.

[35] JW Nickel, 'Group Agency and Group Rights' in I Shapiro and W Kymlicka, *Ethnicity and Group Rights: Nomos 39* (New York, New York University Press, 1997) 235.

[36] Ibid.

[37] Ibid, 235–36.

[38] On the duty to consult as developed in Canada, and with some comment on developing international law, see generally DG Newman *The Duty to Consult: New Relationships with Aboriginal Peoples* (Saskatoon, Purich Publishing, 2009).

[39] Nickel (n 35) 252.

The political community, I will claim, should foster civil society in this sense and thereby empower collectivities to hold rights or, more simply, to pursue their collective interests, which in turn contribute to the lives of members. One question might immediately arise – to what degree must the political community foster subcommunities within? Kymlicka's approach to questions of group-specific rights has an advantage of simplicity in certain respects – though that oversimplicity is part of what has led us to reject his claims – and he had an easy answer to issues of how far group-specific rights should extend. Because his theory derived from an egalitarian premise, he could say that group-specific legal rights should be assigned as necessary to comply with the egalitarian requirement.[40] Within the present framework – one recognising a complex set of values, the value of individual interests and collective interests, and deep epistemological difficulties – the answer is not so simple. Within this section, I will not seek to develop specific claims concerning to what degree the political community should pursue certain policies, but simply to develop claims that it has powerful moral reasons to pursue these aims. In chapter nine, I will return to the issue of degree, after analysing further reasons for interference and reasons for deference, arguing there that it may well be permissible for different political communities to make different choices on what path to follow, a realisation that gives rise to deep, path-dependent divergences.

There are moral reasons for the political community to foster the organisation of subcommunities within because by doing so it serves the members whose lives will be enhanced by the flourishing of those subcommunities. And this may require active steps since the viability of subcommunities is not guaranteed. Indeed, the successful development of civil society groups can be challenging and often has to work against individual incentives to favour individual well-being at the expense of efforts for collective interests that might otherwise contribute more to their lives.[41]

This readily recognised point gives moral support already to policies that might otherwise be questioned. Consider the issue of tax concessions enjoyed by charitable groups and, more broadly, various civil society groups, and those contributing to them. The historic rationale has been that the groups in question provided public services, lessening the burden on the state.[42] For example, religious organisations have a long tradition of providing education, health care, and social services in many contexts. Some of these services have even been in veiled forms; for instance, the pastoral work of religious workers often substitutes for state-provided counselling for those in psychological distress. Yet, such rationales are today

[40] See eg W Kymlicka, *Liberalism, Community and Culture* (Oxford, Clarendon, 1989) 182–91.

[41] *Cf* Nickel (n 35) 253; M Olson, *The Logic of Collective Action: Public Goods and the Theory of Groups* (Cambridge MA, Harvard University Press, 1971); M Walzer, 'The Idea of Civil Society' (1991) 38 *Dissent* 293, 300–301; B Barry, *Political Argument* (London, Routledge, 1965) 234–35.

[42] See eg BI Bittker, 'Churches, Taxes, and the Constitution' (1969) 78 *Yale Law Journal* 1285, 1286; H Hansmann, 'The Rationale for Exempting Nonprofit Organizations from Corporate Income Taxation' (1981) 91 *Yale Law Journal* 54, 71–72 (but elsewhere in the article offering technical reasons for some tax rules based on non-profit organisations' differentiated access to capital).

under challenge from those who question the extent to which some groups which benefit from tax concessions actually promote public aims.[43] And some theorists have even gone so far as to suggest selectively removing tax concessions from particular religious organisations with which these theorists have disagreements.[44]

An alternative, more general rationale for tax concessions for civil society groups could, of course, be developed in semi-economic terms following a recent body of literature. In particular, the powerful arguments in recent years of Robert Putnam and others have focused attention on the concept of 'social capital', with the formation of links within associations grounding broader patterns of trust within society that facilitate cooperation, wealth creation, and other goods.[45]

However, the more basic point that collective interests can contribute in important ways to the lives of members offers a support not founded on the mere worth of belonging to organisations and the social capital it allegedly creates but on the value of what civil society can do for individual persons, thus sustaining a deeper and broader argument that might support a policy of tax concessions. The point is not that any particular collectivity can claim particular tax concessions as an ongoing moral right in perpetuity but that tax concessions may be one appropriate way of meeting the requirement to foster civil society. They will be a deficient way of doing so in certain contingent scenarios, such as where the people in a particular society will form bad collectivities (say, dangerous religious cults and racial supremacy organisations), where something makes it impossible to distinguish between collectivities meriting support and various sham organisations that seek to fit within the incentives, or where there is danger of political capture of the system that will then enable greater wrongs. But they will often be a good way of fostering civil society generally and overcoming some challenges that otherwise distort society in an individualistic direction. In any context, however, they will be only part of a larger set of policies that can foster civil society in a creative, positive manner, with other important elements including a broader policy framework that will provide appropriate regulatory mechanisms empowering individuals to organise civil society organisations (sometimes best promoted by non-regulation, but sometimes by the existence of regulatory frameworks, particularly for larger organisations).

A broad duty falls on the political community to foster civil society because civil society organisations contribute to improved lives for individuals within the political community. This rationale for the duty also explicates limits on the duty. First, so far as it uses state resources, compliance with the duty takes away from the

[43] See eg Bittker (n 42) 1286; OS Thomas, 'The Power to Destroy: The Eroding Constitutional Arguments for Church Tax Exemption and the Practical Effect on Churches' (1991) 22 *Cumberland Law Review* 605.

[44] SM Okin, '"Mistresses of Their Own Destiny": Group Rights, Gender, and Realistic Rights of Exit' (2002) 112 *Ethics* 205, 230n. *Cf* A Gutmann, *Identity in Democracy* (Princeton, Princeton University Press, 2003) 114–16 (arguing generally for subsidising only those associations that are nondiscriminatory).

[45] *Cf* R Putnam, *Bowling Alone* (New York, Simon & Schuster, 2000); F Fukuyama, *Trust: The Social Virtues and the Creation of Prosperity* (London, Penguin, 1995).

political community's opportunity to pursue other objectives improving the lives of the same or other individuals. As with any duty of a political community, complex choices must be made; this book does not purport to offer a complete theory of balancing between different ends but to highlight certain ends that have been disregarded by much political theory. Secondly, because the rationale concerns implications of the humanistic thesis, the political community must foster civil society in a manner fitting with the humanistic thesis and its consequent Community Conditions. Thirdly, the value of collectivities' autonomy will also pose limits to appropriate state action.

It might sometimes seem tempting for the political community to step in to create and define certain civil society organisations where there seems no other effective means of individuals themselves developing the organisations or institutions needed for the pursuit of their collective interests. For instance, earlier in the book, we have seen some defences of the Quebec political community defining the linguistic communities to benefit from francophone or anglophone education.[46] But any such endeavour is fraught with extreme danger. Governmentally-ascribed identities have enabled or even been the source of grave injustices, with the racial definitions of apartheid South Africa being just one extreme example of many one could cite.

Fostering civil society obviously cannot mean generally circumscribing the opportunity of collectivities to define themselves or, indeed, of individuals to develop their own autonomous memberships and identities. But this point equally does not mean that the political community may adopt an entirely hands-off approach to civil society, given the need to promote the effective agency and clear membership of collectivities to facilitate their pursuit of their collective interests. The regulative needs of collectivities may well be substantial. James Nickel describes well the difficulty unorganised collectivities may face in claiming and exercising their rights.[47] As Nickel notes, 'the consequences of making minority groups into capable rightholders may be as large as the consequences of recognizing, implementing, and respecting their rights'.[48] But these efforts to make minority groups into capable rights-holders must proceed in a manner consistent with the rationales behind fostering civil society in the first place.

The viability of a community's self-definitional processes may depend upon governmental support or involvement that brings the coordinative effects of legal authority in at least some form. For instance, as noted in chapter seven, a collectivity's ability to regulate its membership boundaries may be crucial to the integrity of its identity. In contexts where membership rules depend upon familial membership, there is an unavoidable interaction between collective membership

[46] *Cf* ch 5.II, above; S Grammond, *Identity Captured by Law: Membership in Canada's Indigenous Peoples and Linguistic Minorities* (Montreal, McGill-Queen's University Press, 2009) (discussing some of the important membership control issues at stake).

[47] Nickel (n 35); *cf* L May, *Sharing Responsibility: Expanding the Domain of Moral Responsibility* (Chicago, University of Chicago Press, 1992) 109.

[48] Nickel (n 35) 253.

rules and legal authority's coordinative rules on family membership. Family law may effectively determine who is inside or outside a community, with these boundaries being 'a basic aspect of cultural self-determination for all communities',[49] so the political community whose legal authority establishes family law cannot avoid engaging with questions of how to interact with the collectivities at stake.

In confronting such issues, we thus need to draw a fundamental distinction based on the previous distinction between supplantive and supportive regulation. Here, we distinguish *supplantive definition* and *recognitional definition.* Supplantive definition is legally authoritative definition of membership that replaces the definition that the (potential) collectivity's own decision-making processes would yield. Recognitional definition is legally authoritative definition of membership that recognises and reinforces the definition that the (potential) collectivity's own decision-making processes would yield. In the case of a well-ordered collectivity, there are powerful arguments for recognitional definition because it best guards the collectivity's integrity and thus best fosters civil society. However, as implicit in chapter seven, there can be reasons for interference with actual collectivities' self-definitions of membership where there are substantial departures from the Community Conditions or where other powerful moral reasons (such as the opportunities of non-member individuals) weigh heavily in favour of such interference. The tensions between these reasons remain subject to the further analysis of reasons for interference and reasons for deference.

For the moment, though, we can remind ourselves that the political community has a moral duty to foster civil society through appropriate policies, which fall to be analysed in the circumstances and based on further principles we will develop, and that this moral duty does not imply a hands-off approach in any general sense. This moral duty is one of a broader set of duties to encourage compliance with the Community Conditions.

[49] M Boyd, *Dispute Resolution in Family Law: Protecting Choice, Promoting Inclusion* (Toronto, Ontario Ministry of the Attorney General, 2004) 90.

9

Toward a Community of Communities

I. INTRODUCTION

THIS PART DEVELOPS principles related to institutionalising collective rights. Chapter eight set the groundwork by arguing for the approximation principle, a principle making it possible for the arguments of the previous chapters to apply in situations departing from perfect compliance with the Community Conditions. Chapter eight has also indicated the potentially tension-laden implications of our analysis for the duties of a political community. In this chapter, I carry forward the general analysis of chapter eight toward some more specific principles. We can say more about how these tensions are addressed, while, in the process, drawing in yet more complex circumstances with the sorts of epistemic limitations and other needs for deference from chapter seven. Finally, later in the chapter, I will apply the approximation principle to identify a frequently-desirable way of facing up to these tensions, what I will call *principled contestation.*

To this end, the second section of the chapter elaborates a set of reasons for deference to a collectivity's choices and a set of reasons for principled interference with a collectivity's choices. Counterpoising these two sets of reasons makes manifest the difficult dilemmas the political community actually faces. Although I will argue that there can be circumstances in which careful analysis of the two sets of reasons reveals a definitive decision for either deference or interference, we will also see that there can be many circumstances in which a dilemma remains.

The third section argues, however, for a particular approach as often reconciling the competing reasons for interference and deference. Namely, we will see how supporting platforms for what I will call *principled contestation* (principle-based forms of argument concerning the proper accounts of collective interests) can often reconcile many of the competing reasons and interests at stake. We should be clear from the outset that the argument there will be only that providing platforms for such principled contestation can often be an appropriate policy. The complex tensions of the reasons for deference and reasons for interference fall to be considered in complex circumstances, and we clarify some relevant considerations but do not provide a recipe book for political action.

The fourth section will describe briefly some applications to emerging questions involving collective rights. The concluding section sums up with a reminder of the rich vision now opened before us, one in which the value of collective interests is more fully recognised, their possible rights implications respected, the communities and subcommunities of a jurisdiction forming a mutually enriching context for the lives of all individuals. We will there remind ourselves of the accomplishments of the book's theoretical framework in making important claims that groups have rights and in showing that a remarkable range of group rights issues can share a common moral framework. I will conclude simply by noting some new fields of endeavour that this harvest opens for other ploughs.

II. PRINCIPLED DEFERENCE AND PRINCIPLED INTERFERENCE

In institutionalising and operationalising a theory of collective rights, we must recognise that real-world collectivities will do things with which others will disagree. Were utter homogeneity demanded, there would be no point to a theory of collective rights. That said, we have also clearly identified circumstances in which reasons exist for interference with the actions of particular collectivities.

In this section, I seek to further develop reasons for deference and reasons for interference, an effort hopefully shedding light on the right choices for a political community to make. I will develop four general reasons for deference: (1) plural values realised by collectivities; (2) autonomy of collectivities; (3) epistemic reasons for non-interference; and (4) ineffectiveness of interference. I make no claim that this is an exhaustive set of reasons for deference. Many considerations within political morality impact on the decision for interference or deference in any particular circumstances. These include considerations related to the broader effects of greater state power, concerns related to the constitutional structure of the particular communities at issue, and even matters like the effects of interference or deference on any moral requirements related to equality in instances where interference or deference has effects on distribution. I will not develop these considerations further but cite them simply as illustrative of the complex elements at play in factual circumstances. The four reasons I develop here are those most specific to the context of collectivities.

I will then revive the possible importance of interference based on two major reasons: (1) interference to prevent violations of the Service Principle; and (2) interference to prevent violations of the Mutuality Principle. In the process, I will show the tensions between reasons for deference and for interference, tensions not dissipated even by the helpful distinctions some theorists have attempted to draw.

First, then, recall the important argument of chapter five, in which it became clear that the humanistic principle entails a broad principle that a collectivity must serve the interests of its members generally, which is not precisely captured in a suggestion that it must promote the autonomy of its members.[1] We can

[1] Ch 5.III, above.

reiterate here a broader significance to this earlier conclusion. Different collectivities facilitate different aspects of human flourishing. Just as there is no requirement of 'liberalism all the way down', no requirement that each and every collectivity mirror the principles behind a liberal state,[2] there is no requirement that any given collectivity serve particular sorts of human interests, just that it serve interests generally. The corollary is that different collectivities embody service to different interests. This point in itself is a reason for a political community professing the values of autonomy (thus itself having certain content to its own service) to defer to the actions of collectivities serving different interests. In doing so, it actually opens alternative lives to the members of the political community, not – we should emphasise – out of any relativism, but out of a recognition that the modes of human flourishing are diverse. The fact that some of these collectivities' visions differ from those of the political community itself is a reason for the political community to consider deferring to their choices even when it disagrees with them.

Although he would surely acknowledge a range of ways collectivities can serve their members, Will Kymlicka's argument right from *Liberalism, Community and Culture* has been that cultural groups provide 'contexts of choice',[3] meaning contexts setting out the range of options within which individuals may live autonomously.[4] Then, he argues that to the extent that the choices of a particular group do not promote autonomy, there would be reason to interfere with it but there may be pragmatic reasons for not doing so (something to which we will return below).[5]

Kymlicka would thus be ready to see substantial interference with particular communities. For instance, in discussing the United States Supreme Court decision in *Wisconsin v Yoder*,[6] in which the Court accepted an exemption for the Amish from requirements of attendance at the public schooling system after age 14, Kymlicka seems on the verge of suggesting that there should have been greater interference on the basis that the Amish were an autonomy-limiting group.[7] He makes a somewhat surprising claim about the Amish:

> The Amish, like the Hutterites in Canada, *tried to make it difficult for their members to leave the group*, albeit in a different way. They wanted to withdraw their children from school before the age of 16, *so as to limit severely the extent to which the children learn about the outside world*.[8]

Kymlicka thus emphasises the potential autonomy-limiting effects of the Amish mode of life, with his words unfortunately verging on suggesting a malicious intent

[2] NL Rosenblum, 'Civil Societies: Liberalism and the Moral Uses of Pluralism' (1994) 61 *Social Research* 539; *cf* ch 7.I, above.

[3] W Kymlicka, *Liberalism, Community and Culture* (Oxford, Clarendon, 1989) 166.

[4] Ibid, 166–68.

[5] W Kymlicka, *Multicultural Citizenship* (Oxford, Oxford University Press, 1995) 164–70.

[6] *Wisconsin v Yoder* 406 US 205 (1972).

[7] Kymlicka, *Multicultural Citizenship* (n 5) 162–63.

[8] Ibid, 162 (emphasis added).

to the Amish. However, Kymlicka's approach to the Amish simply cannot stand, and there are powerful reasons for deference. One such reason is that in considering the claims of communities that are different, there are important reasons to seek actually to understand those communities and their aspirations without caricaturing them. Kymlicka's rapid presumption of the Amish, apparent also in his writing on certain other religious communities,[9] is that certain sorts of religious denominations must be autonomy-limiting and prevent their members from developing critical thinking skills important to autonomy.[10] Although I will not develop this point at length here, powerful arguments have emerged that members of fundamentalist religious communities develop their critical thinking in ways not acknowledged by secular political theorists, as they need to consider carefully arguments between different accounts of religious texts and to consider arguments they use in defence of their faith against critics.[11] Even were the first point not to apply, the United States Supreme Court itself, when considering the claims of the Amish in American constitutional law, reveals other moral reasons for deference to the Amish. The Amish produced evidence that they accepted the nature of the primary educational system up to age14, that they provided continuing vocational education to their children after age 14, and that they sincerely believed that attendance at secular high schools after age 14 was contrary to their way of life and religion and would endanger their salvation. Chief Justice Burger enumerated some of the ways in which American high school education was argued to be in conflict with Amish beliefs, which included high school's emphasis on intellectual attainment, competition, and worldly success, rather than on goodness, community welfare, and separation in religious community.[12] The very fact the Amish can promote different forms of human flourishing, in ways that may not be possible in a mainstream secular society is a reason for some deference to the community's claims.

Secondly, we can build further on the point implicit earlier that collectivities may have an important claim to a sort of collective autonomy.[13] The degree of collective autonomy necessary, as with several of the reasons for deference, is obviously dependent on the nature of the collectivity and collective interest involved. A hockey club's needs for collective autonomy will presumably be more limited than those vital to the meaningful cultural survival of an aboriginal community or to a religious community with doctrines distinct from those of the larger community. Where some form of autonomy will contribute to the fulfillment

[9] DG Newman, 'Liberal Multiculturalism and Will Kymlicka's Uneasy Relation with Religious Pluralism' (2003) 64 *Bijdragen* 265, 272–76.

[10] W Kymlicka, *Politics in the Vernacular: Nationalism, Multiculturalism, and Citizenship* (Oxford, Oxford University Press, 2001) 304; *cf* R Reich, 'Minors within Minorities: A Problem for Liberal Multiculturalists' in A Eisenberg and J Spinner-Halev (eds) *Minorities Within Minorities: Equality, Rights and Diversity* (Cambridge, Cambridge University Press, 2005) 224–25.

[11] See eg S Burtt, 'Comprehensive Educations and the Liberal Understanding of Autonomy' in K McDonough and W Feinberg (eds) *Education and Citizenship in Liberal-Democratic Societies: Teaching for Cosmopolitan Values and Collective Identities* (Oxford, Oxford University Press, 2003) 179, 185.

[12] *Wisconsin v Yoder* (n 6).

[13] Ch 8.III–IV, above.

of the other collective interests of a particular collectivity, there are reasons to defer to the collectivity so as not to interfere with this autonomy.

William Barbieri has argued for what could seem like a bright-line rule applicable to this reason for deference. He argues for what he calls a lexical priority of non-domination over equal rights to self-determination.[14] By this priority, Barbieri suggests what we may take to be a distinction between two elements to the autonomy of collectivities. We could take him as claiming that domination of a collectivity is always a more serious wrong than limitation of another non-dominated collectivity's ability to determine its ongoing development in more positive ways. This rule's meaning obviously depends on a fuller sketch of how we might distinguish definitively between 'non-domination' and 'self-determination' types of exercises of autonomy. Barbieri does not provide such a distinction in a full-fledged manner, other than to say that domination is a 'lived process' involving damage to a group[15] and to apply his distinction to some examples that might be illuminating. He uses his distinction to claim: (i) that a broader community's architectural aspirations, a sort of self-determination, cannot take priority over a Muslim community's opportunity to build a mosque and thus avoid non-domination; and (ii) that women's rights of non-domination must bar a particular community's exercise of self-determination in having a practice of polygamous marriages.[16] These examples, especially the latter, are of course much more complex (including in certain empirical ways we cannot even begin to explore here) than Barbieri seems to allow, which might at once lead us to question the distinction whose application to these cases he has asserted but not explained.

A different example can illustrate some of the same issues, making clear in the process that Barbieri's distinction cannot be definitive. In the context of indigenous communities that have traditionally depended on and have cultural links to the fishery, for example, the community may have a collective interest not just in fishing rights but in the management of the fishery. This fact does not mean that there is any reason to try to establish a fishery the same as in the past – as Michael Anderson aptly notes, 'The aim of full reconstruction [of tradition] is not to be taken seriously anyway, to do so would be to hypostatize history and replace a living culture with a fossilized one'.[17] But it may mean that there is a powerful claim by that community to manage the fishery. Nothing about this claim depends on whether we characterise it in Barbieri's terms as a self-determination right or a non-domination right. Its priority relative to the claims of non-indigenous economic fishers in the same area depends on the relative moral weight of the claims at stake. We can carry out the appropriate analysis based on the Community Conditions, an analysis recognising the deep-seated interests of members of this

[14] WA Barbieri, 'Group Rights and the Muslim Diaspora' (1999) 21 *Human Rights Quarterly* 907, 919.

[15] Ibid, 914.

[16] Ibid, 926.

[17] MR Anderson, 'Law and the Protection of Cultural Communities: The Case of Native American Fishing Rights' (1987) 9 *Law and Policy* 125, 139.

indigenous community in the ongoing survival of their community, something going to their very integrity as persons. Of course, matters could be different if we were considering the indigenous community's claim to management relative to another indigenous group claiming similarly deep cultural roots in the same fishery, as has arisen in some cases.[18] In such a circumstance, it would, as discussed in chapter eight, be necessary to find a compromise, or, if impossible to do so, it might be that one group ends up with a right allowing it to carry forward with its self-determination while the other faces some constraints. The moral questions are what promotes compliance with the Community Conditions while respecting the nature of the interests at stake; where the interests at stake themselves involve autonomy, there are powerful reasons for deference.

Thirdly, we can return to earlier suggestions that there are epistemic reasons for deference to collectivities' choices and actions. [19] The correct application of the Service and Mutuality Principles assumes a certain sort of objective knowledge of the relevant features of the state of the world. In real life, objective knowledge at crucial points in the analysis can be frustratingly elusive. A political community ought to have humility about its knowledge, adjusted to and tempered by the consequences of interference and deference. Where, for example, interference holds the prospect of limited gains in approximate compliance with the Service and Mutuality Principles at the risk of great loss in the event of error, this balance yields particularly powerful reasons for deference. In a number of contexts, issues have come up concerning revelation of knowledge considered sacred or secret within certain cultural or religious traditions. To take one of these, in *Foster v Mountford*,[20] Australia's Northern Territory Supreme Court was confronted with such issues when the Pitjantjara Council sought an interlocutory injunction against the publication and dissemination of anthropologist Charles Mountford's book, *Nomads of the Australian Desert*, within the Northern Territory. The case was argued in terms of legal doctrines of breach of confidence. The moral questions behind these legal doctrines included the real concern 'that the revelation of the secrets to [the Pitjantjara] women, children and uninitiated men may undermine the social and religious stability of their hard-pressed community'.[21] The Court granted the injunction, and there seems not to have been subsequent publication of Mountford's book in the area.[22]

Behind a moral claim that the Court's decision was normatively justifiable, there is of course a presumption that some reason implies that certain sacred or secret knowledge ought not to be generally disseminated; this presumption may be backed by the spiritual beliefs of a particular community typically not meeting wide agreement in the political community. There is no denying that there are

[18] See eg *Hwlitsum First Nation v Canada (Minister of Fisheries and Oceans)*, 2001 FCT 936 (with rival First Nations claiming the same fishing rights).

[19] *Cf* ch 5 V, above.

[20] *Foster v Mountford* (1976) 29 FLR 233.

[21] Ibid, 236.

[22] See discussion in MF Brown, *Who Owns Native Culture?* (Cambridge MA, Harvard University Press, 2003) 33–37.

serious arguments for the diffusion of anthropological and other scientific knowledge. But the prospect of destroying a living culture must raise powerful reasons for the political community to restrain its membership from interfering in a potentially irreversible way, even if members of the political community do not themselves believe that there is any objective reason behind the moral claims at issue; in the absence of compelling reasons otherwise, they ought to be humble about these beliefs. In this example, as in many actual contexts of deference, there are of course arguably overlapping reasons for deference. There would be a cultural autonomy argument for deference. Insofar as humility about what we know must commend caution in taking action that interferes with a culture that has lived and thrived, there is also an epistemic reason for deference.

Fourthly, introducing an even more pragmatic argument, we can raise the effectiveness of interference. Even Kymlicka has accepted the possibility of this reason as a basis not to interfere in specific instances.[23] If interference with a collectivity will not be effective in attaining the aim of the interference, then the aim provides no rationale for the interference. As Jeff Spinner-Halev puts it more directly: 'Attempts to reform (formerly) oppressed groups may very well backfire.'[24]

A much-discussed example on this point is the *Shah Bono* case concerning application of family law to Muslims in India.[25] The Indian Supreme Court ruled that duties existed beyond those provided by traditional interpretations of Muslim family law, both on the basis of other laws and, going farther, on the Indian Supreme Court's interpretation of the Qu'ran. This latter aspect of the decision in particular created such a backlash in traditionalist elements of the Muslim community that the cause of Muslim reformers was set back, now being perceived as a cultural threat in cahoots with the interfering threat seen as being posed to Muslim culture by the Indian Supreme Court.

The case has given rise to a literature beyond what I could conceivably survey here. But we can note two concerns. First, the Court's decision is particularly intrusive because it purports to interpret a religious text. Second, with or without that element, interference with an autonomous system of Islamic law by outsiders to that system has the potential to cause counterproductive effects. Reform may well be more successful if it proceeds from internal debate and choices amongst members of a community itself, and this point will give a reason for deference to some choices of a collectivity.[26]

Of course, admitting such a reason for deference may seem to justify ongoing burdens on traditionally disadvantaged 'minorities within minorities', with particular individuals or groups within a collectivity facing ongoing infringements on their interests simply for the sake of so-called pragmatic reasons for not interfering. This reason for deference is not the only one raising this concern, as it could equally express the broader concern with deferring to the purported

[23] Kymlicka, *Multicultural Citizenship* (n 5) 164–70.
[24] J Spinner-Halev, 'Feminism, Multiculturalism, Oppression, and the State' (2001) 112 *Ethics* 84, 95.
[25] *Mohd Ahmed Khan v Shah Bono Begum* AIR 1985 SC 945.
[26] Spinner-Halev (n 24) 99–102, 110.

interests of real-world collectivities. There seems always a danger that the burdens of deference fall more harshly on some than on others. In a report on religious arbitration in Ontario in the context of Shari'a-based arbitration, Marion Boyd described what some saw as a problem of individuals 'bearing the burden of the protection of the culture . . . [and being] sacrificed for the sake of group survival'.[27] However, there can be real dangers in interference. After Boyd's report, which had recommended space for religious arbitration with certain safeguards for individuals, Ontario's legislature chose instead to ban all religiously-based family law arbitration.[28] The effect has been that such arbitration continues but is now outside any state scrutiny.[29]

We saw in earlier chapters arguments that collective interests may warrant protection and have the status of rights even though the fulfillment of collective interests has differential effects on different members. This argument does not cease to apply even when we institutionalise collective rights, unless something about the non-ideal world we now confront makes such differential effects more problematic. In accepting the epistemic limits of the political community concerning collective interests, we must realise that there may be epistemic limits concerning the situation of individual members within. This point can weigh in favour of deference, insofar as we properly avoid interfering with collectivities when we will not improve matters and when we do not know that we will improve matters. On the other hand, it may weigh in favour of interference on behalf of individual members at risk; in this third section, we will face up further to these tensions. For the moment, however, we can note that the reasons for deference do remain powerful and compelling in general terms and will be so in many circumstances. But they are certainly not all-determinative.

Indeed, there is an internal relation (of the sort discussed in chapter four in the context of conflicts of rights) between these reasons for deference and reasons to interfere. Both reasons for deference and reasons for interference are ultimately grounded in the humanistic principle with which we began, and we must abide ultimately by its implications. It can also present powerful reasons for interference. I will not restate here the reasons for interference that emerge from the two fundamental principles elaborated in Part II, the Service Principle and the Mutuality Principle. In pinpointing these principled reasons for interference, I again do not set out an exhaustive list of reasons for interference. However, the principles to be discussed are those particularly important in relation to collectivities.

First, interference may be an important means of preventing violations of the Service Principle. There remains no reason to defer to and every reason to interfere with a cult that wishes to carry out human sacrifice on its brainwashed members. And there can be clear conclusions even on real examples. For example, we might consider issues related to the breakaway sect in Bountiful, British

[27] M Boyd, *Dispute Resolution in Family Law: Protecting Choice, Promoting Inclusion* (Toronto, Ontario Ministry of the Attorney General, 2004) 92.

[28] Family Statute Law Amendment Act, 2006 SO 2006 c 1 (Canada).

[29] Harvey Simmons put this claim in various newspaper commentaries in September 2010.

Columbia formed by men excommunicated from the Mormon Church.[30] This sect implements a practice of polygamous marriage. In 1992, provincial government authorities contemplated prosecuting two men from the community under Canadian anti-bigamy legislation but eventually decided not to do so because of suggestions that this law was unconstitutional as contrary to religious freedom. Others have since challenged that conclusion, and indeed it has now gone back to the courts. There is no doubt generally that polygamy raises complex issues and not ones we will resolve in some simple way here. Some writing on the Bountiful community specifically, such as that of Angela Campbell, discusses it as an eminent example of how complex and misunderstood significantly different communities can be.[31] There would have been a clearer conclusion for the authorities on how to proceed had certain initially-raised allegations of not just polygamy but trafficking and sexual abuse of young girls, stood up. The violation of human integrity in such acts would clearly be sufficient to call for serious interference with a community and any members perpetrating such abuses.

Dramatic violations of the Service Principle can make out a clear case for interference. But more complex cases also arise, in which any case for interference is more nuanced. Those who feel troubled by various collectivities' claims for greater control of family law, particularly by claims for control of adoption procedures, are rightly on guard for the interests of young children. However, whether there should be interference by any political community having power over the collectivity with its decisions on adoption is a more complex question – more complex than admitted by those who reach simply for stock phrases about the 'best interests of the child' being of sole relevance.[32] In the context of Canadian aboriginal communities, there have been suggestions that the communities might reasonably be recognised as having powers to implement adoption procedures which would serve the interests of children, and not only the interests of children analysed in a culturally sensitive manner, but also the aims of cultural preservation.[33] Although self-government agreements in Canada seem ambivalent on this point,[34] the American Indian Child Welfare Act already implements such a policy, granting jurisdiction over the placement of Indian children in many circumstances to tribal courts, with the legislation's dual purposes being to promote 'the best interests of Indian children' and 'the stability and security of Indian tribes and

[30] The case has been described in various contexts. See eg 'Hunting Bountiful' *The Economist* 8 July 2004; 'Wives galore: Just part of being free?' *The Economist* 22 January 2009.

[31] See eg A Campbell, 'Bountiful Voices' (2009) 47 *Osgoode Hall Law Journal* 183.

[32] On the complexity of the best interests of the child consideration in this context, see eg M Kline, 'Child Welfare Law, "Best Interests of the Child" Ideology, and First Nations' (1992) 30 *Osgoode Hall Law Journal* 375. See also R Snow and K Covell, 'Adoption and the Best Interests of the Child: The Dilemma of Cultural Interpretations' (2006) 14 *International Journal of Children's Rights* 109.

[33] D Russell, *A People's Dream: Aboriginal Self-Government in Canada* (Vancouver, University of British Columbia Press, 2000) 53.

[34] The recent Tlicho Self-Government Agreement provides for a power in the Tlicho government to make laws concerning 'child and family services for Tlicho Citizens on Tlicho lands or in a Tlicho community, provided that such laws provide for standards, including standards for the application of the principle of acting in the best interests of the child' (Tlicho Agreement (25 August 2003) art 7.4.4).

families'.[35] Thus, in a case in which an Indian mother deliberately gave birth off-reserve and sought to give her child up for adoption off-reserve, thinking the child would have greater opportunities in life without an Indian heritage, the United States Supreme Court upheld the jurisdiction of the tribal court to decide on the appropriate adoption based on the legislation.[36] The case has evoked controversy, not for its legal decision on what the technical issue of domicile (which determined jurisdiction under the legislation), but for the moral issues and for concerns by some that it undermines child welfare and women's liberation.[37]

The interesting moral question concerns the instance where a child would, hypothetically, be individually better off by being stripped from his or her cultural heritage group, but where the ongoing effects of such policies work against the survival of the cultural community.[38] The morally acceptable adoption policy in such circumstances will actually depend on matters of degree. I have earlier made out a moral case for the value of cultural survival,[39] so there is no reason to think that allegations of negative effects on the interests of children are an all-determinative reason. In other contexts, nobody thinks that a wealthier individual automatically has a right to adopt a child simply in virtue of claiming to offer greater life opportunities – there is no such sale of children to the highest bidder. So, there may be very good moral reasons for an adoption policy having goals that include cultural flourishing.

That said, were some community to act in violation of the Requirement of Sufficient Regard (which procedurally enacts the Service Principle) or otherwise clearly in violation of the Service Principle, there could rightly be interference. For instance, if a community, counterfactually, were genuinely insensitive to the interests of children and put them knowingly for adoption in families where they suffered abuses (actions deliberately directed against the interests of the children, as compared to those with some limited negative effects on the interests of the children), there would be reason for any political community with the power to do so to interfere with this violation of the Service Principle and protect the interests of our most vulnerable individuals.

The Service Principle can establish reasons for interference in complex cases, though they need to be considered with all the wisdom we can muster. Indeed, we must be wary of any assumptions as to what kind of 'interference' is appropriate; in the sort of case we are discussing, powerful arguments also suggest that the real problem in some aboriginal communities has been that they struggle to deal with holistic dimensions of child welfare because they have *too few* powers over, for

[35] Indian Child Welfare Act 25 USC §1902. Even when the tribal court does not have jurisdiction, any placement under state law must give preference to extended family, the tribe and other Indian families: §1915.

[36] *Mississippi Choctaw Band of Indians v Holyfield* 109 S Ct 1597 (1989).

[37] See discussion in DJ Goldsmith, 'Individual vs Collective Rights: The Indian Child Welfare Act' (1990) 13 *Harvard Women's Law Journal* 1.

[38] Ibid.

[39] Ch 5.V, above.

instance, economic development matters.[40] The appropriate response to tensions with the Service Principle will, in some circumstances, actually be to give a collectivity more powers, but in a coherent set such that they are able to achieve approximate compliance. Difficult policy questions obviously remain, but the Service Principle can, in any, case help to provide an analytical framework on our approach to these questions.

Second, reasons for interference can also arise from the Mutuality Principle. Again, dramatic violations of the Mutuality Principle can ground clear action. When the Ku Klux Klan or some terrorist organisation seeks to engage in violence or to act in other ways not in conformity with the Mutuality Principle, there is no reason to defer to it and every reason to interfere with it. And, again, different sorts of cases can give rise to more complex challenges. When a linguistic-cultural community, such as the Québecois, legislates to protect its language and culture from being submerged, questions could arise about its compliance with the Mutuality Principle if the terms of the legislation, in the particular circumstances that existed, interfered with the viability of other cultural, linguistic, or religious groups.[41] The larger political community of which Quebec is a part would then have a reason to interfere, to be considered carefully along with important ongoing reasons to defer. Again, difficult policy questions would remain, but the Mutuality Principle would provide a tool for analysing the appropriate interactions between collectivities and structure our analysis of challenging questions.

It is not a weakness but a strength of this book's account that it admits tough questions. Accounts that provide simple distinctions and dichotomies fail to account for the tortuous moral dialogues in which real individuals and societies are immersed regarding how to accommodate diversity, other than through the implicit suggestion that everyone else has failed to grasp the simplistic nature of reality identified by the theorist. Issues around appropriate interaction with collectivities are difficult ones, and one should not hesitate to make the courageous admission that they will remain difficult, even if the account at hand sheds significant light.

Indeed, a further attractive feature of this account is that it allows for the possibility that different political communities might act rightly while pursuing very different paths of development. We discussed in chapter seven the possibility of epistemic differences between different political communities grounding legitimate differences in responses to the practices of subcommunities within,[42] and we could generalise that point. Even without epistemic issues, we could add that the nature of our account obviously makes room for significant differences in decisions in different contexts. And, finally, though the argument of chapter three made clear that theoretical conclusions about incommensurability do not affect

[40] See eg F MacDonald, 'The Manitoba Government's Shift to "Autonomous" First Nations Child Welfare: Empowerment or Privatization?' in AM Timpson, *First Nations, First Thoughts: The Impact of Indigenous Thought in Canada* (Vancouver, University of British Columbia Press, 2009).

[41] *Cf* ch 6.V above.

[42] *Cf* ch 7.IV, above.

the force of the argument for our account of collective rights, we can add that if incommensurabilities of values exist, they open room for communities to make different value-based choices about complex issues of what violations of the Service and Mutuality Principles are more or less serious and about when interference and deference are preferable. This point is no embrace of a general relativism, and there will be limits on what could be tolerated even under such a possibility (arguably, there could never be deference to certain practices, such as human sacrifice), but any possible plurality of incommensurable values would make clear yet another way in which the account could endorse a variety of societal approaches.

We must respectfully reject accounts that would, at this stage, seek to implement any simplistic recipe on how to adjudicate between reasons for deference and reasons for interference. We have seen repeatedly reasons to reject Kymlicka's attempt to distinguish simply between internal restrictions and external protections, and we need not repeat those again.[43] We saw in chapter five reasons not to adopt, whatever the temptations, any simplistic rule that individual interests always take priority over collective interests.[44] There cannot be a simplistic adjudication between interference and deference, although, at the same time, there must be a principled consideration of reasons for each possible course of action.

The tensions cannot simply be set aside. The political community is unlike all other collectivities precisely because it holds power. Indeed, in a context where the political community has power to develop legally authoritative coordination, it frames the very terms of existence of civil society organisations.[45] It has the power to affect significantly the human lives it is bound to serve and cannot avoid making difficult choices between deference and interference with the subcommunities within. Moreover, given the existence of collective moral rights, as established in chapter three, there is an all-pervasive issue of how to respect these rights. There is no dodging the challenging questions of appropriate interactions with collectivities. And we have one more question to address, which will, in the process, reveal an often-preferable means of reconciling these tensions. Let us turn to whose voices we recognise as delineating the collective interests at stake.

III. PRINCIPLED CONTESTATION

1. Introduction

In this section, we will identify an important mode of engagement with the tensions arising from competing reasons for interference and non-interference. The mode of engagement by the political community that we will argue is often an

[43] *Cf* eg ch 1.III, above.

[44] Ch 5.II, above.

[45] *Cf* M Walzer, *Spheres of Justice: A Defense of Pluralism and Equality* (New York, Basic Books, 1983) 78–79.

appropriate policy is actually one involving support for the ability of individuals to contest collective interests through what we will call *principled contestation.* This policy can thus entail a less interventionist role for the political community itself, thus fitting with many of the reasons for deference. At the same time, we will see that principled contestation has the possibility of making a real difference to the actions of many collectivities in encouraging them to comply with the Service and Mutuality Principles in at least an approximate way, thus often fitting with the reasons for interference.

The concept of principled contestation, however, will develop out of one final critique that might be levelled against the analysis. The objection is often made that intra-group differences on group interests undermine arguments for group representation or group rights. The argument thus begins by clarifying this objection and showing how it elides an important distinction between what we have called 'dissenters' and what we can call 'contesters'. The failure of the objection to attend to this distinction robs it of much of its force, at least as against the present argument. Attending to the distinction reveals that earlier chapters have already addressed the dissent issue and lays the groundwork for principled contestation as a means of engagement with collectivities.

2. Responding to the Intra-Group Difference Objection

The objection at issue can take different forms. As put at one point by Phillips, it sometimes focuses on ambiguities in groups' preferences: 'It is hard to see what counts as "representing" a group, for there are few mechanisms for establishing what each group wants.'[46] However, this first expression of the claim is not a propos this book's argument. The argument concerns interests rather than preferences, with interests sufficient to ground duties not inherently dependent on the holding of any particular preferences, unambiguous or otherwise. As put elsewhere by Phillips, Young, and others, however, the objection focuses on claims that theories of group representation risk wrongly assuming a unified group interest, thereby mistakenly essentialising group identity[47] and freezing group development.[48] Questioning group interests leads to questioning group representation: 'If there is no clearly agreed woman's interest, can this really figure as a basis for more women in politics?'[49] For Iris Marion Young, such objections are so serious that she argues that representation of groups ought to represent not interests but perspectives.[50]

[46] A Phillips, *Democracy and Difference* (Cambridge, Polity Press, 1993) 97. *Cf* A Phillips *The Politics of Presence: Issues in Democracy and Group Representation* (Oxford, Clarendon, 1995) 55.

[47] See eg Phillips, *Politics of Presence* (ibid) 104; Phillips, *Democracy and Difference* (ibid) 99–101. *Cf* IM Young, *Justice and the Politics of Difference* (Princeton, Princeton University Press, 1990) 47; IM Young, *Inclusion and Democracy* (Oxford, Oxford University Press, 2000) 88; M Williams, *Voice, Trust, and Memory: Marginalized Groups and the Failings of Liberal Representation* (Princeton, Princeton University Press, 1998) 6.

[48] See eg Phillips *Politics of Presence* (n 46) 114; Phillips *Democracy and Difference* (n 46) 99–101; C Mouffe, 'Feminism, Citizenship, and Politics' in *The Return of the Political* (London, Verso, 1993).

[49] Phillips, *Politics of Presence* (n 46) 68.

[50] See ch 4 of Young, *Inclusion and Democracy* (n 47).

Various forms of the objection may run together in the same theorist. In writing against collective rights generally, Yael Tamir puts the following claims with an apparent intention that they be synonymous: (1) 'It is in these moments of transition that we ought to decide whether to side with the community or with its individual members (especially with those who wish to dissent from the traditional way of life)'; and (2) '[I]n periods of social and cultural transition, when collective rights are most needed to protect a community from external pressures, they pose a threat to social reformers'.[51] Tamir does not make clear here whether her concern is with the opportunity of individual members to dissent from community practices and engage in different individual practices, or with the opportunity of individual reformers to change group practices. And these two concerns are very different.

A *dissenter* is a member of a collectivity whose individual interests differ from the collective interest, either *subjectively* (that is, from the dominant account of the collective interest) or *objectively* (that is, from a necessary account of the collective interest).[52] A *contester*, by contrast, is an individual who argues for a different account of what is in the collective interest than that based on which the collectivity currently acts. It is possible for a contester to be a non-member, and we will see later that this possibility is important for contestation in relation to the Mutuality Principle, but it will, of course, more commonly be the case that contesters will be members.

The distinction, of course, may seem more complicated. The same individual, first, might be both a dissenter and a contester. For example, a religious reformer seeking to change accounts of a religious group's collective interests might simultaneously be a member of a subgroup within the religion disadvantaged by the dominant account of the group's collective interests. Indeed, perhaps she is a reformer partly based on her experience of disadvantage; her experience of subjective dissent might have led her to become a contester, now arguing that better account of the collective interest need not leave so many members in dissenting positions. Or perhaps, even if she was never a dissenter before, she has become a dissenter in virtue of being a contester; if the collectivity represses contestation based on (perceived) harms to its collective interests from the presence of contestation, its actions may impose disadvantages on contesters, thereby rendering them into objective or subjective dissenters. There can thus be interactions between dissent and contestation.

Nonetheless, there remains a principled difference between the two concepts. Dissent concerns the relation of a particular individual (or set of individuals) to the collectivity; contestation concerns the account of the collective interest. We can put the objections at their strongest by accepting that both dissent and contestation are endemic, thereby escaping any claim that we have made a wrongful 'essentialist' assumption. However, the distinction enables a response to the objections.

[51] Y Tamir, 'Against Collective Rights' in C Joppke and S Lukes (eds) *Multicultural Questions* (Oxford, Oxford University Press, 1999) 184, 188.

[52] A 'dissenter', for these purposes, can be a silent dissenter.

First, we have already dealt with the argument that dissent is endemic. Individuals in groups differ and have differing interests, so some will not have individual interests in accord with particular collective interests. However, for the reasons elaborated in chapters two and five, this reality does not undermine the existence of, or moral importance of, collective interests.[53]

Secondly, the presence of contestation says only that some believe different accounts of particular collective interests and does not undermine the existence of collective moral rights. Importantly, the argument for the existence of collective rights, and the subsequent analysis of principles flowing from this justification, was not based on perceptions of collective interests but on objectively existing collective interests. We can perhaps recognise this point more clearly by noting how Young's definition of 'interests' diverges from this approach. Young defines 'interests' as 'what affects or is important to the life prospects of individuals, or the goals of organizations'.[54] In other words, she writes asymmetrically of individuals and of groups, granting that the former may have interests in the sense of things that make their lives go better and implicitly denying the same proposition for groups by referring only to the 'goals of organizations'. Yet, as argued in chapter three, some objects can make the life of a collectivity go better, can make it flourish, and it is these objects that are properly recognised as collective interests. Such collective interests can ground rights on the basis argued in chapter three. It is, then, strictly speaking, irrelevant that there is debate about what these collective interests are.

Of course, the objection arguably does pose challenges to the procedural expression of collective interests. Although dissent in the absence of contestation would leave a collective interest unambiguous, one might wonder if the presence of contestation does not create inherent ambiguities around collective interests, thereby robbing their expression of accuracy and usefulness, and undermining our practical ability to respect collective rights. Attending to the dissenter/contester distinction thus clarifies the real issue, revealing that it is whether the representation of collective rights as discussed earlier can be accurate and useful when there is contestation around collective interests. Indeed, to her credit, Ayelet Shachar asks the right question: '[W]hich voices from within an identity group should be recognized by the state as representative of the "integrity of a group's culture"?'[55] Martha Nussbaum would give an answer warning of grave dangers in the entire endeavour to respect collectivities, stating that 'what gets to parade as "the traditions" of "the group" is typically a matter of power, and to the extent that homogeneity prevails, it is likely to result from the success of power in putting down dissenters'.[56] In realising that this is the real question, we have laid the

[53] Ch 2.IV, above; ch 5.VI, above.

[54] IM Young, 'Deferring Group Representation' in I Shapiro and W Kymlicka, *Ethnicity and Group Rights: Nomos 39* (New York, New York University Press, 1997) 363.

[55] A Shachar, *Multicultural Jurisdictions: Cultural Differences and Women's Rights* (Cambridge, Cambridge University Press, 2001) 38.

[56] M Nussbaum, 'The Complexity of Groups' (2003) 29 *Philosophy and Social Criticism* 57, 61.

foundations for the next subsection, in which we can seek a less dangerous answer, one in which the Community Conditions govern contestation, thereby maintaining the accuracy and usefulness of representation on collective rights and establishing a basis for ongoing consideration of collective rights in legal and political decision-making.

3. Principled Contestation

If we had only a variety of assertions about collective interests and no cogent means of distinguishing accurate from inaccurate accounts, representation of collective rights would be in a troubled position. We will sometimes be able simply to identify what amount to collective interests in terms of the earlier account; however, what collective interests are often depends on matters on which knowledge is uncertain or highly internal to collectivities, so we may be in a position of seeing only contesting accounts. However, if moral principles guide us to at least some degree in distinguishing between accurate and inaccurate accounts of collective interests, then contestation means only that there is conflict in life and does not undermine representation of collective interests. In this section, we will see that the Community Conditions provide the necessary guidance, at least enabling distinctions between accurate and inaccurate accounts of collective interests. We cannot, of course, claim that the Community Conditions will immediately provide clear answers, but we can see that they provide guidance for analysis of contesting accounts.

We will see first that the Service Principle of chapter five and Mutuality Principle of chapter six provide fundamental guidance for the identification of collective interests but that they do not necessarily identify unique sets of collective interests. We will reach no conclusion that we can always adjudicate between contesting accounts, but we will see that these principles can set much of the framework. Other factors may also be relevant in cases of underdetermination, and we will refer specifically to when *authenticity* – fit with the traditions and past accounts within the collectivity – is and is not helpful. We will conclude that there exist principled bases for contestation and for sometimes adjudicating between contesting accounts.

First, an account of a collective interest is subject to a fundamental test. As discussed in chapter five, a collectivity not complying with the Service Principle, not serving its individual members in a broad sense, cannot claim collective rights. As between different accounts of a collectivity's set of collective interests, one that leads to non-compliance with the Service Principle is thus to be avoided and one promoting compliance with the Service Principle to be preferred. The same may be said of chapter six's Mutuality Principle, with compliance with the principle again marking an account as more defensible. In both cases, chapter eight's approximation principle makes clear that the principles do not resolve every question with a bright-line test, but they offer significant guidance, with fuller compliance with the principles marking out not only better moral action by collectivities but better accounts of their own collective interests.

The determination that the Community Conditions can guide contestation leads immediately to some important conclusions of great help in particular contestations. Consider for a moment contestation within some cultural/religious group on the issue of clitoridectomy.[57] Let us suppose that a faction we will call the traditionalists maintains that the practice of clitoridectomy is a collective interest of this group because it promotes the preservation and ongoing flourishing of their culture, thereby serving members of the cultural group. A faction we might call the reformists offers an alternative account of the collective interest, claiming that the collective interest is actually in a reformed tradition. The reformists argue that cultural tradition can be maintained while causing less harm to female members of the culture by developing a modified, essentially symbolic form of female circumcision where the physical harm to women becomes trivial.

To allay any doubts about the realism of this example, note that such a modified form of female circumcision was actually developed as a compromise between a group of medical practitioners and the Somali immigrant community in Seattle; the symbolic circumcision there became simply a small incision with no lasting physical effects.[58] That compromise was undone when feminist critics later characterised it as a concession to patriarchy and an authorised subordination of women on American soil.[59] Were the policy one of committing one evil to prevent another, to put it in the terms on which some would defend it,[60] these criticisms would have more weight. However, we will here see the grounding in justice for the reformist position.[61] As between the two contesting accounts of the collective interest, the reformist account has powerful support in the Service Principle.

Indeed, the reformist account of the collective interest maintains the culture while minimising harm to members, thereby marking a clear improvement in terms of the Service Principle. Some might respond that it does not remove all of the gendered power dynamics giving rise to clitoridectomy in the first place. If such a criticism were right, it might call for us to offer a different example making the same point, such as one involving what we might call the 'abolitionist faction' calling for an end to even symbolic circumcision.

However there are reasons to think that a shift to a merely symbolic operation removes many of the power dynamics with which such critics would be concerned; the reformist account ends physical harm to women and simultaneously removes from the culture a requirement that women's bodies be physically modified in a

[57] The issue is in fact contested, including on issues around any religious basis in Islam for the practice (DL Coleman, 'The Seattle Compromise: Multicultural Sensitivity and Americanization' (1998) 47 *Duke Law Journal* 717, 731–33), further making the earlier point that the rich cultural and religious traditions of the world are open to a variety of competing accounts.

[58] Ibid.

[59] Ibid, 738, 783.

[60] Ibid, 768–69.

[61] *Cf* J Carens, *Culture, Citizenship, and Community: A Contextual Exploration of Justice as Evenhandedness* (Oxford, Oxford University Press, 2000) 150–51.

manner fitting with men's patriarchal demands. There is no longer a male power to change women's bodies. That said, a symbolic operation may continue to preserve some power in the elders and in the tradition, giving some possible arguments for the abolitionist position.

So, the reformist account has powerful support in the Service Principle. In other words, the account here empowers the reformists to engage in principled contestation of the collective interest and gives reasons for the reformist account. Of course, one difficulty might be that the Service Principle does not seem to identify a reason to choose the reformist account over the abolitionist account. But we obviously cannot ask the Service and Mutuality Principles to determine everything about collective action; there remains underdeterminacy and space for cultural (or, more generally, collective) development. The point remains that these principles can engage with accounts of collective interests in a manner enabling the political community to respond appropriately to collectivities and enabling members to engage in principled contestation.

This example, of course, presents a fortunate case in which one option better addresses the interests of some and is less preferable for none. Although we cannot question that such cases arise, since precisely this debate occurred in Seattle, an objector might argue that they arise in limited circumstances and that the account does little to resolve more complex problems. However, we should note that the objection itself implicitly pertains to simplistic cases, without richness of interpretive possibilities. In sophisticated cultural traditions, for example, it is often possible to reinterpret traditions without endangering cultural or other collective identity.[62] Realising this, we open ourselves to the morally compelling possibility of empowering members to transform their membership conditions,[63] which may in turn enable escapes from zero-sum conflicts. We should not begin by assuming that possible accounts of traditions are irrelevant and without possible scenarios achieving more for all. Where there are zero-sum conflicts, their resolution may again be underdetermined by the Community Conditions. Nonetheless, our analysis of the issues in terms of the Community Conditions has yielded progress by narrowing the potential range of plausible accounts of the collective interest and by providing guidance on the ways in which contestation may proceed.

Outsiders responding to claims of collective rights from those claiming to represent a cultural community also gain guidance from my account. Representations on behalf of a traditionalist account on this issue, claiming some exemption from laws that would otherwise prevent the practice of clitoridectomy in non-symbolic form can rightly be contemplated with great scepticism, since this account of the collective interest fails to meet the Service Principle as fully as a plausible alternative account. Outsiders may struggle more on representations on behalf of a reformist or abolitionist account. Which provides an accurate account of the actual collective interest is a matter of contestation within the community and is certainly no easier for outsiders to resolve.

62 *Cf* Shachar, *Multicultural Jurisdictions* (n 55) 40.
63 *Cf* ibid, 150.

Our discussion of deference has revealed reasons for outsiders to defer to an internal account of a collective interest that can be advanced reasonably in terms of the Service Principle. Insiders have advantages in the closer understandings they will have of the actual significance of practices to the survival of culture and so forth. But there is no reason to defer to a manifestly unreasonable internal account, such as a traditionalist account on the clitoridectomy issue arguably would be, given the presence of an alternative clearly better justified on the Service Principle. As stated in chapter eight, there is also no reason to defer to an account that would violate the Mutuality Principle, since insiders have no inherent advantage in evaluating their impacts on other collectivities of which they are themselves outsiders.[64]

The Mutuality Principle, too, can guide accounts of morally legitimate collective interests that can warrant respect. As discussed in chapter six, an asserted collective interest in secession is subject to moral analysis and attains moral legitimacy only when it complies with the Mutuality Principle. The same will be true of other issues evoking the Mutuality Principle. The Mutuality Principle, too, can affect our respect for asserted accounts of collective interests.

Contestations are thus subject to adjudication based on theoretical weakness in particular accounts, notably where there are manifest departures from the Service Principle or departures from the Mutuality Principle. Those examining contestations might appropriately look to other aspects of the Community Conditions. One example would be a conclusion that widespread internal dissent within a collectivity parallel to the contestation might also lead to a questioning of an account of the collective interest against this dissent. If leaders who advance a widely rejected account cannot give a reasonable account that explains why they are in a better position to evaluate the interests of the dissenting individuals,[65] then the presence of this dissent must raise questions about the account.

We must note a remaining challenge, that of underdeterminacy of the principles and the wide range of possible accounts presumably permitted. We say 'presumably' because we must also imagine the complex problem of compliance with the Mutuality Principle by the wide range of collectivities within a political community, and the achievement of harmony amongst these collectivities might conceivably impose some limits beyond those immediately ascertainable. However, assuming that there remains still a range of accounts, the possibility exists of collectivities having wide scope to define themselves – arguably not a problem but part of the very sort of flourishing of many forms of which we have spoken.

We can, however, note that there will sometimes be other moral factors that come into play. One particular issue will concern the place of tradition and *authenticity* to tradition and past accounts within a collectivity of its collective interests. I have argued in this book against any endorsement of tradition for tradition's sake and have maintained that collectivities must not be frozen but free

[64] Chapter 8.II, above.
[65] *Cf* ch 7.III, above.

to evolve, grow, and flourish in new ways.[66] However, there will sometimes be circumstances in which authenticity has a role to play. If individual members' choices as to membership have been structured around certain expectations, there may be something morally illegitimate in uprooting those expectations in a rapid, disruptive manner.

If, for instance, in a campaign for the leadership of a left-wing political party, a right-wing candidate (so right-wing as not properly to fit within the spectrum of the party) joins the party and drafts new members so as to have sufficient numbers to take control, we would properly describe the result not as a change but as a hijacking. Where expectations of members have moral force, and appropriately so as against other considerations as in chapter seven, there might then be morally legitimate use of membership control to prevent such a result. We might then speak of authenticity as helping us to determine the appropriate account of a collective interest.

Thus, we have concluded that contestation of collective interests can be analysed with the Community Conditions. This conclusion, all complexities aside, supports a claim that there are identifiable collective interests. The Community Conditions can contribute to principled contestation and can sometimes enable definitive adjudications between rival accounts. Where they do not, then other factors may enter. There are also complex analyses to be undertaken on a contextual basis of reasons for deference and reasons for interference. But we have a framework for principled contestation of collective interests.

4. Platforms for Contestation

If the political community could empower and draw on principled contestation of collective interests without undue interference in collectivities, we can see that it would often find a reconciliation of reasons for deference and reasons for interference. In circumstances where principled contestation can work to facilitate reforms internally, the rationales behind reasons for interference can be met while also complying with the reasons for deference. Such circumstances will not always exist; there will be circumstances where internal principled contestation will simply never be effective, and there are circumstances where empowering principled contestation will itself be too much of an interference. But we give collectivities too little credit if we assume that doing so is always problematic and never effective. Empowering principled contestation is a viable means of reconciliation in many circumstances, and we can now contemplate how to establish what we can call 'platforms for contestation'.[67]

[66] *Cf* ch 5.V, above.

[67] Although she does not offer the same extensive analysis to support the practice, the term is Oonagh Reitman's: O Reitman, 'Multiculturalism and Feminism: Incompatibility, Compatibility, or Synonymity?' (2005) 5 *Ethnicities* 216.

In advocating such a policy as often viable, we implicitly limit the application of Ayelet Shachar's widely-discussed model of what she calls 'transformative accommodation'.[68] As we discussed in chapter seven, Shachar's preferred approach to addressing issues makes use of a division of jurisdictional powers as between the state and groups to attempt to give patriarchal groups incentives to transform themselves so as to be more respectful of individuals' citizenship rights.[69] Several problems arise with Shachar's seemingly appealing approach. First, as Reitman has noted, the approach privileges those most able and ready to invoke the threat of exit and thus those least attached to the group, thereby simply relocating the problem. [70] Secondly, the approach depends on the use of exit, something which Shachar herself has critiqued as forcing people into a choice of 'your culture or your rights'.[71] Thirdly, Shachar's approach involves a significant interference with the groups in question, which may have complex cultural patterns related to something like the distribution of assets. Interference on this issue might be warranted, but it needs to meet a full analysis of reasons for deference.

Moreover, Shachar's approach also assumes that threats of exit will be an effective means of promoting reforms. It is far from clear that this claim is true, and it is certainly a contingent one. As Reitman has also noted, the threat of exit may be least effective against the very sorts of groups with which Shachar purports to be most concerned.[72] Certain conservative religious denominations may respond to the individual who threatens to exit by encouraging him or her to either set aside the apparent apostasy or to leave so as not to further contaminate other members, achieving precisely the opposite effect to what Shachar seeks, and reinforcing divisions. It is a contingent matter whether facilitating threats of exit is an appropriate strategy to empower individuals to contest accounts of collective interests. It may often be better to empower them to act within existing interpretive communities. Shachar's proposal seems tragically amiss in execution in many relevant circumstances, but it also has something right in spirit in its orientation to enabling internal reforms, something that overcomes many of the reasons for deference while finding a way to improve compliance with the Service and Mutuality Principles.

We are better to admit that there may be a range of policies that might establish platforms of contestation from which individuals may seek to transform communities needing to improve their compliance with the Service and Mutuality Principles. In some circumstances, establishing realistic exit rights might be a way of doing so. However, there are many contingencies around exit rights. We must contemplate a fuller range of possible policies, any one of which must be carefully tailored to the relevant circumstances, taking into account all of the principles we have elaborated. In some circumstances, there might be nothing wrong with implementing initiatives that could be seen as having liberalising effects, such as

[68] See ch 6 of Shachar, *Multicultural Jurisdictions* (n 55).
[69] Ibid, 140. *Cf* ch 7.II, above.
[70] O Reitman, 'On Exit' in Eisenberg and Spinner-Halev (n 9) 189–90.
[71] Shachar, *Multicultural Jurisdictions* (n 55) 41.
[72] Reitman 'On Exit' (n 70) 201–204.

by providing education to disadvantaged group members – although such a policy must be considered carefully for the full range of effects it has on a particular collectivity, and may not be the ideal policy in other circumstances. In some circumstances, it may be appropriate to implement independent advice requirements on certain legal steps individuals might take; for example, Marion Boyd has defended requirements of independent legal advice before Muslims in Ontario may engage in private arbitration based on Shar'ia law.[73] In some circumstances, it might be appropriate to develop regulatory frameworks that facilitate the establishment of bodies within civil society organisations that make the case for different accounts of collective interests.[74] In each case, the appropriate steps must be subject to careful analysis for their compliance with the reasons for deference and reasons for interference, but some such steps will often be possible reconciliations of these reasons.

In contexts where the Mutuality Principle is at stake, there may be less interventionist ways of promoting compliance with the Mutuality Principle, such as through encouraging intercultural or interfaith dialogue directly between cultural or religious groups. They may be able to strike reconciliations that the political community could not impose. Indeed, where particular powers are being granted to subcommunities within the political community, there will often be arguments for some form of consociational structure within which different subcommunities must reconcile their disputes.

Because authenticity can be a guide in cases of underdetermination, approaches permitting collectivities themselves to engage in principled contestation may well be able to reconcile the tensions we saw in the last subsection with less difficulty than any other means. If so, empowering principled contestation through the establishment of platforms for contestation may present a range of viable, solidly justified policies. Where circumstances do not permit such an approach, however, the political community must face up directly to the reasons for deference and reasons for interference and make difficult choices, any one of which will involve the loss of something valuable. We cannot pretend here to give easy answers and recipes for the complex task of governance subject to many contingencies,[75] but we can offer principles that offer moral guidance. In this book, I have presented an argument that clarifies what is at stake and morally acceptable ways of approaching it, thereby both recognising the complexity of the world and declining a simple surrender to pragmatism. At the same time, fields of study related to political institutions, group behaviour and so on would serve as necessary supplements to the full application of the theory.[76] In the last two sections, I will turn briefly to some emerging fields of application for these sorts of theoretical accounts and then seek to sum up what we have accomplished and gesture toward some of the new lands that await intrepid explorers and pioneers.

[73] Boyd (n 27) 105–106, 134

[74] Reitman 'Multiculturalism and Feminism' (n 68).

[75] *Cf* J Raz, *The Morality of Freedom* (Oxford, Clarendon, 1986) 419.

[76] *Cf* ibid, 428–29.

IV. EMERGING APPLICATIONS

The purpose inherent in this book has been the presentation of a general theory with application across a range of different issues. Although I have referred briefly to specific examples that have helped illustrate different points or implications of the argument, the book has not been principally concerned with showing all of the applications of the theory so much as offering the theory that can be applied in more specific work addressing all of the factual details of different scenarios. Nonetheless, it is worth mentioning, again, the emergence of certain applications, simply for sketching how larger parts of the book's argument apply to these contexts than has been apparent in quicker references to them along the way. I will mention one domestic law example and one international law example.

The Supreme Court of Canada's freedom of religion jurisprudence over recent decades has shifted toward a very individualist account of religion.[77] More specifically, the test in relation to religious exemptions from particular legal norms that overly limit expression of religious belief through religious conduct has come to depend not on any community interpretation of the requirements of particular religions but on the genuine and sincere beliefs of the individual believer. Thus, for example, in the *Amselem* case, a slim majority of the Supreme Court of Canada upheld an exemption from condominium rules for individual Jews claiming the right to construct individual succahs on their balconies over a dissent that would have focused on expert evidence about the religion which showed that the use of a communal succah would meet the religious precept while causing less disruption to neighbours.[78] Chief Justice McLachlin restated the pertinent test in the more recent *Hutterian Brethren* case:

> An infringement of s. 2(*a*) of the *Charter* will be made out where: (1) the claimant sincerely believes in a belief or practice that has a nexus with religion; and (2) the impugned measure interferes with the claimant's ability to act in accordance with his or her religious beliefs in a manner that is more than trivial or insubstantial.[79]

The claimed exemption test remains subject to a balancing against other societal interests. For the majority, this particularist claim of a small number of Hutterian Brethren to be exempt from having photos on their driving licenses then lost out against state security concerns.[80] So one arrives at a combination of an individualist-focused test for the claim to manifest a religious practice that may not hold up well precisely due to its individual focus.

[77] For some discussion on this point and how it fits in with some other phenomena in Canadian freedom of religion jurisprudence, see generally BL Berger, 'Law's Religion: Rendering Culture' in R Moon (ed) *Law and Religious Pluralism in Canada* (Vancouver, UBC Press, 2008) 264, 267–72.

[78] *Syndicat Northcrest v Amselem* [2004] 2 SCR 551, 2004 SCC 47.

[79] *Alberta v Hutterian Brethren of Wilson Colony* 2009 SCC 37, [2009] 2 S.C.R. 567, [31].

[80] Ibid. On balancing of security concerns and religious freedom, see eg AN Guiora, *Freedom from Religion: Rights and National Security* (Oxford, Oxford University Press, 2009).

The dissenting judges in *Hutterian Brethren* focused not on the particular belief of some individual Hutterites that they should not have their photos taken but on the impact on the Hutterite community of a new, rigid enforcement of photos on them. Justice LeBel described the impact of these believers not being able to have driving licenses and the role of religious freedom rights in supporting

> the maintenance of communities of faith. We are discussing the fate not only of a group of farmers, but of a community that shares a common faith and a way of life that is viewed by its members as a way of living that faith and of passing it on to future generations.[81]

Defining the religious freedom concern partly in community-oriented terms might, as it would for LeBel J, limit the right in *Amselem* to something facilitating good relations between communities, but it would have expanded the recognised right in *Hutterian Brethren* because the Court would have identified the real harm of the restriction.

The religious freedom context is obviously a complex one that would bear a full treatment of its own. But what becomes apparent even from this short example is that having a real language of community rights could enable new possibilities within a religious freedom jurisprudence such as that in Canada. Those judges ready to identify the relevance of religious freedom not just to individuals but to communities open legal possibilities.[82] A moral theory of rights held by groups can have a supportive relationship with these legal arguments. Opening the possibility of religious freedom being significant to communities makes it possible to see certain claims as religious freedom claims, notably claims to opportunities to create and maintain religious institutions and claims by religious communities to exercise elements of jurisdiction.[83] At the same time, these approaches would also make explicit why the state could legitimately take steps to ensure, for instance, the presence of institutions facilitating principled contestation within religious communities making such claims. A theory of collective rights can inform new religious freedom claims and principled moral tests on these claims.

In the international law context, the new Declaration on the Rights of Indigenous Peoples advances many significant rights.[84] Amongst these are rights by indigenous communities to consultation and participation in a variety of state decisions, particularly those impacting on their indigenous rights. James Anaya, acting as the Special Rapporteur on the Situation of Human Rights and Fundamental Freedoms of Indigenous People, has made great efforts to highlight the significance of these provisions and also to offer an interpretation of them

[81] Ibid [182].

[82] On arguments for using freedom of association arguments conjunctively with freedom of religion arguments, see generally D Schneiderman, 'Associational Rights, Religion and the *Charter*' in Moon (ed) (n 77) 65.

[83] Alvin Esau traces exercises of jurisdiction by religious communities in Canadian and American contexts and discusses some judicial responses in A Esau, 'Living by Different Law: Legal Pluralism, Freedom of Religion, and Illiberal Religious Groups' in Moon (ed) (n 77) 110. These claims have experienced limited legal possibilities so far as religious freedom tests have been individually based.

[84] Declaration on the Rights of Indigenous Peoples, GA Res 61/295, UN Doc A/RES/47/1 (2007).

geared to facilitating their realisation.[85] Notably, the 2009 Special Rapporteur's Report engages in great efforts to work the relevant provisions of the Declaration into a well-structured spectrum analysis making clear the relevant type and level of consultation in different factual scenarios.[86]

A theory of collective rights has important things to say about this sort of community-held right to be consulted on certain decisions impacting on the rights of the community. It offers, first, of course, a moral explanation of there being rights held by that community in the first place. At the consultation stage, it will be attentive to concerns that might arise in relation to how the community's views are to be represented and, indeed, how to individuate the particular communities holding these rights. On the latter, this theory accepts the possibility of different historical formation processes, subject only to the moral requirements of the Service Principle and the Mutuality Principle, and thus accepts that the individuation of communities holding rights may well differ in different places within the rich diversity of the human family. The Service Principle and Mutuality Principle provide important guidance on representation of the community, providing means of assessing that presumed representatives do indeed speak for the community in legitimate ways and providing a possible language of principled internal contestation within the community itself.[87]

This book's theoretical account provides for a deep relation of communities and individuals of a sort that can provide analysis of innovative rights issues emerging in both domestic and international law contexts. Each context will present significant factual complexities that relate to parts of the theoretical account, and it is important to go through the actual detailed work to analyse the application to specific contexts. But if the aim has been partly to reorient 'rights talk' in a manner that makes it fit more accurately many real issues, the book has done that, and the book hopefully provides a platform for ongoing discussion of these and other issues involving collective rights.

[85] Special Rapporteur on the Situation of Human Rights and Fundamental Freedoms of Indigenous People, *Report of the Special Rapporteur on the Situation of Human Rights and Fundamental Freedoms of Indigenous People*, Human Rights Council, 12th Sess., Agenda Item 3, UN Doc. A/HRC/12/34 (15 July 2009).

[86] Ibid. The analysis ends up looking much like the Canadian duty to consult analysis (which I have detailed in my book, DG Newman, *The Duty to Consult: New Relationships with Aboriginal Peoples* (Saskatoon, Purich Publishing, 2009)). This is paradoxical since Canada ended up voting against the Declaration partly because of concerns about the wording of the consultation provisions within it. As I have argued in some presentations, the Special Rapporteur's reframing of them may even have helped facilitate Canada's recent reversal of its prior rejection of the Declaration. .

[87] It is, as Jeremy Webber notes, important not to try to reconstruct communities into a political theorist's preferred form, as has all too often happened in, for instance, liberal attempts to assimilate indigenous communities: J Webber, 'The Meanings of Consent' in J Webber and CM Macleod (eds) *Between Consenting Peoples: Political Community and the Meaning of Consent* (Vancouver, UBC Press, 2010) 1, 23. Applying the Service Principle and Mutuality Principle to an assessment of representation does not, of course, do that. It simply applies moral standards of legitimacy to the choices and historical processes of communities in a manner that cannot morally be avoided, in the same way that legal standards on the related doctrines will contain legal requirements.

V. A COMMUNITY OF COMMUNITIES

In this book, it has proved possible to address a wide range of collective rights issues within one common moral framework. The book's extended analysis of collective moral rights has gone beyond previously limited discussion. I have challenged, and overcome, the notion that collective rights cannot be discussed within a unified framework. I have argued that collective rights exist, developed moral conditions necessary to their consistency with individual rights, and offered some principles related to institutionalising collective rights.

I have also left many questions unanswered, not because I have declined to answer them but because they invoke matters going beyond the ken of moral or political theory. I have reached many complex questions by going farther than previous theories. It is, however, part of the richness of my account that I acknowledge its limits.

I began by arguing against accounts like that of Kymlicka that would force groups' arguments into a different form than they would argue them. I have not made room for every group's argument, but for many more. It would be another project altogether to analyse whether an account such as presented in this book, one more attuned to the way others might put their claims, opens more room for intercultural dialogue on rights issues. But the present account does one very important thing. It sees a diverse variety of groups, of different natures and different values, as being able to live together in ways one might not have thought before, in a sort of community of communities.

Achieving this community of communities is a shared project, one toward which the political community as a whole, subcollectivities within, and each of us as members, can contribute. Those often thought not to be participating in a citizenship mission have a full role in the project. The Amish on their farms, the First Nations on their territories, the book clubs in members' kitchens, the churches in our hearts, the cultural-linguistic communities that feel threatened, the community as a whole – those of every shade and tongue, faith and culture – all have a place in our community of communities.

Index

www.ingramcontent.com/pod-product-compliance
Ingram Content Group UK Ltd.
Pitfield, Milton Keynes, MK11 3LW, UK
UKHW020803290926
15470UKWH00003B/940

9 781841 132280